Pelican Books
Divided Ulster

Liam de Paor was born in Dublin in
1926 and educated there at Irish-
speaking schools and at University
College, from which he graduated in
archaeology and early Irish history;
he then spent two years doing
postgraduate work in central Europe.
A member of the Royal Irish
Academy, he has served as UNESCO
adviser to the Government of Nepal,
and since 1964 he has been College
lecturer in History at University
College, Dublin. He is a member of
the Irish Labour Party and has
broadcast in Irish and English, on
radio and television, on current
affairs. In 1955 he married Máire
MacDermott, also an archaeologist
and writer, with whom he wrote
Early Christian Ireland (1958). He
has also written *Archaeology: An
Illustrated Introduction* (a Pelican
Book), has edited *Great Irish Books*,
and has contributed to *The Course of
Irish History*, an *Encyclopaedia of
Ireland*, *The Gentle Revolution* and
*Conor Cruise O'Brien Introduces
Ireland*. Liam de Paor has five
children and lives in Dublin.

LIAM DE PAOR

Divided
Ulster

SECOND EDITION

PENGUIN BOOKS

Penguin Books Ltd, Harmondsworth,
Middlesex, England
Penguin Books Inc., 7110 Ambassador Road,
Baltimore, Maryland 21207, U.S.A.
Penguin Books Australia Ltd, Ringwood,
Victoria, Australia

First published as a Penguin Special 1970, 1971
Reissued in Pelican Books 1971
Reprinted 1972

Made and printed in Great Britain by
Cox & Wyman Ltd,
London, Reading and Fakenham
Set in Intertype Times

Contents

For Máire

And the LORD your God, he shall expel them from before you, and drive them from out of your sight; and ye shall possess their land, as the LORD your God hath promised unto you.

Be ye therefore very courageous to keep and to do all that is written in the book of the law of Moses, that ye turn not aside therefrom to the right hand or to the left;

That ye come not among these nations, these that remain among you; neither make mention of the name of their gods, nor cause to swear by them, neither serve them, nor bow yourselves unto them:

But cleave unto the LORD your God, as ye have done unto this day.

Joshua, 23.5–8

List of Abbreviations

A.O.H.	Ancient Order of Hibernians
C.R.A.	Northern Ireland Civil Rights Association
C.S.J.	Campaign for Social Justice
I.R.A.	Irish Republican Army
I.R.B.	Irish Republican Brotherhood
P.D.	People's Democracy
R.I.C.	Royal Irish Constabulary
R.U.C.	Royal Ulster Constabulary
U.V.F.	Ulster Volunteer Force

Introduction

In Northern Ireland Catholics are Blacks who happen to have white skins. This is not a truth. It is an oversimplification and too facile an analogy. But it is a better oversimplification than that which sees the struggle and conflict in Northern Ireland in terms of religion. Catholics and Protestants are not quarrelling with one another (most of them) because of matters of theology or faith. There is no burning urge on either side to convert the other to the one true faith, nor does a member of one side strike a member of the other on the head with a club in the hope that he will thereby be purged of his theological errors and become a better candidate for heaven.

The Northern Ireland problem is a colonial problem, and the 'racial' distinction (and it is actually imagined as racial) between the colonists and the natives is expressed in terms of religion. It goes perhaps somewhat deeper than that; for it is necessary to maintain the distinction in order to maintain the colony as a colony. It is true that the colonizing of Northern Ireland took place a long time ago; it is true too that there was a time when it seemed that distinctions might be merged in a happy integration of the descendants of settlers with the descendants of natives, but for historical reasons this tendency was reversed almost two centuries ago, and it has always since seemed to be to the advantage of somebody to keep Ulster divided.

The outbreak of fierce fighting in 1969, which within a few days had brought British intervention and the replacement of the forces of law and order of the Stormont government by British soldiers, began on 12 August. It began on that date be-

cause it is the date of a great annual celebration in Londonderry. What is being celebrated is the raising of the siege of that
city in 1689. In Belfast, and over most of Northern Ireland, on
the other hand, the great day for Orange celebrations is 12 July –
the anniversary of the victory of William III over James II at
the battle of the Boyne in 1690. It is plain that events in the
seventeenth century have a special meaning for the Protestant
people of Northern Ireland, and indeed they are not mistaken in
attaching a great significance to these events. In the happenings
of the seventeenth century lies some – a good deal – of the
meaning of the events of the last few years. Perhaps it would be
more true to say that a good deal of the meaning of these events
lies in the ideas that Ulster Protestants have today about what
happened in the seventeenth century.

The whole Northern Irish problem is complex, and its complexities are entangled in history. This book attempts to sketch
not a history of Ulster, but a view of the problem of the divisions of Ulster as these appear in its history. The emphases
throughout, therefore, are placed where it is hoped they will
best bring out the meaning of what has been happening in
Northern Ireland; thus it is that many interesting and important
aspects of the history of that area have been passed by.

Introduction to the Pelican Edition

This book was first written as a Penguin Special, and the original version was completed at the end of 1969. It has now been revised and the last chapter, dealing with events and developments in Northern Ireland since 1968, has been rewritten and expanded, to cover the period down to the election of Mr Brian Faulkner as leader of the Unionist party and Prime Minister of Northern Ireland in the spring of 1971.

The years since about 1965 have been a time of very rapid change in Ireland, especially in Northern Ireland. The Civil Rights movement of the late 1960s was a symptom of the breakdown of the system of sectarian rule which, in response to the rebellion of Ulster Unionists, supported by an extra-Parliamentary agitation by British Conservatives and by a mutiny in the British army, Britain had imposed in 1920. An area of six thousand square miles was arbitrarily carved out of the province of Ulster and given the anomalous status of being at once an integral part of the United Kingdom, like Scotland and Wales, and, unlike those nations, a self-governing statelet. At no time was any serious attempt made to negotiate a settlement directly between the Protestant and Unionist minority in Ireland and the Catholic and Nationalist majority: instead an artificial majority was created for the Protestant and Unionist party by drawing the boundary of the new province to suit them. Appeal was then made to the principle of democratic government and majority rule. The Nationalist population of the six counties of Northern Ireland have always felt entitled to ask, 'Majority of *what*?' A full third of the inhabitants of the new statelet bitterly resented its existence and wished it to be merged in a self-governing Ireland. The response of the Orange rulers of Northern Ireland was to treat one citizen in three as a politically suspect and therefore under-privileged person. As I have suggested in the course of the book, a state so constituted and so fundamentally divided simply cannot function as a normal western democracy, which must be founded on some general consent to the existence and institutions of the state. Northern Ireland in fact has been a system of government imposed by external force. The force is British: the problem is a colonial problem.

At the end of 1969, in the first version of *Divided Ulster*, I wrote of the British army, which had then been but a few short months on the streets of Belfast and Derry, that 'an occupying army could not be expected to sit for too long on its bayonets'. It did not. At the beginning of July 1970 the British forces began to abandon their 'peace-keeping' role in Northern Ireland and to show themselves as a force whose central function was the maintenance of the Stormont regime, when they carried out an extraordinary (and illegal) operation against the population of the Falls area of Belfast. Early in July 1971 the British Prime Minister, Mr Heath, in a broadcast on the terms agreed for Britain's entry into the E.E.C., had chosen to revive dreams of England's vanished imperial past, and later in the month the Home Secretary, Mr Maudling, declared that a state of all-out war now existed between his country's army and the Irish Republican Army. By early August, as I write, this has come to resemble more nearly a state of war between the British army and the Catholic population of Northern Ireland, as the soldiers carried out mass arrests, for internment without trial, of civil rights leaders, and as they opened fire with less and less discrimination on houses and people.

Both in the Republic of Ireland and in Great Britain, public opinion has swung to and fro during the years of trouble in Northern Ireland. Undoubtedly, to many people in Britain the whole business must seem wearisome and inexplicable. *The Spectator* and other conservative journals have referred to 'the Irish mess' in terms which suggest that the whole situation is due to some defect in the Irish character. This is to miss the point. It is a British mess.

A good deal of British impatience in these years has been directed at the Unionist rulers of Northern Ireland, especially since the situation has been over-simplified by presenting it as little more than a conflict of religious bigotries. There is indeed religious bigotry in plenty in Northern Ireland, as elsewhere, but that is not the root of the matter, and to suggest that it is is to be unfair in particular to the Protestants of Ulster. These prefer the British connection to being ruled by a largely Roman Catholic parliament in Dublin, and this, of course, is a perfectly valid political aspiration. It derives, I believe, in the first instance from fear, a fear of the 'native' majority in the island which is rooted in the colonial past. It is expressed in the intransigence summed up in such catch-cries as 'Not an inch!' and in the carefully cultivated myth of Protestant superiority. It is however backed by the massive force of the British army and by the bland British support of such absurdities as that what happens in Northern Ireland is a matter in which the government of the Republic of Ireland is not entitled to concern itself, or that a mass movement like that which developed in Northern Ireland in the late 1960s is due to either a handful of 'extremists' or an international communist conspiracy. Because of the support of British force the Unionist party in Northern Ireland has been enabled to ignore the point of view of their opponents – a point of view which is at least as legitimate as their own – and to insist that the constitution of Northern Ireland is not open to discussion. This in fact, if there is to be any solution, short of sectarian massacre, to the problem, is just what must be open to discussion and negotiation. But, as Mr Maudling indicated in July 1971, it had by then become a function of the British army to 'maintain the constitution of Northern Ireland'.

All lines of argument about the Northern Ireland situation in fact lead back to the central question of the use of force and violence. The process begun by Protestant Ulster in 1911, the process of disregard for established institutions and resort to force, is still working itself out, and must continue inevitably to work itself out in violence and turmoil until the way is opened to negotiation. This will involve a recognition on the one hand that the Dublin government has a legitimate interest in Northern

Ireland, and on the other hand that the nine hundred thousand or so of Ulster's population who reject Dublin rule are entitled to a special political provision. These are the two parties to solve the problem. A British solution, imposed by British guns, has failed, is failing and will continue to fail.

It is obviously difficult to assess the Ulster situation objectively at the time of writing, August 1971, just as it is difficult in narrating events which had a large illegal or clandestine element to provide an exposition which is at once balanced and reasonably full. The account here provided of the events of the period 1968 to 1971 is brief and is based as far as possible on printed and verifiable sources. In this connection it is perhaps worth remarking that two types of source of information have proved especially useful in the attempt to discern what has been happening in the extremely confused and often obscure Ulster situation. One is the proceedings of commissions of inquiry, of which there have been several; the other is the ephemeral literature, Protestant and Catholic, republican and unionist, of the Ulster revolution. This ranges from established weekly or monthly papers like *The United Irishman, The Protestant Telegraph* or *The Ulster Protestant* to the hand-bills, posters and other occasional statements and pro-clamations which appear briefly on the streets. For the future documenting of the revolution of 1968 onwards these will prove to be extremely useful. Fortunately, a comprehensive, or near-comprehensive, collection is being made by the Linenhall Library in Belfast.

Several unofficial inquiries have been made into episodes of the Ulster trouble, and published. While these have tended to serve one interest or another they are useful to the extent that they provide verified accounts of the facts which supplement or correct the reports available in newspapers or the (usually highly un-reliable) recollections of participants and eyewitnesses. Of such accounts I wish to acknowledge in particular the help I have received from *Burntollet*, by B. Egan and V. McCormack, which provides a fully researched narrative of the Belfast–Derry march of January 1969 and of the ambush at Burntollet, and *Law and Orders*, introduced by Michael Dolley, which investigates the

British army's curfew in the Falls area of Belfast in July 1970.

There have also been several general works dealing with aspects of the modern Ulster situation. *The Sins of Our Fathers*, by Owen Dudley Edwards, which was published simultaneously with the first version of this book, investigates in depth the origins of the present crisis. *Holy War in Belfast*, by Andrew Boyd, gives a detailed account of sectarian conflict in Belfast from the middle of the nineteenth century down to the present. Martin Wallace's *Revolution in Ulster* and Max Hastings's *Ulster 1969* provide narratives of the events of the first year of the northern troubles. A work in Irish, *Géar-chéim in Éirinn*, by Dick Walsh of *The Irish Times*, brings the story down to the end of 1970 and includes a fairly detailed account of the events in the Republic of Ireland which arose from the northern situation in 1970. Admirers of admirers of the military mind may also find something to instruct them in Patrick Riddell's book, *Fire Over Ulster*, a work which sets out to argue the unionist case but strays into racial theories and regimental histories. There *is* a unionist case but it has not so far found a worthy present-day exponent, although those who are interested in understanding its basis are recommended to read a work of 1912, *The Ulster Scot*, by J. Woodburn.

Most commentators on the Ulster position, whether they speak as observers or as participants in politics, address themselves explicitly or implicitly to the question of partition of Ireland and the re-unification of the country. This question appears to me to be secondary, although it concerns the more intractable part of the problem. I have therefore laid the emphasis on the British connection, since it is British attempts to govern in Ireland through a colonial regime which seem to me to have given rise (not only in the case of Ulster) to most of the difficulties in what for long was known as 'the Irish question' (although an Irishman might well think that it were better called 'the British question'). British statesmen have not been prepared to devote to Ireland the amount of time and attention its good government required. They have attempted, in all Ireland in the more distant past and in Northern Ireland in the recent past, to rule Ireland through a colony. This has failed. 'Planters and natives' can undoubtedly come to an agreement in Ireland, perhaps an agreement to continue in some form the partition of the country, but it seems to me essential that those who are responsible for government in Ireland should be rooted in the country and committed to it – and ultimately dependent on Irish resources and initiatives to solve Ireland's problems. What keeps the sterile quarrel of Orange and Green alive is the constant presence of the third party, Great Britain.

Great Britain is and has been an interested party, and has therefore been unable to intervene successfully in the Ulster disputes in the role of peacekeeper or intermediary. The attempt to do so has produced the situation where the British army confronts and combats whole populations on the streets of cities in what is nominally 'The United Kingdom of Great Britain and Northern Ireland'. The exercise of responsibility in the affairs of other people, however well-meaning, is the essence of imperialism, and it is an activity which has generally proved to be unrewarding to both parties concerned. It has certainly been so in the case of Ireland and Britain: southern Ireland in the early decades of the century, and divided Ulster in the 1970s, bear witness. The responsibility for dealing with Irish divisions should, in my opinion, be returned where it belongs: to Ireland.

1 Settlers and Natives

If the *principles* of the Revolution of 1688 are any where to be found, it is in the statute called the *Declaration of Right*. In that most wise, sober, and considerate declaration, drawn up by great lawyers and great statesmen, and not by warm and inexperienced enthusiasts, not one word is said, nor one suggestion made, of a general right 'to choose our own *governors*; to cashier them for misconduct; and to *form* a government for *ourselves*.'

This Declaration of Right (the act of the Ist of William and Mary, sess. 2. ch. 2.) is the cornerstone of our constitution, as reinforced, explained, improved, and in its fundamental principles for ever settled. It is called 'An act for declaring the rights and liberties of the subject, and for *settling* the *succession* of the crown.' You will observe, that these rights and this succession are declared in one body, and bound indissolubly together. *Edmund Burke*[1]

By heroic magic, by single combats, by turning the chariots only sunwise (to the right), the frontiers of Ulster were defended against the armies of Queen Maeve and the men of Ireland in the earliest Irish saga, *Táin Bó Cuailgne*. The saga faintly preserves the memory of the kingdom which had held all the north in the period at the end of prehistory – the kingdom of the people known as the *Ulaid* – and of its downfall. The royal seat of the Ulaid at *Emhain Macha* (now Navan fort just outside Armagh) was overrun, but their kingdom was not wholly destroyed. It had once extended across the whole north of Ireland from the Irish Sea to the Atlantic, and its southern boundaries had been the Erne and the Boyne, but from the sixth until the twelfth century Ulster was a small, not very important, kingdom lying east of the Bann in the north-east corner of the island.

All that lay north of Erne and west of Bann was ruled by dynastic groups who claimed descent from the legendary Niall of the Nine Hostages, and were known therefore as the Uí Néill, the Descendants of Niall. A southern branch of the dynasty held the midlands and the ancient sacred site of Tara, in Meath. From the northern and southern Uí Néill were selected the kings of Tara, who claimed also to be emperors of the Irish.

The men of the north-east remembered their ancient glories, and never fully acquiesced in the possession of most of Ulster by the Uí Néill, but they directed much of their attention, in the early centuries of Ireland's history, eastwards to Scotland. Here a sub-kingdom of Ulster named *Dál Riata* had established a colony, which gradually over the centuries won territory from the Picts and Britons. Here too a scion of the Uí Néill, Columba, sailing from his church at Derry, had established his monastery of Iona, from which the conversion of the northern Picts and, ultimately, the northern English was undertaken. The *Dál Riata* colonists had brought their native Irish language with them. In time it replaced British as the tongue of northern and western Scotland. It is the Gaelic still spoken today in parts of the Hebrides and the Highlands.

When the Anglo-Normans invaded Ireland in the twelfth century, north-east Ulster was one of the first areas to be conquered, by John de Courcy. Strong castles, abbeys, and towns consolidated the conquest, but west of the Bann the Normans failed to penetrate the lands of the Uí Néill, whose descendants, the O'Neills of Tyrone, the O'Donnells of Tyrconnell, maintained with their people an ancient way of life which, except for the adoption of Christianity, had not changed fundamentally since before the dawn of history. Even east of the Bann the Norman imprint was superficial – and Scotland was not very far away. The Hebrides in the thirteenth century supplied professional soldiers, the gallowglasses, to fight in Irish wars, and early in the fourteenth century Edward Bruce, followed soon by his brother Robert, king of Scots, landed in east Ulster with an army. Edward Bruce was crowned king of Ireland, he marched up and down the country, burning and ravaging, he was defeated and killed. The power of the English in Ireland, already diminishing before his time, shrank still further. Late medieval Ulster was for the most part Gaelic, conservative, and beyond the English law. O'Neill 'took his seat upon the fern', reckoned his thousands of head of cattle and listened to his poets. The ancient, rich, complex culture of Gaelic Ireland, driven back on itself in Ulster, pretended that the late medieval world of towns, national monarchies and nascent capitalism did not exist, and continued to pretend until in the late sixteenth century Hugh O'Neill came home from London.

O'Neill was the product of an immemorial tradition and of the age of Machiavelli. Tudor policy had added to his kingly title of 'O'Neill' the vassal's title of 'Earl of Tyrone'. It had educated him in London (as later generations of Indians, Africans, Malays, and indeed Irishmen were to be educated at Eton, Harrow, Cambridge, Oxford) to make of him an instrument of policy. From the streets of London he came to the windy hillside of Tullaghoge, the inauguration-place of the kings. He was a Renaissance statesman come to rule an Iron-Age tribal state. At first O'Neill, while ruling his people in the old ways, yet seemed content to be the instrument of Tudor policy he had been fitted to be. He served the Queen in the war that broke the great Earl of Desmond and reduced Munster. But in his 'deep dissembling heart' he pondered the meaning for him and his people of the English reconquest of Ireland, and the meaning of the Reformation which Elizabeth came to represent, while the agents of the Counter-Reformation worked in conservative Ireland. He raised against the Queen one of the greatest and fiercest of Irish wars, and was beaten after nine long years. At Mellifont, beside the Boyne, O'Neill and O'Donnell signed the terms which left them their earldoms but opened Ulster to the administrators of the Crown. And a few years later, in 1607, finding themselves no longer masters in their own houses, and fearing for the future, they slipped away, from Tyrone, from Tyrconnell, from the heritage of the past, and sailed down

3

Lough Swilly for the open sea and exile in Spain and Italy.

Ulster at the beginning of the seventeenth century was the most conservative, indeed archaic, part of Ireland, the last Gaelic area to come under the control of the English administration. Its economy was pastoral. It had no towns. For a thousand years its people had lived under Irish law and had served the descendants of Niall of the Nine Hostages. For a thousand years they had, in their own fashion (for in this every European people had its own fashion), been Christian – Catholic. There were ancient churches, there were medieval friaries and abbeys. There were some, a few, stone castles, but lake-dwellings and raths were still inhabited and had been defended in the war. The Reformation had made as little headway as other innovations among the Ulster forests. The long war had brought hunger, disease, and, with the flight of the earls, despair.

England now had a king who was king of Scotland, and early in the century lowland Scots from King James's northern kingdom began to change the whole character of Ulster. This came about partly through the renewal of a policy which Tudor administrations had tried without marked success in other parts of Ireland, the policy of plantation.

Through the Middle Ages the English administration had coped with the alien Gaelic culture largely by holding it at arm's length, since preoccupations in France and elsewhere prevented the formulation of any whole-hearted Irish policy. The government appointed as governors of Ireland members of the great Hiberno-Norman families who held vast lands in Gaelic areas and had accommodated to Irish law, language and custom. At the same time successive administrations denied English law to the Irish, but attempted to impose on the small English Pale and on the handful of English-speaking towns prohibitions against Irish language, dress and manners. The 'king's English' in Ireland were especially forbidden to follow Irish law (they showed themselves false English and king's enemies if they did so) and to observe such dangerous native customs as 'alterage' – sending one's son to be fostered in another man's house, thus creating an alliance which in practice was often stronger than ties of blood. Laws to impose the separation of the two cultures were passed again and again, but always the rising tide of Gaelic culture threatened to engulf the little English islands. As a Palesman of the fourteenth century put it:

> By granting charters of peace
> To false English, without lease
> This land shall be much undo;
> But gossipred and alterage
> And losing of our language
> Have mickly holp thereto.[2]

The Tudors tried new policies, which were all the more necessary when a religious difference was added to the cultural division. From early in the sixteenth century on, attempts at colonization by English settlers were made, attempts in other words to extend the bridgehead of English rule and law from the towns into the hinterland. The early attempts met with little success. Under Philip and Mary the midland areas bordering on the Pale were chosen for English settlement, and two new counties, Kings County and Queens County, were created, with chief towns at Philipstown and Maryborough. Other attempts were made later in the century, on a very small scale in east Ulster, and on a very large scale in Munster. The Munster plantation, in which Spenser and Raleigh were involved, was planned in the same way as the colonies being attempted at this time in Virginia and elsewhere in America. It was overwhelmed in the nine years war at the end of the sixteenth century. Ideas for planting English colonists were, however, in the air at the end of the century – some proposing that the native Irish should be disarmed and kept as helots to work on the lands granted to the new English colonists, but that the strict legal separation of the two cultures be maintained and indeed given the force of a racial segregation; others recommending that the Irish should be expelled from Ireland altogether – some of those found suitable being shipped perhaps to America to help in colonizing that wilderness under firm English control.

It was found impracticable to replace the native inhabitants

of the country wholly with new settlers – these were not forthcoming as readily as were the capitalist speculators interested in
quick profits – and there remained the two problems at the turn
of the century, of effectively disarming the Irish and of preserving such new settlers as might be planted in the country
from succumbing to the customs and cuture of the natives.
Mountjoy, the victor in Elizabeth's long war against O'Neill,
summed it up:

Because the Irish and English–Irish were obstinate in Popish
superstition, great care was thought fit to be taken that these new
colonies should consist of such men as were most unlike to fall to
the barbarous customs of the Irish, or the Popish superstition of
Irish and English–Irish, so as no less cautions were to be observed
for uniting them and keeping them from mixing with other than if
these new colonies were to be led to inhabit among the barbarous
Indians.[3]

After the departure of the earls in 1607, the head of the Irish
government, Sir Arthur Chichester, put forward a scheme (initially very moderate but strengthened as a result of a further,
abortive, uprising in Ulster in 1608) for the settlement of the
lands over which the earls had exercised control. The area
affected comprised the counties of Donegal, Tyrone, Fermanagh, Cavan, Armagh, and Coleraine (now Derry). All this
territory, although much of it had been under only a vague
Tyrone or Tyrconnell suzerainty, was treated as confiscated
land. In each county some land was set aside for native Irish
who were thought to be 'reliable', but most was held for grant-
ing to new settlers. The City of London, on the proposal of the
Crown, undertook to plant the county of Coleraine and to re-
build and defend the cities of Derry and Coleraine in return for
extensive privileges. Derry was now renamed Londonderry, and
tracts of land in the county were set aside for different city
companies, new towns planned, and the county – in theory –
colonized by Londoners.

Antrim and Down, east of the Bann, were not included in the
scheme for the plantation of Ulster, since they were not involved in the confiscation of lands which followed the flight of

6

the earls. However, they lay close to Scotland, there was a Scottish king on the English throne, and there were not wanting lowland lairds and tenants who for one reason or another were interested in settling in a new home in Ireland. By means which were, as often as not, unscrupulous, a great deal of land in the two counties was acquired from its Irish proprietors and a determined immigration and energetic colonization by lowland Scots followed.

From the government's point of view, the colonization of Ulster in the period after 1609 suffered from the same defects as had earlier attempts at plantation in Ireland. Not enough of the natives were driven out: not enough settlers came in to take their place. Although the plantations were state-sponsored enterprises, they were also essentially private enterprises, fairly typical of the mercantilism of the time. The government provided land, acquired by conquest and confiscation, but the necessary investment to exploit the land by supplying and maintaining a colony was provided by entrepreneurs known as 'undertakers' – companies like the Irish Company set up by the City of London to settle the county of Coleraine, landed gentlemen with money to spare, and other speculators – who sought a profitable investment. The quickest and highest profits could be made by allowing the Irish to stay on their own land, which they were willing to work, and for which they were willing to pay a high rent. This, in practice, is what was done in most areas. However, there was a good deal more genuine settlement and colonization in Ulster than there had been in the Elizabethan plantations, and what developed over most of the province was a patchwork of alien and hostile cultures. The natives, Catholic and Irish-speaking, clung miserably to the land, where they now worked as labourers, or retreated to the forests and hills, where the living was poor and where they were a constant threat to the newly settled colonists. In east Ulster, however, beyond the Bann, there were large areas which were densely settled by the Scots, better husbandmen than the pastoralist Irish whom they had replaced, and with a hungrier grip on the land than most of the English settlers. Many of the

Scots were Presbyterians, and if they had little in common with the Anglican English, they had no more in common with the Catholic Irish.

The situation thus established in early seventeenth-century Ulster was an uneasy one. Colonization and the building of towns and defences were slower than policy would have them, and those who did settle the confiscated lands lived among a hostile people who harboured a deep sense of wrong. The situation has often been compared to that of the early colonists of North America, whose little settlements lived under threat of Indian attack.

This too was the time when religious extravagance possessed men like a madness and when a constitutional and economic struggle was causing upheaval in the English policy. These had their effects on Irish affairs, and Irish affairs had some effects on them. The native Irish, dispossessed, waited for an opportunity to recover what they had lost. The 'Old English' – the families who had been the English colonists of the Middle Ages and who had mostly remained Roman Catholics – while they were hostile to the natives, were yet uneasy at the threat presented to their own lands and declining position by Protestant planters, an arbitrary government and a new age. Plans for extending the Ulster method of plantation to other parts of the country met with little success. And after the accession of Charles I, discontent with government policies gradually spread to virtually all groups in the country. Sir Thomas Wentworth, who arrived in Ireland as lord deputy in 1633, achieved in a long term of office the establishment of a firm administration and a rising revenue, but he did so at the cost of antagonizing the Presbyterian settlers in Ulster by his application of the Government's ecclesiastical policy and his strict enforcement of the terms of their land-grants. His rule was also resented by most other groups and classes.

The pressure which was felt by the Ulster Presbyterians was also felt by the Presbyterians of Scotland. When the National Covenant was renewed at Edinburgh in 1638, many of the Ulster planters signed it – there was much traffic and communication across the North Channel – and when the quarrel between the king and the Presbyterian Scots turned to war, the sympathy of the Ulster planters lay with the king's enemies. This same war forced the king to recall parliament, which proved to be hostile to him and to his power. All parties in Ireland combined to undo Wentworth's system of administration, and indeed to undo Wentworth himself (now Earl of Strafford), for he was executed in 1641, but the Roman Catholic groups in Ireland (including the Old English) became apprehensive at the tone and character of the parliament. Of these groups, the most aggrieved were the Ulster native Irish, and it was they who planned to seize the centre of Irish government, Dublin Castle, as well as other centres and strongholds, in 1641. Their plans in Dublin were betrayed, but the rising went forward in Ulster, led by Sir Phelim O'Neill, who claimed that he and his followers were not rising in rebellion against the crown, but were in arms to defend the king against parliament.

The insurgents soon controlled most of Ulster, and then they marched south towards Dublin, defeating a small government force, and besieged Drogheda. They were now joined by the Old English of the east midland and coast area, and their cause became distinguished as that of the Roman Catholics, of whatever origin, in the country. Their army became known as the Catholic Army. The rising spread, meeting, however, with no major military successes, and a form of Roman Catholic parliament was convened to meet at Kilkenny late in 1642. The king, who was now at war with his English parliament, maintained an army in Ireland, as did the English parliament. An indecisive muddle ended with the execution of the king in 1649, and the arrival in Ireland of Oliver Cromwell with an army by which the Irish were, as Marvell put it, 'in one year tamed', not a few of them being massacred in the process. After this there followed major confiscations of land all over Ireland, and the establishment of a new landlord class to replace those who, whether Irish or Old English, had held most of the land outside Ulster.

In Ulster itself, something like the Irish rising of 1641 had been long awaited by some observers, who had from time to time criticized what they regarded as the inadequacy of the plantation settlement. Their prophecy had been that one day the dispossessed native Irish, too many of whom had been kept on the land for the profit of speculators and undertakers, would rise and cut the throats of the colonists. Fear, contempt and hatred animated the opinion held by the planters of the ragged native Irish who worked on the land, or passed homeless on the roads, fear, and a deep-seated uneasiness compounded of cant, guilt, and a determination to hold what they were building where before there had been nothing. Like white farmers in Kenya watching their Kikuyu workers and thinking of the midnight advent of the Mau-Mau, the English and Scottish planters watched and waited.

Expectation was fulfilled when the rising came. It was more than fulfilled; it was justified by being fulfilled, and that the rising had happened at all could be used to justify any tall tale that might be told of it. The policy of the Irish leaders was directed against strong points held by the government in Ulster, not against the dispersed colonists. But their followers, burning with a long-damped sense of wrong, drove out the planters from the homes they had established on confiscated land, and murdered many of them. There was no wholesale or concerted massacre of the planters, but in the confusion of the time and in the willingness of the colonists to believe that their worst expectations had in full measure been fulfilled, it became an established conviction that the Ulster Catholics had risen and slaughtered the Ulster Protestants to plan, a plan worse than that of St Bartholomew. Fear and hatred were intensified, and lent added bitterness to the vengeance which was exacted by Cromwell's puritans.

The policy of government by colonization is at best a short-term one, for colonists soon enough develop a sense of their own interests as being distinct from those of the home government. This had already appeared in Ulster in the resentment shown by the planters to the policy of Charles I as executed by Wentworth; against that lord deputy they had to some extent cooperated with Roman Catholic groups in Ireland. But the very time and nature of the plantations of British settlers in Ireland had made religion one of the distinguishing marks of the dispossessed on the one hand and of the invaders on the other – and this in a matter which closely concerned home, land, livelihood, and often life itself. Sixteenth-century Ireland had remained Roman Catholic – the Old English families of the Pale and the people of the towns as well as the Gaelic Irish to whom they had been opposed in policy, language, and culture. The colonists given land in Ireland – land which had been taken from the Irish – by Elizabeth and James were Protestants. The contrast of religions, however, was only one among many contrasts between these planters and the dispossessed natives, since they differed also in language, law, custom, economy, thought, and art. But the complexities of religious conflict in seventeenth-century England, interwoven as they were with the complexities of class conflict and of the struggle for power between different economic and ideological groups, combined, when extended to Ireland, to give a special prominence, not so much to the religious issue as such, but to the religious denomination as the badge distinguishing exploiter from exploited. That important propertied class, the Old English, who had language and culture in common with their fellow royalists in England, found themselves by force of seventeenth-century circumstance (being as they saw it constantly threatened in their power and in their property) allied with the native Irish, and with them defeated and dispossessed. What they had in common with their allies, by way of motivation, was a desire to hold the land that their ancestors had held, but in many respects their interests were incompatible. What they had in common with their allies that would serve as a simple identification in time of war was Roman Catholicism. So the rising of 1641, a complex struggle for power and property in Ireland, as the civil war was in England, manifested itself as a religious war.

The Cromwellian settlement did not in practice involve colonization on the model of the Ulster plantation. The confiscations of land were much more extensive, but they involved a change of ownership rather than a displacement of population. Catholic landowners were transplanted westward across the Shannon to smaller holdings – if they could demonstrate innocence of participation in the rising. The confiscated land, much of it in fairly large holdings, was distributed to 'Adventurers' and disbanded soldiers. The mass of the working population did not change, and the chief effect of the settlement over most of the country was to establish a Protestant landowning and ruling class, small in numbers, in a countryside which remained Irish and Roman Catholic.

The 1641 rising, although it began in Ulster and was in part a reaction to the plantation there, made no fundamental change in the Ulster situation. Distrust between the main elements of the population was deepened, and the colonial character of the province was advanced by the further confiscations of the Cromwellian settlement. However, this settlement as it affected the rest of Ireland also had some effects on Ulster, and served to point up a number of growing contrasts between the northern province and the other three. These were mostly due to the character of the colonial settlement in the north, and to the fact that the rest of Ireland was now treated, without compunction, as conquered territory.

It seems clear that in the later seventeenth century Ulster was the most prosperous part of Ireland, and that the industry and skill of the settlers, many of whom were of urban origin, caused it to be distinguished by a flourishing of craftsmanship not to be found to the same extent elsewhere. The abject poverty which characterized the conquered Irish made a poor basis for any kind of economic development, but the Protestant settlers in the north were not equally exploited and afflicted, even the small men among them. They practised their weaving, linen-making, tanning, and other home-crafts in an atmosphere which was wholly different from that of Munster or Connacht at the time. On the land, too, there were important differences, due partly to the special concessions in terms of leases which had been made as inducements to immigrant tenants, since these were required to fulfil the conditions of plantation land-grants. Leases tended to be long, and the interest of the tenant in his holding was recognized, in what became known as the 'Ulster custom'. Security of tenure had important economic effects. The tenant was not penalized for improving his output or his holding, and productivity was in his interest. So too was the practice of a craft (such as linen-making), which was often combined with farming. These conditions encouraged industriousness, and to a large extent overcame the discouragement provided from time to time by acts of the English government designed to protect English producers from Irish competition.

Ulster remained, as it had been early in the century, a patchwork of cultures – for the towns and farms of the settlers were surrounded and intermingled with the fragments of the ruined Gaelic society. This Gaelic culture was deprived in defeat of its aristocracy, its texture, its basis of subsistence, although the tradition of Irish poetry and learning was to live on in Ulster for many years yet. While even the ruins of this society remained, the plantation must continue in a state of defence, repairing the limestone towers and the musket-looped farmyard walls that had been over-run in 1641.

The restoration of Charles II in 1660 brought about no more than a modification of the Cromwellian settlement. Promises had been made to those who had fought for his father, but it was also necessary if Charles was to be permitted to return to the throne at all that the land-grants made by Cromwell should not be too seriously upset. In the outcome, some Cromwellian land-holders were required to relinquish a part of their grants of land, and a few Catholics, mainly Old English, had a part of their lands restored to them. The Gaelic Irish received virtually nothing, and some of those who had been landowners abandoned hope of recovering their lost possessions and were driven to leave the country or to exact private revenge by preying on the planters who had replaced them. Others bided their time and hoped for a further opportunity to displace the settlers and restore the old owners.

The Stuart restoration was not received with joy by the Ulster

Presbyterians, and Catholic hopes were matched by Protestant fears. These came to a head, however, only with the accession to the throne of James II, the Roman Catholic brother of Charles, in 1685. Catholic hopes and Protestant fears now combined to see the land-settlement undone, in spite of the king's reassurances – which he knew to be very necessary if he were to retain his throne – that the settlement would not be changed. His recall of the Duke of Ormond, Charles's lord lieutenant, immediately after his accession caused disquiet among the Protestants; his appointment of the Catholic Richard Talbot, Duke of Tyrconnell, as lord lieutenant in 1687, caused the explosion of feeling which is expressed in the Protestant war-song *Lillibulero*:

> Ho, broder Teague, dost hear de decree,
> Lillibulero, bullen a-la,
> Dat we shall have a new Deputee,
> Lillibulero, bullen a-la,
>   Lero, Lero Lillibulero etc.,
> Ho, by Shaint Tyburne, it is de Talbote,
> Lillibulero, bullen a-la,
> And he will cut de Englishman's troate,
> Lillibulero, bullen a-la . . .[4]

Tyrconnell was known to be opposed to the maintenance of the settlement, and his acts on arriving in Ireland indicated that he proposed to undo it: he recruited large numbers of Roman Catholics into the army and began to replace Protestants by Catholics in positions of power or influence throughout the country. In response to the king's call for troops in England, Tyrconnell withdrew soldiers from Ulster, thus causing alarm simultaneously among Protestants in Northern Ireland who took fright to see the English army go and among Protestants in England who took fright to see the Catholic army arrive. In England the Protestant constitution was at issue; in Ireland the constitution too, but also the ownership of the land.

Tyrconnell held Ireland for King James while that monarch was deprived of England by William of Orange at the end of 1688. But the Protestant colonists in Ireland, both those in a small minority in the south whose recently granted lands were in danger and those in larger numbers in the north who saw the towns which they had built and the lands which they had tilled in danger of relapsing into what they thought of as barbarism, now took scattered initiatives against the lord lieutenant. Londonderry and Enniskillen closed their gates against his troops and defied his authority, and maintained their defiance through the following spring, even when he had reduced all the rest of Ulster with his forces. James himself landed in Ireland in March, proceeded to Derry, and negotiated there with the governor, Robert Lundy, who was prepared to open the gates to him on terms. Lundy was overthrown, however, and the citizens now defied not the lord lieutenant but the king, who began a siege which lasted for three months. His army was not equipped to breach the stout walls of Derry, but they encircled the city and barred the wide river Foyle with a boom so that no supplies could reach the garrison and the civilian population – many of whom were refugees who had crowded within the protecting walls. The city was starving when a relief ship broke the boom and brought in supplies, forcing James to raise the siege.

Enniskillen, the other Protestant stronghold which had held out against the lord lieutenant, played an active rather than a passive part during the months of the siege of Derry, sending its forces out to attack, successfully, the Stuart troops and communications. By the defiance and resistance of the two towns, colonist Ulster had refused James an undisputed base in Ireland, and by their success in withstanding him the Protestant settlers made Ulster available as a base for King William in the summer of 1689.

Shortly after the raising of the siege of Derry, King William's commander, Marshal Schomberg, landed near Belfast, took Carrickfergus, and proceeded to establish the Ulster base for the winter. In the spring 7,000 French troops landed in the south to aid King James, who, however, remained in Dublin, and in June King William arrived at Carrickfergus and joined Schomberg. James marched northward from Dublin to meet them. decided to hold the line of the river Boyne, and there awaited the Williamite army. The battle, still annually celebrated in Northern Ireland on 12 July, was fought on 1 July according to the old-style calendar then still in use in England. It is the major feast in the Orange calendar, and the theme for two and a half centuries of Ulster Protestant legend and song:

Now, praise God, all true Protestants, and heaven's and earth's Creator,
For the deliverance that he sent our enemies to scatter.
The church's foes will pine away, like churlish-hearted Nabal,
For our deliverer came this day like the great Zorobabel.[5]

Schomberg was killed, but the crossing of the river was forced and James's army fell back in defeat towards Dublin, which could not now be held. The war, however, continued for another year. The Stuart cause suffered another disaster at the battle of Aughrim, in Co. Galway, in July 1691, and finally the forces supporting King James were driven back to Limerick where they were besieged by Ginkel, the victor of Aughrim. The city was surrendered, on terms, in October by the Jacobite commander Patrick Sarsfield, Earl of Lucan, who sought and obtained transport to France for such of the defeated army as wished to go, some guarantee of protection against further confiscation of land for those who wished to stay, and a measure of toleration for Roman Catholics. The terms, especially those relating to toleration for Roman Catholics, were not ratified by the Protestant Irish parliament, and further extensive confiscations followed the surrender of Limerick. By the end of the century almost all the land of Ireland was in the hands of new owners, and the old landowning class, the Old English and native Irish gentry and aristocracy, were dispossessed.

In Ulster, all Protestants, all the colonists, felt that they had earned and shared in a victory, which they saw as one for 'freedom, religion and laws' over royal absolutism, popish superstition and Gaelic barbarism. In the rest of the country, a much more dispersed colonial class, of English origin and Protestant religion, landowners and townsmen, found themselves in a position where they could exploit freely the great mass of the people, defeated, alien in religion and culture, leaderless. They proceeded to do so.

The Williamite settlement ended for a long time to come the possibility that a Catholic property-owning class would dominate Ireland. It established instead a Protestant ascendancy which proceeded to consolidate its position by enacting a penal code against Roman Catholics designed essentially not to punish Catholics for their beliefs, nor to convert them to any form of Protestantism, but to prevent them from obtaining, as a group, property, position, influence or power. The penal laws ratified, as it were, the identification of opposed classes in terms of religion. They secured the privileges of planters, settlers, speculators, and adventurers in land and ensured that the great mass of the native stock of the country should be deprived of land, property, education, and the prospect of advancement. No serious attempt was made to stamp out Catholic religious worship, but this for most of the eighteenth century was restricted to being a hole-and-corner affair, in rough shelters, little thatched chapels, or back alleys in the towns. The laws on the statute books directed against Roman Catholicism were sufficient, had they been fully applied, to stamp it out, but their application was erratic and selective, designed to convert or ruin landowners, to restrict the numbers of the clergy, and to fix the association of Roman Catholicism with poverty, humiliation, and servitude. Some efforts at new small-scale plantations of Protestants which were attempted round the turn of the century were not encouraged by the planters already established, who preferred to have their estates inhabited by hewers of wood and drawers of water who were deprived by the code of virtually all civil rights.

These larger landowners themselves were mostly of the established church and were seventeenth-century planters whose titles dated from the Cromwellian or Williamite settlements. In Ulster, titles in many of the large estates went back to dates earlier in the century. But in general the new Protestant ascendancy, north and south, belonged to a new class, an aristocracy and gentry of wealth rather than of ancient blood, which had

17

emerged as the eighteenth-century synthesis from the dialectic of seventeenth-century struggle in England: they represented in Ireland the oligarchy of landed and mercantile proprietors who ruled England. In the peace which ensued after the warfare of the seventeenth century, they built handsome houses, laid out their estates, and drew their rents, honouring by portraits and emblems in their houses the memory of William of Orange. These magnates were everywhere in Ireland now, but only in Ulster (apart from the towns) was there any sizeable Protestant population of lower degree. The poets and other scattered custodians of the Gaelic tradition who had the ear of great numbers of the poor people of the country express at this time not only resentment at the dispossession of their old patrons, but also contempt for the Smiths, Browns, Greens, Blacks, Joneses, and others who had taken the place of, as one poet put it:

... na flatha fá raibh mo shean roimh éag do Chríost.

... the chieftains my people served before the death of Christ.

As a result, the impoverished tenants did not even yield their new masters a grudging recognition of legitimacy, but comforted themselves with dreams of a Jacobite restoration when a golden age would return again – although indeed it made little difference to the lot of the ordinary tenant whether he served a Catholic Irish or a Protestant English master. The threat of a restoration remained, although it was a fading one, especially after the failures of the Jacobite cause in 1715 and 1745. The soldiers who had sailed in defeat from Limerick after its surrender in 1691 remained in the service of King James, and an Irish Brigade in the French army fought in the eighteenth-century wars wearing the uniform of the Stuart pretenders. The Irish contingent who stood to die at Culloden while the broken Highlanders swept by them in rout saw the final downfall of the Stuart cause, but throughout the eighteenth century the presence of the 'wild geese' on the Continent was remembered both by the government and by the oppressed people of Ireland, but above all by the Gaelic poets, whose writings are filled with that whining sentimentality about an imagined past which is one of the recurring vices of conservative traditions.

Not only Roman Catholics suffered disabilities in eighteenth-century Ireland. Dissenters also – and there were Quakers, Huguenots, and others as well as Presbyterians – were discriminated against although in much smaller measure than the Catholics (especially after 1719). They had made common cause with the established church against King James, and would continue to do so against Stuart pretenders, but they were not part of the ascendancy or the establishment, and they were given no more toleration or acknowledgement of their rights and needs than was deemed expedient. English policy in mercantile and industrial matters operated against them to the advantage of English products. At the same time, for most of the eighteenth century, they had little inclination to make common cause with the oppressed Catholics. Very large numbers of Ulster Presbyterians indeed escaped from their dilemma in the eighteenth century by migrating to America as their forefathers had migrated to Ireland from Scotland, seeking the democratic freedoms which dissenters in general so often sought in the seventeenth and eighteenth centuries, and which so often they were reluctant to extend to others. Ulster Presbyterians, or 'Scotch Irish', played their part later in the century in establishing, in the name of freedom, the United States, a slave-owning republic like those of antiquity.

This migration to some extent counteracted the effect of the inward flow of migration from Scotland in the seventeenth century. The Scots-Presbyterian bridgehead east of the Bann was not extended westward at full strength, and much of Ulster remained Gaelic-speaking through the eighteenth century. Indeed, on a local scale, Irish poetry and culture even flourished at times, especially in the south-east of the province, and in Antrim itself there were many Irish speakers. The mixture of English-language and Irish-language cultures, the development of the 'Ulster custom' in land tenure, the spread and development of the tradition of home crafts, all combined to give Ulster a more distinctive character than it had possessed in its now distant Gaelic past, while at the same time the plantation and settlement culture had over the years and decades gradually adapted itself to its environment. The northern Presbyterians were no longer Scots, but 'Scotch-Irish', Ulstermen – a distinctive kind of Irishmen, but still increasingly conscious of being Irishmen, with interests distinct from those of the English.

In the later eighteenth century the population of Ireland was increasing rapidly, and with this rise pressure increased on the land. In Ulster the pressure accentuated the division on the one hand between Protestant landlords and Protestant tenants and on the other between Protestant and Catholic tenants. Excessive rents and tithes (for Catholic and dissenter alike were required to contribute to the upkeep of the established church), enclosure, and the refusal to renew leases on reasonable terms added to the agrarian grievances which were widespread throughout the country from the middle of the century on. Agrarian secret societies were formed to impose, by threats and terror, moderation on the landlords and the parsons. Such societies in Munster were commonly known as 'Whiteboys' from the custom of wearing white shirts over their heads, and their methods there were extremely violent in the 1760s, provoking savage methods of suppression by the ascendancy class. In Ulster the 'Oakboys' and 'Hearts of Steel', who went about their activities in large bands, burning and terrorizing, were Protestant, but their resistance too was to the exactions of the landlords. In the meantime the ascendancy class itself, taking the example of the colonists in America who had asserted their rights against King George, were chafing at the restrictions on Irish trade imposed for the benefit of the English and at the control over Irish affairs exercised by the British parliament, which left the colony in Ireland in a position where it could not improve itself.

The war in America gave the colony the opportunity to assert itself. When France and Spain entered the war in support of the American colonists, the English government found itself without available troops to defend Ireland against invasion, and the Protestant ascendancy throughout the country met the emergency by forming volunteer corps. Having armed to defend the government's policy, they found themselves in a position to emulate the Americans and take effective action on their own grievances. At a great volunteer parade in Dublin in 1778 a cannon was displayed with a placard reading 'Free trade or this', and after the British surrender in America a convention of the Ulster volunteer corps at Dungannon demanded legislative independence for the colonists in Ireland. The Whig government which replaced Lord North's made concessions: the Dublin parliament was freed from the control of the Westminster parliament, Irish trade was freed from some of the restrictions which had hampered it. But while legislative independence was thus achieved by the colony, the London government in effect retained full control over the Irish executive. And 'divide and rule' remained the instinct of the executive in Dublin Castle, an instinct which had long been successfully acted on in practice.

In Ulster a renewal of sectarian feeling had already been provoked by clearances, enclosure, and the non-renewal of leases on reasonable terms. In many instances, Presbyterians, who had established a fair standard of living for themselves, were cleared from their holdings, when their leases fell due for renewal, in favour of native Irish Catholics, who were prepared to pay much higher rents and tolerate a bare subsistence-level standard of living. Protestant landlords, like the Marquess of Donegal, did not scruple to see their Protestant tenants driven out to make their way to America to be replaced by Catholics creeping wretchedly back to the lands where their ancestors had grazed the great herds. Thus the misery of the natives was exploited to undercut the livelihood of the smaller settlers, and the backwardness of rural Ireland at large threatened to drag down the relative prosperity established in the 'Ulster custom'.

The arming of the volunteer corps in Ulster when these economic tensions and grievances were at their height provoked outbreaks of violence. The volunteers who were armed to resist a French invasion and who then imposed their demands on the government were, with few exceptions, Protestants. There was a

21

general reluctance among the colony to see arms in the hands of the Catholic natives, but after the volunteers had achieved legislative independence, indeed after many of the corps had disbanded, a small minority of radicals in Dublin and Belfast favoured keeping them in being to take up the cause of giving some relief to Catholics. The 12th of July 1784 was celebrated by the Belfast volunteer corps with a parade at the Catholic chapel in that city, after which they presented a petition on behalf of the Catholics to Lord Charlemont, commander-in-chief of the volunteers and governor of the county of Armagh. Offers were also made to accept and train Catholics in the volunteers, and considerable quantities of arms were available, which, if these proposals were followed, would soon be in trained Catholic hands. It was, however, illegal, under the penal code, for Catholics to possess arms, and Protestant organizations, resembling the Oakboys, were now formed to raid Catholic houses at dawn and search for hidden arms. These were known as Peep O'Day Boys, and they became active in the middle 1780s, especially in the mixed county of Armagh.

In 1784 a Catholic intervened in a fight between two Presbyterians in Markethill, Co. Armagh, and the defeated Presbyterian in revenge raised a band, known as the Nappach Fleet, which began raiding Catholic houses. Although strong efforts were made to prevent a violent division on sectarian lines, conflict rapidly spread. A Dissenting minister raised a group known as the Defenders to protect Catholics, and this band succeeded in defeating the Nappach Fleet and compelling them to accept a Catholic leader. Other bands of Defenders were formed, however, and these soon became purely sectarian Catholic groups conducting a private war against the Peep O'Day Boys. The Presbyterian tenants and craftsmen were not prepared to tolerate the arming of Catholics, whether in volunteer corps or in agrarian secret societies, but their basic fear was of economic competition from the Catholics. The willingness of the Catholics to pay extravagant rents had been a grievance for some time and there were other sources of economic grievance also. In Armagh there were Catholic weavers and, although the

Peep O'Day Boys ostensibly carried out their raids to ensure the enforcement of the law forbidding Catholics to possess arms, their early raids singled out these weavers.

Disorder spread through Co. Armagh and continued, although two troops of horse were sent to the affected area in 1787 to restore order. Charlemont then raised a new force of volunteers, from among the Protestant population, to act as a police force, and declared his intention to exclude Peep O'Day Boys, in order to preserve the impartiality of the force. The new volunteers, however, paraded with Orange (Williamite) emblems through Defender areas, and made a display of Protestant ascendancy which was provocative in itself. They also became involved in anti-Catholic incidents, and in the upshot the formation of the corps added to the conflict it had been intended to curb. The Defender movement spread to many other counties, including those in the south where Protestants were in a small minority, often taking on the old character of an anti-landlord agrarian secret society. It was centrally organized as a federated society, which could concentrate fairly large bodies of men from different districts if they were required. It was concerned solely with agrarian and sectarian matters, and its secret oath affirmed loyalty to the crown. The Defender activity was successful by the 1790s in forcing down rents and tithes in some areas.

The volunteers were dissolved in 1793 and replaced by a militia, which was largely Catholic, Catholics being also given the franchise. These measures, which originated with the British government, were connected with the outbreak of war with revolutionary France and were intended to secure Ireland partly by making some concession to the mass of the people. This further alarmed Protestants throughout the country, but especially in the north, since the Defenders infiltrated the militia just as in the preceding decade the Peep O'Day Boys had infiltrated the volunteers. A federate league of Protestants was now attempted to counter the Defender organization more effectively than could the merely local organizations like the Peep O'Day Boys. James Wilson, a Presbyterian farmer of Co.

Tyrone, formed an oath-bound group at Benburb in 1793. They called themselves Orange Boys, and he proposed extending the organization on federated lines, but this extension did not take place in fact until 1795.

In that year Defenders were active in many parts of the country, causing great alarm and disquiet to the government as well as to the Protestant tenant-farmers and landlords. An assembly of their forces in September near Loughgall in Co. Armagh, to loot Protestant farms, led, after a week's skirmishing, to a pitched battle between them and Protestants who came with arms from the surrounding districts to engage them. The Defenders were driven off, with thirty or forty dead, from the crossroads known as the Diamond where the battle was fought. Immediately afterwards the victorious Protestants formed an oath-bound league on the lines which had been suggested by James Wilson, but his Presbyterian radicalism was rejected and he left the Diamond without joining the new association, which was wholly or largely composed of members of the established church. Its first head was the innkeeper at Loughgall, James Sloan. This was the origin of the Orange movement, which has played an important part in Ulster to the present day. It came into being to counteract the Catholic Defenders, who in Ulster directed most of their activities against the Protestant tenant-farmers and craftsmen, although in the south they had chiefly acted against landlords and parsons of the established church. They in turn had come into being to counteract the Protestant Peep O'Day Boys.

Another society had in the meantime been formed, under the influence of the French Revolution. This was the Society of United Irishmen, founded in Belfast in October 1791 by Theobald Wolfe Tone and a few others. These were middle-class radicals from Dublin and Belfast, representing a movement which had continued since the Dungannon convention of the volunteer corps. The main supports of the movement had been Ulster dissenters, in sympathy with the American colonists, but there were some Catholics and numbers of established churchmen, aiming at an extension of the gains made in 1782, and at equality for Catholics. The earlier leaders of the movement had been moderate Whigs like Lord Charlemont, but the events of the French revolution encouraged middle-class radicals like Tone (a Dublin Protestant by origin) to seek much more drastic changes. The new society was founded to establish the 'rights of man' in Ireland by means of parliamentary reform and full religious equality. It was in touch with the Paris Jacobins and with similar societies in Britain, and it was, although not overtly at first, revolutionary in intent. By the time the battle of the Diamond was fought, Tone had already moved to the stage of illegality, through dealings with a French agent (who was arrested and convicted of treason and committed suicide in the dock in Dublin), and had gone to America on his way to France. Societies of United Irishmen were being organized throughout the country to prepare for revolution with French help, and were preaching the rights of man, and urging all to forget religious differences and rejoice in 'the common name of Irishman'.

In Co. Armagh, however, the formation of the Orange order was followed by a violent campaign by Protestants designed to drive Catholics from their homes and into the province of Connacht, where indeed some thousands of refugees fled, abandoning their houses and holdings to be taken over by the Protestants. The reaction of the government and of the landlords to this new outbreak of violence was ambiguous. Co. Armagh was in a state of considerable disorder and one of the effects of the violence and the expulsions was to lower rents, while Orangeism itself was essentially a lower-class movement at this stage. However, at a time when revolutionary and radical ideas, some of which had a strong appeal for the Presbyterians of Ulster, were being widely disseminated, when the dangerous conjunction of the peasant-based Defender movement with the urban-based United Irishmen was becoming a revolutionary reality, the conservative interests in the country who wished to maintain the Williamite settlement and the Protestant ascendancy were slow to move against the Orangemen. These showed their strength in 1796 by a parade of about 5,000

25

unarmed men to the Diamond, and the gentry began moving cautiously towards support of the movement. It was at this time that Thomas Knox, a magistrate of Dungannon, wrote:

As for the Orangemen, we have a rather difficult card to play; they must not be entirely discountenanced – on the contrary, we must in a certain degree uphold them, for with all their licentiousness, on them we must rely for the preservation of our lives and properties, should critical times occur.[6]

Numbers of 'loyal associations' were now organized by the gentry, and these from the beginning were closely connected with the Orange lodges: they were forerunners of yeomanry regiments which were raised with government consent in 1796 and 1797 to meet the growing danger of invasion and rebellion, the militia being regarded as not sufficiently trustworthy after the relief of 1793 had failed to satisfy Catholic demands. In the meantime the reports of Orange excesses in Armagh and Down, exaggerated by rumour and carried far from Ulster by refugees, had given force to the recruiting now being secretly carried on by the United Irishmen, who everywhere were now winning Defenders into their ranks and thus bringing their Jacobin ideas to the aroused and by now revolutionary masses of the country people. In the winter of 1796, Tone returned to Ireland, or rather to within sight of the coast, for in December of that year he sailed into Bantry Bay, with a French fleet carrying an expeditionary force under the command of General Hoche. Weather and mischance prevented a landing, and the fleet sailed away again. Had the French landed it would have been the signal for a general rising, but as it was the country remained relatively quiet.

In this complex and dangerous situation, it was Ulster that caused the government most concern, and it was recognized that the situation was drastically different in different parts of the province. The overwhelmingly Protestant areas, east of the Bann in Antrim and Down, were the most disaffected, and Belfast, now a vigorously growing town, was the centre of revolutionary sentiment. This was where the United Irishmen had been founded in 1791, and it was here that they were strongest and had most support. Here they published their radical newspaper, the *Northern Star*. In Belfast, almost simultaneously with the adoption of French revolutionary libertarianism, the radicals had made their appeal not only to the grievances of the Catholics, which they proposed to remedy, but also to the Gaelic past. A remarkable festival was organized in the city in 1792, to provide an opportunity of recording something of Ireland's music and traditions. This was the harp festival held on 11, 12, and 13 July, which was promoted by Henry Joy (uncle of Henry Joy McCracken) and Dr James McDonnell, who engaged Edward Bunting, then a young organist, to take down the music. Harpists were invited and ten of them performed, six of whom were blind and one of whom was ninety-seven years old. Wolfe Tone, watching and listening in the gallery of the assembly hall, was impatient – 'strum strum, and be hanged!' – but the assembly showed an effort on the part of these descendants of settlers to understand the ancient native culture, and to achieve a new revolutionary nationalism in which settler and native together would achieve a republic of truly united Irishmen. However, it was probably republicanism rather than any such nationalism that chiefly animated the Presbyterians of Antrim and Down in 1797, when they caused the government so much disquiet.

The policy followed in the north was to foment the conflict between Orangemen and Defenders in mid-Ulster and to proceed firmly but cautiously towards the disarmament of east Ulster. Lieutenant-General Lake, who was charged with the security of the north and issued a disarmament proclamation in March 1797, was advised by his subordinate at Dungannon, General Knox:

I have arranged . . . to increase the animosity between Orangemen and the United Irish. Upon that animosity depends the safety of the centre counties of the North. Were the Orangemen disarmed or put down, or were they coalesced with the other party, the whole of Ulster would be as bad as Antrim and Down.[7]

The real issue which now emerged in the crisis of 1797 was whether the Ulster Protestants – but especially the Presbyterians

27

– would support the government (and the landlords) against the Catholics, or the Catholics against the landlords (and the government). The dilemma was not confined to the Protestant tenant farmers. Now that the United Irishmen had been driven underground and were plotting revolution, the middle-class radicals who had joined the United Irish societies and other such organizations, and had toasted the 'rights of man' in the early 1790s, must either commit themselves beyond the law or lean over backwards from the edge of that precipice to demonstrate their loyalty and respectability. Many of them joined the Orange order, as did many of the suspect militia, moving from the suspected danger of one extreme to the actuality of another. And the disarming of Ulster went ahead, in the most repressive fashion. General Lake's troops, some of them half-trained militia, carried out a campaign of terror, burning, flogging, and torturing. The Monaghan militia and the Welsh fencible regiment known as the Ancient Britons distinguished themselves in this activity. It was the Monaghans who destroyed the printing press of the *Northern Star* and broke the spirit of radical Belfast in a reconstructionist orgy of revenge by Catholic servants of the government against Presbyterian supporters of the Catholic cause.

The middle ground of Irish politics had few occupants by the year 1797. The cautious liberalism of leaders like Grattan and Charlemont which had animated the 1780s had been overtaken by the events of the French Revolution and the hornet's nest of radical ideas which had thereby been released to buzz about the heads of the statesmen of the 1790s. Pitt in 1793 had forced through the concessionary measures of Catholic relief and replacement of the volunteers by militia regiments against the resistance of John Fitzgibbon, Earl of Clare, and his associates in the right-wing 'castle clique' in the Irish executive on the outbreak of the war with France. The half-measures involved in concessions had failed to satisfy Catholics or radicals, who had instead become more radical in their demands and their methods. Those liberals who were not prepared to follow this move to the left must demonstrate their loyalty by moving to the right instead – and moderation perished. In May 1797, the liberal Grattan, on the defeat of a reform bill, following the example of Fox in England, withdrew from parliamentary politics and the scene was set for the politics of violence. The fate of Ulster now turned on the decisions, often made one way or the other by a hair's breadth, of Protestant democrats and radicals, whether to opt for orange or green.

Meantime the government went forward with its policy of disarming and terrorizing one county after another, and also of infiltrating spies and informers into the ranks of the United Irishmen. One of the most effective of these was Thomas Reynolds of Kildare, who became a member of the Leinster directory of the United organization and regularly supplied accurate information to the government, but there were many others. In March 1798, on the basis of its ample information the government struck, arresting most of the leaders of the central organization, and in fact crippling it as an effective military conspiracy. A proclamation of martial law followed and the savage repression of the country by the military proceeded at an enhanced rate. The gentry and agents of the government, having moved from a reprehension of ruffianly Orangemen almost as strong as their reprehension of ruffianly Defenders to the realization that their interests might be served by tolerating or even encouraging the same Orangemen, now began to do more than encourage the Orange lodges: they began to join them. The Dublin lodge was founded on 4 June 1797 and was joined by many people of position and influence. Orangeism, raised from its plebeian origins two years before, was now a national movement sponsored in effect, although unofficially, by the government, and on 12 July in the same year General Lake reviewed Orange parades at Lisburn and Lurgan.

The plans of the United Irishmen for a rising had been linked with plans for a French landing, and Tone and others had long negotiated with the Directory to this end. From their point of view things looked hopeful at the end of 1797 when an expeditionary force began to be assembled in the Channel Ports and Bonaparte was appointed commander-in-chief, but after that they encountered a series of delays and disappointments. Discussions were in progress as to whether revolutionary action should be taken even without the certainty of French help, when the government by its arrests in March 1798 shattered the central organization. The further government action of disarming the counties and terrorizing the population met with a good deal of success – large quantities of arms were handed in – but the uprising took place none the less.

It was now, however, wholly uncoordinated. Late in May bodies of United men assembled in the counties around Dublin, armed largely with pikes. Almost simultaneously the spread of the government 'croppy'-hunt (a cropped head was an expression of republican opinions) to Co. Wexford gave rise to rumours of an impending Orange pogrom in that county, and brought out the Wexford men. Massacres of prisoners by the garrison of Dunlavin and by loyalists at Carnew, inspired by panic, embittered the United men, who defeated a body of cavalry sent to oppose them and soon had almost all of Wexford under their control. After two weeks of fierce and bloody fighting in the south-east, in which the tenant-farmers and journeymen of Wexford showed a remarkable capacity for facing regular troops in prolonged battle, the rising was still spreading, and early in June the United men of Antrim, led by the Presbyterian Henry Joy McCracken, marched on the town of Antrim and occupied most parts of the county. They had not a full muster. Most of the Catholic Defenders of the country, who had been assimilated into the United men, failed to turn out, and McCracken's force consisted largely of Presbyterians who, like himself, were fighting for republican ideas, civil liberties, and social justice. The government commander, General Nugent, won an overwhelming victory over McCracken's forces in the town of Antrim, and then, by a shrewd combination of promises of clemency with threats to life and property, he rapidly secured the suppression of the rising throughout the county – just at the moment when the rebellion spread to County Down. Here the United men's commander was a Lisburn draper named Henry Monroe. Here too, the

Catholic Defenders for the most part failed to join the Presbyterians in the rising, and here too General Nugent's troops defeated the insurgents in battle, at Ballinahinch.

Just as rumours, exaggerated but partly true, of Orange burnings, floggings, and wreckings had helped to spark the Wexford rising, so other rumours, again exaggerated but again partly true, of Catholic atrocities against Protestants in Wexford were now reaching the north, even as the Presbyterians of Down and Antrim rose against the crown. The Irish republic was proclaimed in north and south in those weeks of May and June 1798, the insurgent commanders dated their letters and instructions to 'the first year of liberty', caps of liberty and green banners appeared everywhere, north and south. In Ulster as well as Leinster that 'respectable class' of citizens in whom Tone had placed his trust, the 'men of no property', breathed the heady air of revolution and lived briefly the fantasy of a world where the mighty had fallen and the common people ruled. But the ideal of the union of all Irishmen in a common brotherhood irrespective of creed – which, it may be said, was fostered in the revolutionary movement especially by men like Tone who had no very strong religious conviction of any kind themselves – had not been in the air long enough to overcome the old animosities, and the old fears and distrust between Catholics and Protestants. Tone's religious toleration was easygoing and indifferent – 'to fear the Catholics is a vulgar and ignorant prejudice' – but while his indifference to theology was probably shared by many gentlemen of the ascendancy establishment, their toleration was of a different kind, being extended, in the interest of keeping the lower orders divided, to sectarian bigotry.

After the defeat of the uprisings in Wexford and the north, two small French expeditions did arrive, separately, although the main French invasion force had sailed not for England or Ireland but for Egypt, with Napoleon. Both were defeated, one after a force under General Humbert had landed at Killala in the west and had marched to central Ireland, the other in a naval engagement in Lough Swilly in Co. Donegal, in which

Tone, on board the French flagship, was taken prisoner.

The effects of the risings of 1798 and their bloody suppression were deep and lasting. Pitt decided to deal with the urgent problem of Ireland by forcing through a union of the two kingdoms of Ireland and England with a single parliament in Westminster. On the Irish people, north and south, the rising made a deep impression. It marks the beginning of modern Irish nationalism in the full sense, for it made the first break between the Gaelic past and the era of participation in political mass movements of one kind and another for the Catholic masses of the people. For the Protestant people of Ulster it marks a turning point too: the radical republicanism, the levelling egalitarianism, which seemed natural to the self-reliant Presbyterian spirit and for which Belfast especially was noted in the late eighteenth century, had led the merchants and tradesmen and small farmers of Antrim and Down to open their minds to the ideas of liberty, equality, and, most remarkable of all, fraternity, and to contemplate joining with their Catholic fellows in making another America in Ireland. That spirit was distracted by the remarkable and rapid growth of Orangeism from 1795 (initially largely among Anglicans in the areas where there were large numbers of Catholics); it was cowed and crushed by the brutal pacification of north-east Ulster carried out by General Lake before the risings and by the ruthless suppression of the rebellion; it was dismayed by the stories of vengeance exacted on Protestants in the Wexford rising. The year of terror and misery answered, among others, the question whether the Protestant lower orders in Ulster would combine with the Catholics against landlords and rulers, or would combine with landlords and rulers against Catholics. The Dublin administration divided Ulster and ruled it.

2   Croppies Lie Down

To the glorious, pious and Immortal Memory of King William III,
who saved us from Rogues and Roguery, Slaves and Slavery, Knaves
and Knavery, Popes and Popery, from brass money and wooden
shoes; and whoever denies this Toast may he be slammed, crammed
and jammed into the muzzle of the great gun of Athlone, and the gun
fired into the Pope's belly, and the Pope into the Devil's Belly, and the
Devil into Hell, and the door locked and the key in an Orangeman's
pocket. *Orange toast, early nineteenth century* [8]

In the meantime, however, the Dublin parliament was suppressed by the Act of Union, which came into effect on 1 January 1801. While a separate, and subordinate, executive
continued to function in Dublin Casle, Irish members were now
elected to Westminster, where, of course, they formed but a
small proportion of the total number in the House of
Commons. The peerage, no longer attending the Dublin House
of Lords, tended to move away to semi-permanent residence in
England. The union had been looked on with disfavour or actively opposed by many sections and interests among the colony
in Ireland, especially those like Grattan who had been active in
securing legislative independence eighteen years before and
who felt that again their interests would be neglected or even
discriminated against in favour of English interests. Among
those who were opposed to the union were the great majority of
Orangemen throughout the country, but they found themselves
in a dilemma, for they did not want to go openly or as a body
against the government. Meeting in Dublin, the masters of the
Orange lodges resolved 'that, having associated merely to resist

insurrection, it did not concern them to interfere with respect to any other political concern', and so the Order remained officially neutral on the issue.

Dublin, although it was still the seat of the Irish executive and the place of residence of the Viceroy, had a reduced political connection with the provinces after the union, since these no longer sent members to parliament there, and in Ulster a new provincial capital was emerging with the growth of Belfast. This was already an important city in the eighteenth century, prosperous and handsome, with thriving and growing industries, and at the time of the union it had a population of about 20,000. It continued to grow rapidly, to 70,000 in 1841 and 119,000 in 1861, becoming the largest city in Ulster and the second in Ireland. It was a busy port, outclassing Dublin in volume of trade in the 1830s, exporting large quantities of agricultural produce. Tanning, brewing, and distilling were carried on, and cotton mills had been established in the city and its region by the turn of the century. Fine linen was an important Ulster product which was marketed through the city, although not much was produced there until the great development of mill-spinning of linen in the 1830s.

The liberal tradition for which Belfast had been known in the eighteenth century continued into the opening decades of the nineteenth, although the cutting edge of its radicalism had been much blunted by the events of 1798. However, down to the 1830s the Presbyterians of the town were still distinguished from the Protestants (and Catholics) of mid-Ulster by their willingness to live in harmony with traditions and creeds other than their own. It was, until the end of the eighteenth century, essentially a town of the plantation period, overwhelmingly Protestant in character during the early stages of its growth; its population had been relatively free from the pressures felt by the less densely settled rural descendants of the colonists west of the Bann. The small Catholic population of the town had not been seen as a threat to the livelihood or the dominance of the Protestant inhabitants and they had been treated with the greatest friendliness by the majority. Industrial development changed this situation. Just as in the countryside in the late eighteenth century resentment of Catholics had grown among the lower orders of Protestants largely because of the fear of undercutting in the matter of rents, so now in the early nineteenth century, as poor Catholics crowded into west Belfast to work in the city's developing industries, similar resentments began to arise from similar fears of undercutting and economic competition at the subsistence level. The fear that their rather better standard of living would be undermined remained alive among the descendants of the settlers. By the middle of the century a third of Belfast's population, and this the poorest part of it, was Catholic, and the city was already deeply divided by resentments and fears.

In Ireland as a whole the new century and the Act of Union brought a changed situation. The old nation was now plainly seen to have been not merely conquered but destroyed. Dreams of a Jacobite restoration, cherished in the eighteenth century by the clients of the old aristocratic Celtic order, had long faded. The great mass of the people had a hard and unremitting struggle merely to live: by the Union they were subjected to a new and more efficient system of colonial exploitation. They were rack-rented, and a great part of the rents went out of the country to absentee landlords living in England. The colonial system operated on a number of levels: the maintenance of English political and economic control over the island as a whole: the maintenance of the landlords as the class whose interests had priority in the administration of Irish affairs; the maintenance of the colonial 'Protestant ascendancy', an alliance of the semi-feudal landlord group with an exclusive middle class of merchants, manufacturers, professional people, and 'placemen' of the government. Two opposed and wholly different traditions faced each other in most of the country – settler and native – and there was little more integration of the two than there had been in the seventeenth century. They were kept apart by their economic and political relationship; they were distinguished still by deep cultural differences for which the most convenient label was that of religious denomination.

35

The native culture had, however, suffered mortal wounds, and already in the early nineteenth century the Irish language, which embodied it, was in full withdrawal before the advance of English. There seemed to be two possible ways for the poor Catholic Irishman to make some improvement in his position in the Protestant-English-dominated world: one was to abandon his religion in favour of Protestantism, the other to abandon his language in favour of English. It was the second way which the people chose, largely perhaps because even if they chose the other, they would still find it necessary to abandon their language anyway.

In this colonial system Protestant Ulster was increasingly exceptional in character. Here 'the Protestant ascendancy' is a term which would need further clarification. There was an ascendancy which had the same characteristics as the ascendancy elsewhere in the country, and indeed was part of it. But there were also in the north, and in the north alone, Protestant masses, who, unlike the landlords and placemen, did not maintain a continuing connection with Britain and a colonial relationship to Ireland. They had been assimilated to the country and were themselves an exploited class, paying rent to landlords or, in rapidly increasing numbers, producing the new industrial wealth for factory wages. They had inherited, from the special privileges of their settler ancestors, the 'Ulster custom' in land-tenure, which left them with a feeling that their position was superior to that of the natives of other parts of the country, but with the abiding fear that they might be reduced to the condition of these. The landlords, especially from the late eighteenth century onward, had exploited this fear, fomenting the conflict between poor Protestants and poorer Catholics in competition for land, in a kind of rent-auction where the poorest could make the highest bidding because they could better tolerate poverty, which led to the explosion of violence between Defenders and Orangemen at the end of the century. This conflict was now transferred to Belfast and the growing industrial towns, where it was still a competition for the means of livelihood, and where the Protestant worker, however

wretched he might be, could still be persuaded that he belonged
to the Protestant ascendancy so long as he could keep his Catholic neighbour in a still more wretched state. The alliance between the poor Protestants in the industrial towns with the true
ascendancy was real in the sense that the rulers of Ireland and
of Ulster were not prepared in any circumstances to permit
Catholic domination. A 35 per cent proportion of Catholics in
the population was about right to produce the fullest competition among the workers; this was the proportion reached in
Belfast by the second half of the nineteenth century, and was
the proportion achieved by the Ulster Unionists in this century
when they drew the boundaries of the new state of Northern
Ireland.

The Catholic church, as an organization and institution, was
obviously of considerable importance in this situation. 'Roman
Catholic' in relation to the conflict over land and employment
was almost a racial term, but it also connoted membership of a
church not all of whose members were peasants, and not all of
whose members, for that matter, were Irish. The church as an
institution in Ireland had weathered the eighteenth century and
the popery laws in good shape. Its leaders, the bishops, had
contrived to maintain a supply of clergy, even if the supply was
often inadequate, and to keep close contact with the people,
achieving probably a greater influence over them than in the
Middle Ages, when they were free from religious persecution
and when there were lay leaders to compete with the clerical.
The bishops throughout the most difficult periods had continued to affirm their most subservient loyalty to the established
order and had collaborated, short of acquiescence in the persecution, with the government. They were aware that England's
various alliances with Catholic powers would temper the rigour
of the penal code, apart from the fact that extirpation of the
Catholic religion was not its real object. They were free of
government interference in their internal affairs – if only because such interference would have given them recognition –
and could operate in concert and with a large measure of autonomy to further their ends. These were, in the first place, to

obtain such relief from the penal code as would admit the free practice of the religion, and – almost equally important to them – freedom to provide Catholic education. The Royal College of St Patrick at Maynooth was established by the government in 1795 to be a seminary for Roman Catholic clergy, as one of the conciliatory measures undertaken by Pitt at that time to help secure Ireland after the outbreak of war with the French. Roman Catholics, however, continued to suffer disabilities which deprived them of even a modest share in the establishment: they could not, for example, sit in parliament. It need hardly be said that the institutional church had no sympathy with the French cause or with the 'rights of man', nor was there any church interest which would be served by the success of a separatist movement in Ireland. It is true that some priests, notably in Wexford, had taken part, even as leaders, in the 1798 rising, and that, in the suppression of the insurrection, priests, as well as a number of Presbyterian ministers in Ulster, were hanged, but these were in no way representative of the political church. The objective of Catholic leaders after the relief act of 1793 was, on the contrary, to secure within the colonial system a position for the small but growing Catholic middle-class, as well as protection for such Catholic proprietors as still remained. Nor was 'the common name of Irishman' of any interest to the political church, although there were always individual churchmen with some patriotic or nationalist feelings, and there were times when such feelings affected many of the bishops. On the whole, however, the conservative, anti-revolutionary, and anti-Protestant interest of Rome would best be served by a respectable Catholic voice in Westminster and by Catholic pressures on the English government which would modify but not radically change things, rather than by any intransigent opposition to the political order of things in the new United Kingdom. The main lever the church could use to effect such changes of position, however, was the mass of poor Catholic people in Ireland, who had shown that they were open to influence by radical ideologies and who had more to gain from overthrow of the colonial system than from its modification.

In the early nineteenth century the movement for what came to be known as Catholic emancipation was led by Daniel O'Connell, a lawyer who belonged to one of the rare Catholic families of native Irish stock that had survived as landlords all through the wars, rebellions, and confiscations of the seventeenth and eighteenth centuries. The agitation was sharpened, on the Catholic side, by a feeling of disappointment and a sense of betrayal, for they had understood that the union was to be followed immediately by emancipation; on the Protestant side it was accompanied by a shift of political position, since the Protestant colonists had been deprived by the union of their independence of action in Irish affairs, and they could now defend themselves against Catholic domination and the overthrow of the Protestant ascendancy only through England. Emancipation – seats in parliament and equal political rights for Catholics – was seen as a threat to the ascendancy, and the great majority of Protestants were soon supporters of the union and were concerned to have an effective party in their support among the legislators and ruling class in England. Fear of the very numbers of the Irish Catholics as a threat to the colonial settlement now extended from the lower-class Protestants of Ulster, from whom it had never been wholly absent, to the Protestant establishment in general.

The numbers in the country were growing at a rate which was indeed alarming. At the beginning of the century the population of the island was larger than it is now – about 5,000,000. By 1841 it had risen to more than 8,000,000. Most of these lived on the land, and the increase was not due to industrial expansion or increased employment, but mainly to the way in which the land in Ireland was exploited by the rack-renting landlord system. The mass of the people lived, at the barest subsistence level, on the easily cultivated potato, supplemented with milk or buttermilk. Tenant holdings were divided and sub-divided as numbers grew, marginal lands were brought under cultivation. There was no incentive to thrift, improvement or taking any thought for the morrow: improvement in a man's holding brought an increase in rent; there was nothing for him to save or put by.

They married young. The evils and dangers of the situation were apparent to all, but no effective remedy could be attempted without going against the prevailing *laissez-faire* philosophy, and the chief measures that the government, in these circumstances, found it could take to cope with the misery and distress of Ireland were further instalments of military repression as the situation worsened from famine to famine up to the great mass famine of the 1840s.

Catholic relief, granted in 1793, had come after a period of agitation by a Catholic committee (of which Wolfe Tone was employed as secretary) and with the encouragement of a section of the Irish Protestants. A similar alliance was attempted after the union, when Protestants such as Grattan spoke in Westminster on behalf of the Catholics, whose spokesmen in Ireland were an extremely conservative group including some of the handful of Catholic landlords. A struggle ensued between these conservatives and a group, with whom O'Connell was to be associated, representing the more aggressive emerging Catholic middle class. The issue was the 'veto question', the acceptance or rejection of emancipation on conditions which would give the English government control of the appointment of Irish Roman Catholic bishops, and the middle-class party were successful in having these terms rejected. Emancipation was rejected with them, however, and it was plain that no aggressive Catholic policy on this matter could be forced through by reliance on members of the Protestant colony. The strategy followed, and ably carried out by O'Connell, was to make use of the sheer weight of numbers of the Catholic masses of rural Ireland, although emancipation was a middle-class issue of little if any practical interest to them. O'Connell, however, by his birth and origin and by his legal work, had acquired a knowledge and understanding of the common people, and he realized that, destitute, despised and despairing as they were, they would respond to almost any issue which could give them a sense of involvement on their own behalf in politics – and Catholic emancipation touched at least the faith which they professed. They were involved through speeches at mass meetings, through being asked to contribute a penny a week 'Catholic rent', which gave them a sense of commitment to the cause, and above all through being required to show courage by standing up to their landlords, especially at election times. The demands O'Connell made on the Catholic masses were met, and he was soon leader of a movement of mass democracy whose force and vigour caused alarm to the government, and eventually brought about the bill for emancipation in 1829, and the return of O'Connell himself to parliament in Westminster.

Not only the government was alarmed. Fear of the 'rabble', or the 'mob', was very real and alive among the ruling classes of the eighteenth and early nineteenth centuries, and the prospect of the millions of Irish Catholics, organized as a political force which demanded and might receive equal political rights with minority groups, caused widespread disquiet among Protestants, high and low, in England and Ireland. This fear was met in part by a provision, made simultaneously with the Emancipation Act, which disenfranchised the forty-shilling freeholders, who had borne the brunt of the agitation in confrontations with the landlords, and restricted the franchise to those with freeholds of £10 or over. O'Connell accepted and agreed to this; he was willing to sacrifice these foot-soldiers of his campaign in the interest of the achievement of his central aim, which was the opening of parliament and position to the Catholic middle class. In this, as in his campaign as a whole, he was supported by the Catholic clergy.

Orangeism had suffered a temporary decline in Ulster after 1798, being as it was in its early years a movement against 'insurrection', but there was much to keep it alive, and members of government and ascendancy continued to patronize or at least tolerate it, even while despising it. Robert Emmet's abortive rising of 1803 in Dublin, although it really demonstrated that the spirit and organization of the United Irishmen were no longer a force, gave some stimulus to the Orange movement, but the end of the Napoleonic war in 1815, which was followed by disbandment of the (largely Catholic) militia, marked a period when it seemed for some years to have served its purpose. The Protestant interests, high and low, felt their position to have been made secure, according to the principles of the attorney-general of the time, William Saurin (an Orangeman who had led a movement against the union among the yeomanry at the beginning of 1799):

We ought not to deceive ourselves. Ireland must be either a Catholic or Protestant state – let us choose. But he is a Utopian who believes he has discovered a nostrum by which it can be both, or either.[9]

New agrarian disturbances (of 'ribbonmen') in the south at the beginning of the 1820s, the new administration of Lord Wellesley, who was reputed (an ill-deserved reputation) to favour Catholics, and then the O'Connell agitation for emancipation, all gave renewed vigour to Orangeism throughout the country. The custom had been established since the foundation of the order of making provocative displays of the Protestant ascendancy by holding armed parades with Orange emblems through Catholic areas, in the southern provinces as well as Ulster. These parades were all the more intimidating when those who took part in them were soldiers of yeomanry or other regiments who wore (usually contrary to orders) orange lilies and other supernumerary insignia on the king's uniform. Such parades were now discouraged by the authorities for fear of the effects of their provocation; when to this was added the organization of the Catholic Association, Liberal Clubs, and other associations for furthering the emancipation cause, the fears which were the driving force of the Orange movement revived. The very character of O'Connell's movement, its reliance on the weight of Catholic numbers and on arousing the common people to the realization that, united, they had some power to act politically, its specific connection with the religious question, the close involvement in it of priests of Rome throughout the country, all were calculated to alarm the settler mentality of Protestant Ulster in particular. To add to this, O'Connell, encouraged by the new attitude of the authorities in the 1820s, made a series of speeches attacking Orangeism. When the Orangemen began organizing against him, he planned and tried to carry through a march, with banners and military discipline but without arms or violence, of thousands of Catholics through Protestant Ulster. The non-violent march was led by John Lawless of Belfast, and proceeded northward from Dublin, but was opposed in Co. Monaghan and beyond by large numbers of armed Orangemen – yeomen out of uniform. The O'Connellites lost two dead in the first encounter, and when they reached the outskirts of Armagh they were obliged to abandon the enterprise. O'Connell realized in time the danger of challenging the Orangemen in the areas where they were strong, and he disengaged. By this stage the Orange movement had members in positions of great power and influence in England among Tories who were determined to resist what they saw as an attack on the constitution, and these O'Connell preferred to circumvent rather than confront violently.

The Orange movement by now had moved into a position of alliance with Tories and support for the union. On the two issues which now arose, repeal of the union (the cause which O'Connell took up after emancipation was won) and parliamentary reform, they adopted this new position with few dissidents. The days had gone when Orange lodges could express a general sentiment in issuing a declaration that 'as Orangemen we consider the extinction of our separate Legislature as the extinction of the Irish Nation', and could go on to demand support for 'the independence of Ireland and the constitution of 1782'. The sentiment itself was not altogether dead, and it was not the union as such which appealed to the Orangemen – indeed within their own sphere they remained as anxious as ever to be independent of English domination – but the union was (it now seemed to them) the only safe bulwark against the threat of domination by the Catholic native Irish. The Orangemen in their turn became more aggressive again, and while their excesses continued once more to be an embarrassment to governments, they were now an established part of the working machinery not only of the Protestant ascendancy but of English colonialism in Ireland. The rough-and-ready rank-and-file members who formed the broad proletarian base of the movement were difficult to control at times, but they had repeatedly demonstrated that in time of crisis they could be depended upon to stand by the establishment and the Williamite constitution and settlement, which had in fact been little modified by the union of the two kingdoms. The vigour of their movement could be measured by the processions they held each year on 12 July, the anniversary of the battle of the Boyne. These processions were far more than a mere formal commemoration; they were a central part of the purpose and meaning of the Orange institute:

We also associate in honour of King William III, Prince of Orange, whose name we bear, as supporters of his glorious memory, and the true religion by him completely established; and in order to prove our gratitude and affection for his name, we will annually celebrate the victory over James at the Boyne on the 1st day of July in every year, which day shall be our grand day for ever.[10]

They were meant to be noisy and flamboyant, to intimidate and cow the Catholics, in accordance with the Protestant slogan 'Croppies lie down!', and to assert, often with show of arms, the Protestant ascendancy. At the other end of the social scale, there were now Orangemen everywhere in the military and civil service of the government, among Tory lords and commoners in England, and among the gentry of the countryside. The real Protestant ascendancy, the men of property, wealth, and power, had taken positions of control or influence in the federation of oath-bound lodges, which, spread throughout the country, north and south, played the same part in the machinery of control as the Nazi party did in Hitler's Germany. Unlike the Nazis, however, the Orangemen affirmed loyalty to a constitution which they understood as guaranteeing liberties, and many of them believed that in resisting Catholic domination they were resisting tyranny.

Orangeism by the 1830s had already evolved its potent myths: the plantation, the wilderness settled with bible and sword, the massacres of 1641 and the martyrdom of the settlers by the treacherous and barbarous uprising of the natives; the threat to 'freedom, religion and laws' caused by the accession of the popish James II, the glorious revolution which overthrew him, the sufferings, endurance, valour, and triumph of the cause and Derry, Enniskillen, Aughrim, and the Boyne. There were too the victories of the Diamond and other local affrays where the good Protestants, compassed by enemies, had prevailed and survived, being ultimately delivered, like God's chosen people in the Bible, from the hands of their enemies. This was not, then or at any time before or since, the only tradition of the Protestants of the north, but at this date, in the 1830s, it was making a strong bid to overcome other traditions.

One of these was the tradition of Presbyterian, and especially Belfast Presbyterian, liberalism and toleration. The Orangemen, from the foundation of the movement and down to about this date, had chiefly been Anglicans of English plantation stock; Presbyterian descendants of the Scots who had migrated into Antrim and Down had played little part in the beginnings of the movement, whose strength was centred on the Armagh–Monaghan area. In the 1820s, however, a struggle began within Belfast Presbyterianism, a struggle personified in two ministers of the church, in which the old tradition was represented by Henry Montgomery, two of whose brothers had been with the United Irishmen in the fight at Antrim in 1798, and the new by Henry Cooke, descended from a Calvinist who had fought on the walls of Derry in 1689. Both these men were Presbyterian ministers. Montgomery supported Catholic emancipation: he addressed a mixed gathering of Catholics and Protestants in St Patrick's Catholic church in Belfast in 1829, standing beside the Catholic bishop. Cooke was a Tory, bitterly opposed to relief for Catholics, and also to liberals and radicals within the Presbyterian church. Their opposition came to an issue within their own church on the question of subscribing to the *Westminster Confession of Faith*, in which Montgomery found the description of the pope as anti-Christ repugnant, while Cooke insisted on full subscription to the Confession by all Presbyterian ministers. In 1829, Montgomery, defeated in this dispute, formed the separate Non-Subscribing Presbyterian Church. Cooke formed an alliance with the landlords and the

Orange order. In spite of protests from other members of the Synod of Ulster, he spoke at a rally at Hillsborough organized by the Orange gentry in 1834, at which he pledged Presbyterian cooperation and an alliance with the established church: 'Between the divided churches I publish the banns of a sacred marriage'. Under this new influence, Presbyterianism moved rapidly away from its liberal, republican, and radical past towards a toryism which could run to sectarian extremes. In the 'new reformation' of the mid-century in Belfast, preacher vied with preacher in denouncing the scarlet woman of Rome and the anti-Christ pope. In this competition Presbyterian ministers like Cooke, or Hugh Hanna of Berry Street church, were to the fore. The violent Orange spirit in Belfast led to bloodshed in 1835 when soldiers clashed with celebrants of the anniversary of the Boyne, and two people were shot dead, others injured by sabres.

In these same years Catholic agitation pressed on. Emancipation had brought no benefit to those poor people throughout the country whose force of numbers and persistence had helped to bring it about: having redressed a middle- and upper-class grievance, they now proceeded with new spirit to attend to their own. Agrarian secret societies became numerous again to campaign against the payment of tithes to the established church, which, from the revenues largely of the Catholics, maintained enough bishops, archbishops, deans, canons, and clergy throughout the land to have sufficed had they succeeded in converting the whole population to their own faith. The country people, having learned a little of their own power under political leadership, now on their own began to revive the old savage methods of the Whiteboys to fight against both the payment of tithes and the payment of rents. Indeed they began to combine and organize in the hope of seizing the land from the men of property, lay and clerical. In this agitation they received no support from the 'respectability of the country'. They were met by a harsh coercion act which empowered the lord lieutenant to impose martial law where necessary. This coercion was supported by bishops and other Catholic middle-class leaders, although it was denounced by O'Connell, with whose agitation for repeal of the union it interfered. In the middle of the decade O'Connell suddenly switched from agitation for repeal to support for reformist government within the union, under the new administration of Melbourne, whom he helped to form a parliamentary majority on condition of having some of the benefits of emancipation extended to the poorer Irish Catholics. Drummond, the new under-secretary for Ireland, was the main executive of the policy, which abandoned coercion, reformed the police, and severely restricted the activities of the Orange order. The administration of the late 1830s was remembered with bitterness by Orangemen and conservatives of other shades. The Catholic middle class and the Catholic bishops who supported them, on the other hand, found the Melbourne ministry highly satisfactory and were good unionists under it, but the mass of the people began to withdraw their support from O'Connell. He swung back to repeal again in the early forties, as Peel replaced Melbourne, was supported by Archbishop MacHale of Tuam and won back the people to such an extent that he could hold, and control, peaceful mass meetings attended by hundreds of thousands of people. Repeal had no hope of passing in parliament: it had no English support, and while the monster meetings were a display of a kind of force, alarming to government and ascendancy, O'Connell at no time considered using them in other than a peaceful way, and the movement was suppressed without difficulty in 1843 when a meeting at Clontarf on the outskirts of Dublin was proclaimed and cancelled.

O'Connell was a spent force, and the bogey of the Catholic rabble was at least temporarily laid when, in the late 1840s, the fearful calamity of the great famine struck the rural slums, the mud cabins, the patchwork of sub-divided holdings where millions of people now depended for life (they possessed little more) on the potato. Blight appeared, and the crop rotted, in 1845, 1846, and 1847, and the people starved, especially in the poor lands of the west and north-west. The population, when the famine began, was probably approaching 8,500,000: in 1851 it was just over 6,500,000, and it continued to decline throughout the late nineteenth century. The poorest class of the population, the landless labourers, was almost wiped out in parts of the country, not only by hunger, but by the diseases which followed it. In hundreds of thousands the people fled the doomed countryside to the towns, to America. In hundreds of thousands they survived, changed, however, in body and soul. The colonial status of Ireland, nominally now part of the United Kingdom, was fully revealed in the government's reaction to the catastrophe. Humanitarianism was stirred deeply enough, as it would have been by some calamity befalling an alien and inferior race on the other side of the world, and they took all necessary measures to relieve the distress of the Irish short of treating the famine as a domestic emergency.

The famine affected all parts of Ireland, but it was much more severe in the west, including western Ulster. In Ulster too the population dropped, and continued declining, but the decline was less steep than elsewhere in the country. A good deal of the migration consequent on the famine was not overseas but into the remarkably rapidly growing industrial town of Belfast – from Donegal, Leitrim, Cavan, Tyrone, Derry, Fermanagh, Monaghan, Antrim, and Down. A great deal of this immigration into Belfast was Catholic; the people were in a low and wretched state; they crowded into segregated areas, about half of the Catholics in the post-famine period being in one district of the city. The situation and apprehensions of Ulster Protestants were such that Catholic strength and Catholic weakness were by now equally seen as a threat by the Protestant lower orders. To the Protestant majority of wage-slaves in Belfast the half-starved Catholics crowding in were enemies who would work for starvation wages. The first serious sectarian riots began in the decade after the famine, and the Orange order drew many recruits at this time from workers who listened to the sermons of preachers like Cooke and Hanna but whose devotion to the 'glorious, pious and immortal memory' of William III was inspired by their hope of obtaining protection against the economic competition of hungry Catholics. The city was no longer the handsome Georgian town of the late eighteenth century. Physically as well as in its intellectual character it was a different place: now dirty, overcrowded, and beginning to assume the industrial-revolution ugliness which distinguished it until recent years. The streets of little cottages, new in the 1850s, on the borders of the Protestant and Catholic areas were to be the battle-ground for riots which flared up at intervals throughout the second half of the nineteenth century. In 1857 many were killed and injured in riots which continued for a week, with much use of firearms, after the annual Orange celebrations in July. In 1864 again there were serious sectarian riots which continued for days, until 1,000 policemen and 1,300 troops with artillery had been employed to quell them. Again there were deaths and many injuries from gunshot wounds. There were numbers of dead and injured again in the week's rioting known as the 'battle of the brickfields' in 1872, and there were further serious riots in 1876 and 1878. By this date Orangeism was beginning to revive from the decline it had suffered from the measures taken against it by Drummond in the 1830s. These measures had to a large extent forced it back to its original condition of being a working-class movement of somewhat limited significance, but now it was becoming once again a political force as a result of the patronage of members of the upper and middle classes among whom the manufacturers and merchants of the now industrialized north-east were an important group.

Outside Ulster, the middle years of the century were years in which further movements of resistance to the establishment developed, even in the immediate aftermath of the famine, and the purely local secret agrarian combinations against landlords began to take on a more general and national character, partly because of the scale and extent of the apocalyptic visitation of the forties. A group of romantic nationalists, centred on Dublin and consisting chiefly of middle-class people among whom Protestants like Thomas Davis were prominent, had parted company with O'Connell in the last years of his repeal agitation. They felt that he appealed too exclusively to Catholic opinion (especially on the issue of segregated education) and also that his Realpolitik was not idealistic enough. These 'Young Irelanders' drew their inspiration partly from the example of movements such as Mazzini's on the Continent, partly from the antiquarianism that was much in favour at the time. The pseudo-learned twaddle, emanating from the colony's university in Dublin, which purported to give an account, at the turn of the century, of the early history and culture of Ireland had been replaced by the work of real scholars like Petrie, O'Donovan, and O'Curry (all of whom were employed at one stage by the British government, in the ordnance survey and elsewhere). The picture revealed appealed to the imagination and the pride of those who were not content to see the story of Ireland as simply that of a barbarous nation civilized by the English conquest. The history of Ireland as interpreted to the people by the Young Irelanders through the medium of their paper, the *Nation*, and through other forms of popularization, was simplified and sentimentalized – at times, indeed, silly – but it generated a myth of Ireland which was not confined to their own small circle but was received widely by the people. With nationalistic romanticism there went, in the writings of some men, like the Ulster Presbyterian John Mitchel, a stronger doctrine to appeal to the embittered survivors of the famine.

, . . when a large proportion of the people in any land lie down to perish of want by millions (or were it only by thousands or hundreds), there is no property any longer *there* – only robbery and murder. Property is an institution of Society – not a Divine endowment, whose title-deed is in heaven; the uses and trusts of it are the benefit of Society; the sanction of it is the authority of Society; but when matters come to that utterly intolerable condition in which they have long been in Ireland, Society itself stands dissolved . . .[11]

A developed national consciousness animating a sustained ttack on 'property' – that is, essentially, the landlord system – characterized the second half of the nineteenth century through much of rural Ireland. The Young Irelanders themselves, renouncing the constitutionalism of O'Connell, but renouncing even more vehemently his contribution to the creation of a

Catholic middle class within the existing system, attempted a resort to force in 1848 which ended in little better than farce. Almost without interruption, new groupings and organizations took over from the Young Irelanders. Among the best known were the Fenians, who, in the 1860s, were a large-scale oath-bound secret organization. They had built a network of cells beginning in North America, extending throughout rural Ireland, and penetrating the British army. None the less, this widespread organization, together with other, smaller, armed revolutionary organizations associated with it, failed to bring about another 1798. Far more immediately effective was the banding together of the tenant-farmers in the Land League for the purpose of fighting landlordism.

The Land League and its campaign came as the culmination of developments through the years immediately following the great famine. Efforts in parliament to end the system whereby over most of the country any improvements by tenants on their holdings were penalized by an increase in rent, had been defeated by the landed interest. Even the moderate protection tenants enjoyed under the 'Ulster custom' was to come to an end, it seemed, about the time when the famine spent itself. To meet the threat, a reforming landlord, Sharman Crawford, backed by Presbyterian ministers, formed the Ulster Tenant Right Association in 1847, and they prevailed on the Presbyterian general assembly to associate itself with them. In the south, too, tenant protection associations were being formed. In 1850 a conference of tenant-right groups met in Dublin, mainly under the sponsorship of a group of sympathetic journalists, and formed what was known as the League of North and South – emphasizing in this title the clear recognition by now that Ulster had a distinct social system and also that an effort was being made to join the people of Ulster to the people of the other three provinces in common cause against the landlords. Clergymen were prominent in the League, but in the interests of solidarity it was made a practice for Catholic priests from the south to address tenant meetings in the north and for Presbyterian ministers from Ulster to address the tenants of Connacht, Leinster, or

Munster. The League then came under attack from landlords, Tories, and others, being accused in Ulster of papism and social- ism, and in the south (as by the Roman Catholic archbishop Cullen of Dublin, who forbade his clergy to support it) of social- ism and nationalism. In the election of 1852, only one candidate who supported the League was elected in Ulster, although a number were returned in the south and west. Some of the League's leaders, notably the Young Irelander Charles Gavan Duffy, had wished to associate it with repeal politics as well as tenant-right agitation, and this appears to have been the main reason why northern Presbyterians held back. This was a measure of the extent to which by now they had become com- mitted to unionism as repeal had become associated more and more with the Catholics. It had now become plain, notably in the controversy over university education for the Catholic middle class, that the official Roman Catholic church in Ireland was not prepared to accept the kind of separation of church and state which had been established in the United States con- stitution. It was also clear that in an independent Ireland domi- nated by Catholics the bishops would claim special privilege and status for their church. Looking at the situation in the world at large in the mid-nineteenth century, and at the association of the Roman Catholic church with tyrannical reactionary regimes (not least in the papal states themselves), the Ulster Protestants had good reason to be wary of an independent state in which the institutional Roman church would have the ear of government – and the presence of many priests in the repeal and tenant-right movements gave rise to the suspicion that it might. The sus- picion was exacerbated by all the efforts of landlords in Ulster and of that increasingly powerful class of commercial wealth who had formed strong trading and manufacturing connections with Victorian England.

In fact the influence of the clergy on the mass of the Irish people was not as simple a matter as it must have seemed in the eyes of suspicious Ulster Protestants. Profound and far-reach- ing changes were taking place in the life and culture of the common people, accelerated by the famine. In the middle 1840s there were probably more Irish speakers in Ireland than there ever had been before, but they were no longer a majority of the population, and the greater part of them comprised the most wretched section of it. After the famine, Irish speakers were a rapidly dwindling minority, and the long-drawn-out withdrawal of the language, like an ebbing tide, exposed a new cultural landscape. The process of cultural change involved is as yet little understood. The new nationalism propagated itself through the medium of English. So many cultural patterns are closely involved with language that the new English-speaking Irishman was a different kind of political animal from his Irish-speaking predecessor. He was also a different kind of Catholic: the pattern to which, for social reasons, nineteenth-century Irish middle-class Catholicism tried to conform was that of the Protestant English colonial establishment: the Catholicism represented by the clergy and respectability of late nineteenth-century Ireland was in contrast to the remains of Gaelic culture and was in many cultural respects more anglicized than, say, the Presbyterianism of Ulster. As a result, the relationship of clergy to people was ambiguous: on one level the priests, who had been close to the people since the flight of the Gaelic gentry, were trusted; on another, that of the new nationalist politics, they were not. The ambiguity was manifest in respect of such movements as that of the Fenians: the bishop of Kerry (near the borders of whose diocese they had been first established in Ireland) declared in a notorious sermon that 'hell was not hot enough nor eternity long enough' for the punishment of those who led young men astray in the Fenian movement; yet their aims and methods continued to receive widespread popular support. However, in the mythology of Orange and Green, now at an advanced stage of development, fenianism and popery were equated.

The common ground between southern Catholic tenant-farmer and Ulster Protestant tenant-farmer remained dissatisfaction with the landlord system, and in spite of the growing suspiciousness of the Protestants in relation to Catholic-sponsored politics, collaboration between northerners and southerners continued sporadically on the land question, always watched closely and anxiously by members of the establishment, who more and more clearly set before themselves the objective of preventing, even, if necessary, at the cost of considerable concessions, the union of Orange and Green. The violence organized by the Fenians in the 1860s, although it did not succeed in achieving the planned general uprising, put pressure on the administration to make some such concessions. In 1870 Gladstone carried through a bill to legalize the Ulster custom, an issue which had been the stimulus to form the Ulster Tenant Right Association twenty-three years earlier. The act was so mutilated under landlord pressure that its effect tended to reduce rather than enlarge the rights of Ulster tenant-farmers. At this time too (in 1869) the Church of Ireland was dis-established, an act also put forward by Gladstone, not merely (on his part) as a concession, but on the principle that Ireland should be governed 'like every other free country according to the sentiments of its majority and not of its minority'. The majority here catered for included the Presbyterians and other dissenters as well as Catholics.

In spite of such limited concessions, perhaps because of them, agitation continued. Isaac Butt, a conservative Dublin Protestant, founded in 1870 a Home Government Association, intended to work for Irish legislative independence largely in order to protect Irish landlords, Tories, and others associated with the colonial system, from further English liberal concessions to the lower orders. However, the Association was soon diverted into support of other causes and it was reorganized in 1873 as the Home Rule League, which was to take up the cause not only of legislative independence for Ireland but also of reform of the land system. To these was added the Roman Catholic demand for state-supported denominational education. Thus when, at the end of the decade, Michael Davitt, Lancashire mill-worker, Fenian convict, son of a Mayo tenant-farmer, founded the Land League in Dublin, the Protestant tenants of Ulster were already alienated, even though agrarian discontent was as widespread among them as among their

fellows. Landlords had been screwing higher rents out of their
estates and at the end of the decade a depression, affecting
prices of produce, coincided with a series of crop failures.
Davitt founded his League on what he described as the principles of 'natural justice', and said 'The cause of Ireland today
is that of humanity and labour throughout the world'; the
League was launched with the slogan 'The land of Ireland for
the people of Ireland'. A mass-movement to break the
landlords' grip by refusing to pay rent, backed up by other
militant and concerted action, was met by coercion again, but
also by concession. In the early stages of this campaign the
method of withholding all labour and services was applied to
Captain Boycott, a Mayo landlord, but the 'boycott' was
broken by fifty Orangemen from Cavan and Monaghan who
came to harvest the Captain's crops.

The League met this breach of tenant-farmer solidarity by
opening a special campaign in Ulster to win over the Protestant
farmers to the common anti-landlord cause, and to persuade
them to set aside religious prejudices. By this time Ulster
already had a number of active tenant-right associations (and
radical changes in the laws governing the ownership of land had
been demanded by the Reverend J. B. Armour at a mass meeting in Ballymoney at the beginning of 1880) but on the whole
they went their own way, and the appeal for solidarity failed. It
did cause some alarm, however, to members of the establishment in Ulster, and a number of Irish conservatives voted for
Gladstone's land act of 1881, which granted fair rent, free sale,
and fixity of tenure to the tenants, with the explanation, offered
on their behalf by Lord Derby, that the act was a concession
necessary to keep Ulster out of the nationalist movement. The
1881 act was found by the tenants not to be satisfactory in
practice and the agitation was renewed, the Land League issuing in 1886 a 'plan of campaign' by which rents were to be
withheld from unreasonable landlords. Again Ulster, except in
the Catholic areas, did not cooperate fully, although there were
many indications of the willingness of Protestants to go some
distance with the new campaign. The English prime minister

Divided Ulster

(Salisbury) made further concessions to the demands in the new act of 1887, explaining that this was necessary to hold Ulster to the unionist opposition to home rule.

Protestant Ulster's reluctance to be committed fully in the land war was mainly due to the involvement of land agitation with home rule agitation. In the campaign for home rule the leaders were largely middle-class and Catholic (although their brilliant leader in parliament, Charles Stewart Parnell, was a Protestant landlord). The involvement with the land campaign was to some extent analogous to that of the Catholic middle class in the 1820s with the mass campaign for emancipation. That is to say, the radical, and indeed revolutionary, movement in the countryside was found to be effective in applying pressure to the imperial government – and such gains as the tenant-farmers might make would be at the expense of the Protestant ascendancy whom the middle-class Catholics wished to displace. The home rule struggle was an extremely complex one, of which not the least important part was the struggle by the middle-class leaders of the movement to control and divert the revolutionary force which had been mobilized in the countryside. The split between Davitt and Parnell was a symptom of this. The issue over which they split was Davitt's aim to achieve nationalization (rather than distribution to the tenants) of the land. Another symptom was the home rulers' decision to oppose James Keir Hardie in the Mid-Lanark by-election of 1888, although he supported home rule for Ireland. The most significant indication, however, that revolution had been contained, and the independence movement successfully diverted into a relatively 'safe' struggle for power within a basically unchanged colonial system, was the winning over, from an initially suspicious attitude, of the Irish Catholic bishops to a qualified support for the nationalist movement. Ulster Protestant suspicions of the character of the home rule movement at this time were exaggerated, but they were not, perhaps, wholly unjustified.

The issue of north and south was joined in 1885, when the nationalist movement, led in parliament by Parnell, had taken

56

the way of constitutionalism, and when Gladstone decided to introduce a home rule bill. The election of that year, fought with a reformed franchise which gave the vote to all adult male householders, and with rationally revised constituencies based on a distribution of population, showed clearly for the first time the division of political opinion in Ulster. Of the nine counties of the province, four, Donegal, Cavan, Fermanagh, and Monaghan, returned home rule candidates. Down, Armagh, Derry, and Tyrone were divided between home rule and unionist candidates. Support for the union was concentrated in a small area in the north-east, in Antrim, north Down, north Armagh, north Derry, and west Tyrone, but it was a populous area, and Ulster as a whole returned seventeen members opposed to home rule and sixteen in favour of it. Ulster itself was therefore divided almost evenly, and the division of Ulster divided Ireland. The government Gladstone formed at the beginning of 1886 had a majority over the Conservatives in the house but the disciplined Irish party led by Parnell held the balance, giving their support to Gladstone in return for the home rule bill which he introduced in April. His intention had been known since December, and the powerful interests who wished to maintain the union had been preparing to thwart him, within and without his party, and within and without parliament.

In February, Lord Randolph Churchill, the ambitious Independent Tory member for Woodstock, who had spent three years in Ireland when his father, the Duke of Marlborough, was viceroy there, wrote to the Irish Lord Chief Justice Fitzgibbon:

I decided some time ago that if the G.O.M. went for Home Rule, the Orange card would be the one to play. Please God it may turn out the ace of trumps and not the two.[12]

In echoing the words of Thomas Knox of Dungannon ninety years before, Churchill outlined the basic strategy by which home rule was to be defeated, first in parliament and ultimately, when parliament went against the wishes of the old establishment, outside it. Churchill came to Belfast weeks before the bill, and landed to a tumultuous welcome at Larne, where he made a speech in which he used the slogan, 'Ulster will fight, and Ulster will be right'. In Belfast again he spoke to great crowds, and in the Ulster Hall warned his audience to beware of home rule coming upon them like a thief in the night, but at the same time, playing his 'Orange card', assured them that:

in that dark hour there will not be wanting to you those of position and influence in England who are willing to cast in their lot with you, whatever it may be, and who will share your fortune and your fate.[13]

His disingenuousness in expressing these rousing sentiments is shown in other, private, remarks of his, a little earlier, about 'these foul Ulster Tories'.

Gladstone's own party divided on the matter; the radical, Joseph Chamberlain, split with him on the home rule issue. Chamberlain saw a strengthening of local government, and the building up of a kind of federal system, in Ireland, England, Scotland, and Wales, as the solution to the problem. The bill failed.

In the meantime, Churchill's 'Orange card' turned out to be indeed an ace. His seditious speech in the Ulster Hall had aroused an excitement which did not subside. In June a quarrel broke out between a Catholic dock labourer named Murphy and a Protestant labourer named Bleakley in the Belfast docks, in which Murphy told Bleakley that after home rule none of 'the Orange sort' would get work in Belfast. The quarrel led to blows and both men were dismissed. Bleakley then complained to some Protestant shipyard workers, who descended on the docks and attacked the labourers there with staves, hammers, iron bars, axes, and rivets. A number of men were severely injured and one, attempting to escape by water, was drowned. The rioting which followed was exacerbated by the news of 8 June that Gladstone's home rule bill had been defeated, news celebrated by Orange parades throughout the city, which led to further rioting that went on for days, almost on the scale of civil war. Then, after a lull, it resumed again, and large-scale rioting continued with some intermissions from early June until the second half of September, leaving many dead, many hundreds injured, and many buildings destroyed by fire. The 1886 riots in Belfast were characterized by frequent battles between Orange crowds and Royal Irish Constabulary detachments drawn in from outside the city (most of the rank-and-file being Catholics) and by the inflammatory preaching of Hugh Hanna, who had greeted the introduction of the home rule bill with a call to arms.

The Orange Order now underwent a great revival, bringing it far from the trough into which it had sunk in the middle years of the century. It retained its proletarian base, but middle- and upper-class supporters of the union hastened to don Orange sashes and to march, behind the swaying folk-art of the banners on which King William for ever crossed the Boyne, to the rattle and thunder of the great lambeg drums whose message was 'croppies lie down'. Money and energy went into building an organization that would be ready in the next crisis to oppose home rule effectively, Unionist clubs were established, conventions were held, and the enthusiasm of those young men who thought in terms of opposing a home rule bill, if need be, with arms was winked at by their respectable elders. The English liberals were the danger to be feared: Unionism, which had always been the political creed of the Tory establishment in Ulster, was now, through the use of the Catholic bogey, to make Tories of the Protestant proletarians. When Gladstone, in office again, introduced his second home rule bill in 1893, the unionist establishment was much more ready to meet the crisis. Twelve thousand delegates from the northern constituencies met in Belfast to pledge on behalf of their unionist clubs that they would not accept home rule, and a resolution of loyalty to crown and constitution was passed with the qualification implicit in such speeches as that of the former supporter of Gladstone, Thomas Andrews, who said, 'as a last resource we will be prepared to defend ourselves'. This bill passed the commons but was defeated in the lords, and shortly afterwards the Liberals were out of office again.

There was a lull of ten years before the next home rule crisis came, and with it the rebellion led by the combination of English Tories and Ulster descendants of the colonial settlers of the seventeenth century, who had learned in the course of the crises and adjustments of the nineteenth century that the steadily deepening divisions of Ulster provided them with a means of retaining power and wealth in a changing world. Ireland was now a country of declining population, still economically stagnant outside the north-east, but with its main urban development along the east coast, where the only two cities of any considerable size were situated. Dublin and Belfast were both cities of 350,000–450,000 people at the turn of the century, but very different in character. Dublin, formerly the ascendancy capital where the colonial parliament had met in the eighteenth century, was still the centre of government, and still had the elegant streets and buildings constructed a century before, but it was a city in decay. It had appalling noisome slums – many of them in what had been the handsome houses of the eighteenth-century bourgeoisie – in which a third of its population was crowded in squalor and misery. The ascendancy still dominated, but the city now had a sizeable (and greedy) Catholic mercantile class. Belfast was an industrial city, the only real one in Ireland, much uglier in its architecture than Dublin, but considerably less squalid in the conditions in which its workers had to live, although these were harsh enough.

Elsewhere in the world the spread of socialist ideas of one kind or another was beginning to awaken industrial workers to the possibility of improving their lot by political as well as industrial action. Ireland had had its own socialist thinkers, and many of the political movements of the nineteenth century were of a social-revolutionary character. But most of them were rural-based, and most of them had middle-class leadership which directed their force towards middle-class objectives. In Ulster, where industrialization was more advanced than in any other part of the country, a development of social-revolutionary movements might have been expected perhaps by the end of the century, but the working class in Ulster was divided, and the division was fostered and maintained by middle- and upper-class interests. Especially after the revival of Orangeism, the workers tended to organize either in Orange lodges or in the opposed clubs of the corresponding Catholic organization (which did not, however, have anything like the same significance or force), the Ancient Order of Hibernians.

It was at the time of the second home rule crisis that Keir Hardie came to Belfast to establish there a branch of the Independent Labour party which he had founded the same year; a labour candidate had unsuccessfully fought a seat there eight years before. The Belfast trade unionist William Walker took over from him there, but in circumstances of considerable difficulty, having to contend with his employers, his own union, and a group known as the Belfast Protestant Association, which attacked the new party, often with physical violence. In the years when home rule was not an immediate issue, however, Walker succeeded in building up some support; in 1904 he was elected to the corporation, and in 1905 he fought a by-election in Belfast, his election agent being Ramsay MacDonald. He declared in the campaign that as well as being a labour candidate he was a unionist, but then went on, replying to a list of questions forced on him by the Belfast Protestant Association, to commit himself to a strong pro-Protestant and anti-Catholic position. He was defeated, narrowly enough.

Quite a different approach to labour matters was taken in 1907 in Belfast by Jim Larkin, who, like Davitt, was born of Irish parents in Lancashire, and who arrived in the city as temporary organizer for the National Union of Dockers. An agitator of remarkable power and force, he organized the dockers, brought them out on strike, and produced a chain reaction of sympathetic strikes: he harangued the police who were sent to control the strikers, and brought them out too; but his most remarkable achievement was to bring Protestant and Catholic workers together in a common struggle. He moved on, however, to Dublin, in 1908, having been dropped by the union that employed him, and it was in Dublin that, partly following his lead, the revolutionary organization of the workers took place.

61

In 1911 James Connolly, the son of Irish emigrants born in Edinburgh, an organizer, socialist, and writer of considerable experience at that date, arrived in Belfast as Ulster district organizer of the Irish Transport and General Workers Union. He too denounced the sectarianism of Orange and Green, as he organized the dockers and the mill girls, but on the political issue he was clear, and still adhered to the ideas he had expressed in the manifesto of the Irish Socialist Republican party he had helped to found in 1896:

The struggle for Irish freedom has two aspects: it is national and it is social. Its national ideal can never be realized until Ireland stands forth before the world a nation free and independent. It is social and economic, because no matter what the form of government may be, as long as one class owns as private property the land and instruments of labour from which all mankind derive their substance, that class will always have power to plunder and enslave the remainder of their fellow-creatures.[14]

By 1911, however, many of the Protestant workers of Belfast were already listening to other voices, voices that told them that 'home rule is Rome rule'.

3   The Settlers' Rebellion

All hopes of uniting the workers, irrespective of religion or old political
battle cries, will be shattered, and through north and south the issue
of home rule will still be used to cover the iniquities of the capitalist
and landlord classes. I am not speaking without due knowledge of the
sentiments of the organised labour movement in Ireland when I say that
we would much rather see the home rule bill defeated than see it carried
with Ulster or any part of Ulster left out. *James Connolly*[15]

The Liberals returned to power in the landslide victory of 1906,
which left them quite independent of the Irish vote in the
commons, and therefore under no pressure to revive the
dangerous question of home rule. Ireland was in a strange fer-
ment, changing in unpredictable ways: it did seem, however,
that the country as a whole and the minority in the north-east
were not changing in the same ways. The great land agitation of
the nineteenth century had resulted in a series of acts of parliament by which the tenant-farmers were gradually obtaining
possession of the land. Parnell had died in 1891, after his party
had been split in the bitter quarrel occasioned by his involvement in the O'Shea divorce case, and the Irish party, now
led by John Redmond, had assumed a good deal of the colour-
ing of its Westminster surroundings and was gradually losing
touch with the people at large, although this was not yet reflected in the vote.

The English language had now been firmly established for
some generations in the country as a whole, providing on the
one hand a medium for a talented group of writers, round the
turn of the century, who found that the contiguity of two

linguistic traditions gave an opportunity for striking literary sparks, and on the other hand giving rise to the feeling that something intimately associated with the long cultural history of Ireland had been lost and should be recovered. In 1893, the Gaelic League had been founded in Dublin, a respectable association whose initial object was to keep alive the Irish language still spoken in parts of the west, and then to restore Irish as the spoken language of the nation. The objects were 'non-political', and the league in its early days had ascendancy unionists among its members, but the cultural nationalism implicit in its programme gave it a wide appeal. Its political importance was summed up in 1913 by Patrick Pearse, who had good reason to know what he was talking about:

> For if there is one thing that has become plainer than another it is that when the seven men met in O'Connell Street to found the Gaelic League, they were commencing, had there been a Liancourt there to make the epigram, not a revolt, but a revolution. The work of the Gaelic League, its appointed work, was that: and the work is done. To every generation its deed. The deed of the generation that has now reached middle life was the Gaelic League: the beginning of the Irish Revolution. Let our generation not shirk *its* deed, which is to accomplish the revolution.[16]

Another new organization of the time, but overtly political, was the association known as Sinn Fein, founded in the first decade of the century by the Dublin journalist Arthur Griffith. Sinn Fein held that the union with England was illegal, and that Ireland's elected representatives should withdraw from the English parliament and from participation in the English system and set up a government in Ireland, under the crown, on the model of the parliament of 1782. Griffith also advocated a policy of economic self-sufficiency and protection. This new party, which absorbed organizations in the north known as the Dungannon clubs, and was well established in Ulster, began contesting elections.

Alongside this the underground tradition of the Fenians continued, through the secret oath-bound organization known as the Irish Republican Brotherhood, which had never finally abandoned the hope of armed revolution. There had been times when that hope must have seemed remote, when the organization was most attenuated, when the Fenian leaders were undergoing the terrible test of long periods of solitary confinement, as well as other ill-treatment, in English jails, but in the early years of the century the organization began to build up again.

All of these were to play their part in shaping the Ireland of the twentieth century. But it was the unionists of Ulster who began the Irish revolution. In the British parliament the Liberal government, in the person of the radical chancellor of the exchequer, David Lloyd George, challenged the house of lords, which had rejected his finance bill at the end of 1909. In two successive general elections which followed the Liberals were returned, but in numbers which gave the Irish party the balance of power in the commons. Home rule was mentioned as a prospect by Asquith, the Liberal leader, at the end of the election campaign of December 1910. In the meantime, one of the first acts of the administration was to force through the Parliament Act, which limited the effect of the lords' veto, so that home rule could no longer be effectively blocked in the upper house. The struggle for power within the English establishment threatened now seriously to affect the interests of the colonial establishment in Ireland. The English landlord interest was under severe pressure as a result of the constitutional change effected in the Parliament Act; their Irish wing was in danger; there they resolved to take their stand. The leadership of the Conservative party was in disarray, and the party itself divided, but on the issue of saving the union it now fell in behind a new leader, the Canadian Presbyterian Andrew Bonar Law, who had close family connections with Ulster. In the previous year the Ulster unionist group in Westminster chose as its leader one of the Dublin University members, the Dublin barrister, Sir Edward Carson, who had no Ulster connections but had a firm belief in the necessity of the union. Carson was a man of considerable talents both as a lawyer and as a politician, not least of which was his ability to conceal many of his private views in his

public utterances. He was chosen to lead the political resistance
to home rule, and he came to Ulster in September 1911 to
review his troops.

Captain James Craig, a Co. Down whiskey-millionaire's son,
who had fought in the Boer war, made available for this occasion his house, Craigavon, on the outskirts of Belfast. He
organized there a parade of 50,000 members of Orange lodges
and unionist clubs to greet Carson, who denounced the Liberal
government that was preparing to bring in another home rule
bill, and uttered defiance to them:

> We must be prepared ... the morning home rule passes, ourselves
> to become responsible for the government of the Protestant pro-
> vince of Ulster.[17]

The lead which Carson gave by this declaration was immediately followed, and a commission to prepare for a provisional
government of Ulster was set up by a meeting of Orange and
unionist delegates. There were, of course, many unionists in
Ireland outside Ulster, but, apart from taking the trouble to
devote a phrase or two to their interests, it was plain from the
beginning that the Ulster leaders were prepared to abandon
them and lay down their battle-line where it could be defended
– in north-east Ireland.

The challenge issued at Craigavon was also taken up by the
pugnacious first lord of the admiralty in Asquith's government,
Winston Churchill, who pointed out the weakness in Carson's
reference to 'the Protestant province of Ulster' by jibing that he
had been elected 'commander-in-chief' of only half the province. To expose further the weakness, as he saw it, of the unionist position, Churchill accepted an invitation to speak in the
Ulster Hall in Belfast (where his father had played the Orange
card in 1886) on a platform with Redmond and with Joe
Devlin, the Ulster nationalist who had revived the sectarian
Ancient Order of Hibernians. Churchill had underestimated his
opponent. The home rule speakers were effectively denied the
use of the Ulster Hall, or of any other hall in Belfast, and were
obliged to arrange the meeting for the Celtic Park football

ground in the Catholic area of the city. Churchill was met by
great hostile crowds at Larne; he passed through more hostile
crowds in a city into which thousands of infantry and cavalry
had been drafted to ensure order and his safety; he spoke in a
rain-drenched marquee to a crowd considerably below the capacity of the tent; finally he found it necessary to slip away
quietly to Larne without returning to central Belfast to his
hotel. His demonstration of the insubstantiality of 'these froth-
ings of Sir Edward Carson' displayed only his own mis-
judgement.

Bonar Law, the leader of the Conservative opposition, now
came to Ulster with seventy Conservative members of parliament, at Easter 1912, to address a gathering of 100,000 and
commit his party to the unionist cause which was openly threatening to defy parliament. He added his own defiance at a
further unionist rally in England in July, at the Duke of Marlborough's palace:

I can imagine no length of resistance to which Ulster can go in
which I should not be prepared to support them, and in which, in
my belief they would not be supported by the overwhelming majority of the British people.[18]

In referring to the Liberal government, he said:

In our opposition to them we shall not be guided by the consideration, we shall not be restrained by the bonds, which would
influence us in an ordinary political struggle. We shall use any
means – whatever means seem to us likely to be the most
effective.[19]

And at the same meeting, Carson said:

They may tell us, if they like, that this is treason. It is not for men
who have such stakes as we have at issue to trouble about the cost.
We are prepared to take the consequences and in the struggle we
shall not be alone, because we have all the best in England with
us.[20]

In the meantime, the bill was introduced in the house of
commons in April. It provided for an Irish parliament under
the English crown, having a federal relationship to the imperial

parliament, which retained control of military and (for a period) police affairs, and reserved certain functions in respect of finance, education, and law. It was a very moderate devolution, greeted with joy by Redmond's party, who saw it as the culmination of the political efforts of more than a century, but with considerable reserve by members of the I.R.B., Sinn Fein, and other groups in Ireland, who read a different history into the same century and regarded the bill as at best an instalment.

An important amendment was proposed to the bill in June by two Liberal members, proposing to exclude from its operation the counties of Antrim, Armagh, Derry, and Down, all of which had unionist majorities. This immediately raised the question which had been briefly discussed at the time of the 1886 bill, whether Ulster unionists would consider accepting less than all of Ulster if it came to the point of dividing Ireland. After taking counsel, the unionists for tactical reasons supported the amendment, and as a result the Ulster aspect of home rule was debated for three days. The amendment was defeated, but the extremist determination of the unionists was beginning to have its effect on the minds of the government, and in August Churchill wrote privately to Redmond:

I have been pondering in my mind a great deal over this matter and my general view is just what I told you earlier in the year – namely, that something should be done to afford the characteristically Protestant and Orange counties the option of a moratorium of several years before acceding to the Irish parliament.[21]

Carson, Craig, and the other leaders in Ulster were meantime pushing ahead with their extra-parliamentary campaign, and had by now a mass-movement of impressive dimensions. They now devised, as a means of committing their supporters fully to resistance to home rule, a solemn covenant (inspired by the Scottish Covenant of 1580) to be signed in ceremonial circumstances on an appointed day in the autumn. 28 September was designated Ulster Day, but a series of parades and mass meetings was held beforehand in various towns, at which Carson and others explained the terms of the solemn declaration which was to be signed. On 27 September, at a rally at the Ulster Hall in Belfast, Carson was handed a silken banner which, it was said, had been carried before King William at the battle of the Boyne, and he unfurled it before the great crowd, saying:

May this flag ever float over a people that can boast of civil and religious liberty![22]

On Ulster Day itself, which was a Saturday, religious services were held in the morning, and then, all over Ulster, with great ceremony and solemnity, the crowds lined up to sign the covenant, which read as follows:

Being convinced in our consciences that Home Rule would be disastrous to the material well-being of Ulster as well as the whole of Ireland, subversive of our civil and religious freedom, destructive of our citizenship, and perilous to the unity of the Empire, we, whose names are underwritten, men of Ulster, loyal subjects of His Gracious Majesty King George V, humbly relying on the God whom our fathers in days of stress and trial confidently trusted, do hereby pledge ourselves in solemn Covenant throughout this our time of threatened calamity to stand by one another in defending for ourselves and our children our cherished position of equal citizenship in the United Kingdom, and in using all means which may be found necessary to defeat the present conspiracy to set up a Home Rule Parliament in Ireland. And in the event of such a Parliament being forced upon us we further solemnly and mutually pledge ourselves to refuse to recognize its authority. In sure confidence that God will defend the right we hereto subscribe our names. And further, we individually declare that we have not already signed this Covenant. God save the King.[23]

Women signed a separate but similarly worded declaration, and when the forms were gathered in and a total was made it was found that altogether 471,414 people had subscribed to the covenant.

In spite of this massive display of support for the union in Ulster, Asquith, when parliament reassembled, proceeded to force through the home rule bill in a disorderly house of commons, where shouts of 'civil war' prevented members of the government from obtaining a hearing. In the uproar, Churchill was struck on the head by a leather-bound order book flung by an Ulster unionist. After further prolonged debate the bill passed the commons and was rejected by the lords at the end of January 1913.

While parliament was debating the home rule bill in these months, unionist magistrates were issuing licences to Orange lodges all over Ulster to practise drilling, route-marching, and other military activities, most of which were carried on at this stage with wooden staves or dummy rifles. In January 1913 the Ulster Unionist Council decided to form a body to be known as the Ulster Volunteer Force, of up to 100,000 men who had signed the covenant, to bring together all the separate drilling groups into a single centrally commanded military organization. The import of arms was not at the time illegal, and rifles began to be purchased in England and to flow in some quantity to Ulster, into the hands of the U.V.F. The landed gentry of Ulster could now devote their time, energies, and money to a task congenial to them, that of commanding the new force, which not only satisfied their sense of the inherent genius of their caste, but also placed them in a proper relationship to their social inferiors which they had not always freely enjoyed in the past. To the chief command, on the advice of the eighty-year-old Lord Roberts of Kandahar, was appointed an Englishman, Lieutenant-General Sir George Richardson, K.C.B., veteran of the Afghan, Waziri, Tirah, Zhob, and Kunnan campaigns, who on 14 August 1900 had led his Indian troops to the storming and looting of Peking.

As matters now stood, the home rule bill would become law after three sessions, without the assent of the lords, under the terms of the Parliament Act – that is, in 1914. It was to meet this that the U.V.F. continued drilling and acquiring such arms as it could and that the Tory establishment in England and Ireland pressed on with its preparations to circumvent, if not defy, parliament. In September 1913, Lord Loreburn, lord chancellor until June 1912 and closely associated with the Liberal policy on home rule, wrote to *The Times* suggesting that, to prevent civil war, a conference should be held behind closed doors to reach agreement on the Ulster question – thus opening up the whole question of home rule again. To Redmond, already being outbid, in nationalist terms, by the new groups in Dublin, this was a dismaying betrayal; to Carson an opportunity to press his advantage. Later in the same month he said:

I tell the government that we have pledges and promises from some of the greatest generals in the army who have given their word that, when the time comes, if it is necessary, they will come over and help us to keep the old flag flying.[24]

Behind the scenes the Liberal government, flinching before the defiance of the unionists, and taking the Loreburn letter as its text, began tentatively to bargain with the Irish party and with the unionists, to exclude Ulster or some part of it from the provisions of the bill. Ulster as a whole, as it happened, had a home rule majority of one in parliament at this time, as the result of the capture of the Derry City seat from the unionists (by a tiny majority) in a by-election. The province was almost exactly evenly divided between Orange and Green. The king became involved in the private negotiations, his influence in practice being used on the unionists' behalf, since he too spoke of the need for avoiding (which in effect meant yielding to the threat of) civil war. His concern was expressed especially for the officers of the army, on whose Tory sympathies too great a strain would be placed if they were asked to take action against the landed gentry of Ulster, who were at the head of *their* private army. Of 'our soldiers', he wrote to Asquith privately in September, the day after Carson had claimed the support of 'some of the greatest generals in the army', that:

... by birth, religion and environment they may have strong feelings on the Irish question; outside influences may be brought to bear on them; they see distinguished retired officers already organizing local forces in Ulster; they hear rumours of officers on the active list throwing up their commissions to join this force.[25]

Redmond entered into these negotiations, disposed to give no ground on the matter of partition, although he indicated that 'home rule within home rule' was a possibility – that is some special provision under an Irish parliament for providing autonomy in some matters for the four north-eastern counties. He insisted that all his information from Ulster – which, he pointed out, came from those who would be the first to suffer if they were in error – indicated that Carson was bluffing and that when it came to an issue the unionists would not fight – nor could he envisage the English Tories supporting them. However, in Dublin in November, the leader of the Conservative party, Bonar Law, now went to the stage of calling on the army (that is, on its Tory officers) not to obey orders should they be called on to enforce a home rule act. Having compared Asquith to James II, he went on to remind him of what had happened in 1688:

> In order to carry out his despotic intention the King had the largest army which had ever been seen in England. What happened? There was no civil war. There was a revolution, and the King disappeared. Why? Because his own army refused to fight for him.[26]

There were others in Dublin besides Bonar Law in 1913, watching with interest the developments in Ulster. In the same month of November, Patrick Pearse wrote in the I.R.B. paper *Irish Freedom*:

> It is symptomatic of the attitude of the Irish Nationalist that when he ridicules the Orangeman he ridicules him not for his numerous foolish beliefs, but for his readiness to fight in defence of those beliefs. But this is exactly wrong. The Orangeman is ridiculous in so far as he believes incredible things; he is estimable in so far as he is willing and able to fight in defence of what he believes. It is foolish of an Orangeman to believe that his personal liberty is threatened by Home Rule; but, granting that he believes that, it is not only in the highest degree common sense but it is his clear duty to arm in defence of his threatened liberty. Personally I think the Orangeman with a rifle a much less ridiculous figure than the Nationalist without a rifle; and the Orangeman who can fire a gun will certainly count for more in the end than the Nationalist who can do nothing cleverer than make a pun.[27]

This was an open expression of the opinion formed by a group of whom Pearse, a member of the I.R.B., was one, that the example of the Ulster unionists should be emulated by nationalists who should form their own volunteer force, since it was becoming clear on the one hand that the home rule bill was to be mutilated, and on the other that the English government would yield to force. Almost simultaneously with Pearse's publication in *Irish Freedom*, Professor Eoin MacNeill, a founder member of the Gaelic League, published an article on the same lines, entitled 'The North Began', in the Gaelic League paper *An Claidheamh Solais*, and he was immediately chosen by the activists to be invited to head the new organization, the Irish Volunteers, founded in Dublin at the end of the year. Another conflict, taking place in Dublin in the same year, had led to the formation of yet another military force. Jim Larkin and James Connolly had organized the Irish Transport and General Workers Union to fight for improvements in the appalling conditions of the Irish working class, and in 1913 the Dublin capitalists led by William Martin Murphy organized in a federation and attempted to break the union by locking out its members. A struggle, which at times was literally to the death, ensued, and extended for months, with the full weight of the colonial establishment, allied with the Catholic middle class, being thrown against the workers to starve them into submission. Appeals were made for solidarity to the workers in England; at one stage arrangements were made, in order to help the Dublin workers endure the months of lock-out, to send their children to board with workers' families across the Channel, but church leaders intervened at this point, preferring to feed the children rather than see them exposed to the dangers of temporary fosterage in non-Catholic homes. Because of attacks made by the police on mass meetings, resulting in some deaths, Larkin proposed that since Carson was advising Ulster unionists to arm, he did not see why Dublin workers should not do so. Larkin, however, unlike Carson, was charged with seditious libel and conspiracy. One of his supporters, Captain J. H. White, who had been campaigning (with Roger Casement) against Carson, followed

73

Larkin's suggestion and formed, shortly before the Irish Volunteers came into being, the Irish Citizen Army, modelled on the U.V.F., from among the striking workers. By the end of 1913 there were three private armies in Ireland, as well as the crown forces, which were shortly to show that there was something private about their position too.

The government now, at the end of the year, issued a proclamation prohibiting the importation of arms and ammunition into Ireland, an act which seemed to the nationalists to be designed to deny to them what had been freely available to the unionists. Redmond continued his negotiations with Asquith and the intransigent Carson, realizing more and more clearly that he had lost control of the situation, since the politics of home rule had now in reality moved outside parliament to a harsher real world which was unfamiliar to him. Still no compromise had been reached when the year in which the bill was to become law, the year 1914, began.

Now Asquith too began to realize fully that he had no real control of an extra-parliamentary situation, as he began to receive clearer indications that the army could not be relied upon if it became necessary to enforce the law should the home rule bill be passed. In the meantime he continued into the early months of 1914 pressing Redmond and the parliamentary nationalists to concede more and more modifications to the bill. The final compromise, made public on 9 March, was agreed to by Redmond but by few other nationalists. It provided that those counties which had a majority for so doing might opt out of the provisions of the home rule act for a period of six years only, the boroughs of Derry and Belfast being treated for this purpose as if they were counties. Counties which opted out would continue, as before the Act, to be administered under the Westminster parliament. Carson's reaction was forthright:

> We do not want sentence of death, with a stay of execution for six years.

Carson and Bonar Law indeed by this date had virtually dropped all pretence of dealing with the matter in parliament, which they treated perfunctorily: the open military preparations for resistance to the bill went on in Ulster, but secretly they were involved in a military intrigue which was designed to spare them the necessity of having to fight, by revealing to them the government's military plans and by providing them with the means to prevent their going into operation.

In the preceding months various people in high places had communicated with Carson and had offered him help of various kinds. Lord Milner had been organizing actively in private since December when he wrote Carson a letter in the course of which he said:

> I don't think the Government are serious in their advances. I think they are just passing the time. If they are not serious, there must very soon, certainly in less than a year, be what would technically be a 'rebellion' in Ulster. It would be a disaster of the first magnitude if that 'rebellion' which would really be the uprising of unshakeable principle and devoted patriotism – of loyalty to the Empire and the Flag – were to fail! But it must fail unless we can *paralyse the arm* which might be raised to strike you.[28]

Milner helped in England to assemble military help and munitions for the U.V.F., and he co-operated with a group called the British League for the Support of Ulster and the Union, which was enrolling volunteers to go to Ulster to join the U.V.F. if it came to fighting. He also tried to establish an organization which could paralyse the government's action before it reached Ulster, muster public support in Great Britain, Canada, Australia and elsewhere for the Ulster unionists, and secretly collect money from wealthy acquaintances to help arm and equip the U.V.F. Waldorf Astor and Rudyard Kipling subscribed £30,000 each to this secret fund, Lord Rothschild, Lord Iveagh, and the Duke of Bedford £10,000 each.[29]

The Director of Military Operations, Major-General Sir Henry Wilson, was also an ally of Carson's, functioning mainly as a purveyor of military information to the unionists and of advice – of a character calculated to benefit the unionists – to the military. The close network of military officers' gossip and intrigue, indeed, linking as it did those officers who had retired from regular service to command U.V.F. units with those who, as regular serving officers, might be expected to come into conflict with the U.V.F., helps to explain in part what happened in March 1914.

The U.V.F. had a plan for the contingency that would arise should the government move troops against them or should home rule pass. It involved cutting the lines of communication into Ulster by striking suddenly and simultaneously at approach railways, roads, bridges, telephone and telegraph lines; seizing all military depots of arms and munitions and other supplies, and capturing where possible the guns of any field artillery units, 'either by direct attack or else by previous arrangement with the gunners concerned'. It was not felt that a 'Boer' type of campaign could be waged successfully by the U.V.F. in Ulster conditions, and therefore the fighting that would follow such essentially defensive initial measures would be some form of positional warfare. This was really a reserve plan: Carson, and some at least of the U.V.F. officers, realized that the regular army would achieve a rapid victory in such circumstances. Their working plan therefore was to prevent the regular army from striking by subverting it from within. This was successful.

In March 1914, when Carson peremptorily rejected Asquith's compromise proposals on the second reading of the home rule bill, a special cabinet committee was formed to deal with the worsening Ulster situation. Intelligence had been received which indicated that raids for arms for the U.V.F. were to be expected on military supply depots in Ulster, and the committee, whose most active members were Churchill and Colonel John Seely, secretary of state for war, decided to move. General Sir Nevil Macready was appointed General Officer Commanding the Belfast district with authority over both Brigadier-General Count Gleichen, commanding the infantry brigade in Ulster, and over the police. A secret and sudden move of troops into Ulster was planned – two battalions of infantry – and garrisons were to be reinforced and placed on full alert through the province, while battleships and other naval vessels were to be assembled in the Firth of Clyde, opposite the Antrim coast, with orders to support the army if necessary. All the forces were to be in position by dawn on 21 March.

French, who was present at the cabinet committee meeting which made the basic decision, passed on the information to Wilson, who passed it on to Lord Milner and Carson at dinner that evening, 18 March. The following day, speaking on a vote of censure of the government put down by Bonar Law, Carson said:

> Having been all this time a government of cowards, they are going to entrench themselves behind his Majesty's troops. They have been discussing over at the War Office in the last two days how many men they require and where they should mobilize.[30]

Immediately afterwards, Carson left London for Belfast, where rumours of imminent arrests of U.V.F. leaders were producing a state of tension. Carson, however, was aware of the government's timetable and plans. The U.V.F. stood ready and alert, with alarm-signals prepared.

The troop movements began as planned, and units began arriving in Ulster. On the morning of Friday, 20 March, Lieutenant-General Sir Arthur Paget, Commander-in-Chief in Ireland, who had just arrived in Dublin from London spoke to his senior officers and told them that the government's plan was to go into operation the following morning with the occupation of public buildings in Belfast; if any trouble should ensue, massive force was to be used to convince the U.V.F. of the futility of resistance. Then he explained that he had, with the help of French, obtained from the secretary of state for war the concession that officers domiciled in Ulster would be exempt from involvement in the operation and would have permission to 'disappear' without prejudice to their career for the duration of the operation. Resignations of officers who stated they were unwilling to serve would not be accepted: these would be dismissed from the service. Brigadier-General Hubert Gough, commanding the 3rd Cavalry Brigade at the Curragh in Co. Kildare, who was present, said he could not bear arms against the Ulster unionists, because of his birth, upbringing, and personal friendships. He departed for the Curragh, and later that day news reached London that fifty-seven other officers of his cavalry brigade had refused to serve.

Asquith, who had not personally been involved in the detailed plans for the move against the U.V.F., now decided that Churchill and Seely had gone beyond their brief, and countermanding orders were issued.

As with Churchill's 1912 visit to Belfast, it was not the Ulster unionists', but the government's, bluff that had been called. The fifty-eight officers in the Curragh who had preferred dismissal to obeying the government's orders when it seemed that these would involve moving against the unionists, retained their commissions, and indeed received a written undertaking from the government that they would not be called upon (in the government's exercise of its right to maintain law and order) 'to crush political opposition to the policy or principles of the Home Rule Bill'.[31]

The Ulster situation was watched with interest by the European powers, and the weakness and deep division it seemed to reveal in the British policy played some part in influencing decisions being made in 1914 which were to lead to the outbreak of war in the late summer. Wilson, who had been engaged for some years in consultations with the French general staff in relation to the forthcoming war with Germany, of whose imminence he was convinced, found it necessary to go specially to see General Castelnau to reassure him about England's fitness to fight. The Kaiser's agents too were observing the Ulster scene, and must have taken a particular interest in the shipments of rifles which were being loaded in Hamburg for various destinations. A businessman and ex-artillery officer, Major Frederick Hugh Crawford, who had been dabbling in anti-home-rule adventures since the 1890s, had been engaged since the formation of the U.V.F. in organizing the supply of arms. In 1914, he had the money, opportunity, and backing to do this on a larger scale, and he acquired in Bergen a Norwegian vessel, the *Fanny*, and in Hamburg a cargo of German guns. By transhipping at sea to another vessel, he succeeded, with the aid of Carson and Craig, in avoiding interception by the navy, and on the night of 24 April arrived at Larne with 25,000 rifles and 3,000,000 rounds of ammunition for the U.V.F., who mounted a special operation to meet, unload, and protect the arms. The unionists were now more nearly in the state of readiness they desired to put into operation the *coup d'état* which they planned to carry out as soon as home rule came. Carson openly took credit for the gun-running but, feeling now more secure, he moderated his tone in response to clear indications that the government was now prepared to give way still further, and to go beyond the 'final' compromise of 9 March on home rule.

Nationalist sentiment in the country was moving away from Redmond and there was a great increase in recruitment to the Irish Volunteers. Redmond, in an effort to retain his influence in Ireland, demanded, and received (because his position was still relatively strong), a majority of places on the executive of the Volunteers for his nominees. In July, Erskine Childers arrived, also from Germany, on board his yacht the *Asgard*, with 900 rifles and 25,000 rounds of ammunition, which were landed at Howth and were taken over by Irish Volunteers waiting at the quayside. Troops and police sent to take the arms from the Volunteers failed to do so, but later in the day the soldiers fired on a jeering crowd at Bachelor's Walk in Dublin, killing three and wounding thirty-five.

In the meantime the home rule bill, at last, had passed, on 25 May. On 23 June Lord Crewe introduced in the lords the government's amending bill, which embodied the compromise of 9 March. The lords amended it to exclude all of Ulster permanently from the bill's provisions, and sent it back to the commons. The bill finally became law (without the lords' amendment) on 18 September. It was too late: it was accompanied by a bill to suspend its operation until the end of the war with Germany in which England had been engaged since the evening of 4 August.

The European war came at a point when there seemed to be

no peaceful way out of the Ulster issue. The government were committed, by late July, to the home rule bill; the Ulster unionists were committed to oppose it by force; England was deeply divided, and Ireland had a nationalist, a unionist, and a socialist army, as well as the British occupying forces.

The leadership of the Ulster unionists was tested in its professions of loyalty to king and empire by the outbreak of war. Carson was reluctant to see the U.V.F. leave Ireland (although he declared immediately that large numbers of them would be available for home defence) without guarantees against home rule, but he was faced almost immediately by a demand for them from Kitchener, the newly appointed war minister. After failing to get any satisfactory conditions, he committed 35,000 of the U.V.F. unconditionally, on Craig's advice, when it seemed in the opening weeks of the war that the need for men would be great. Kitchener agreed that the title 'Ulster' might be used in units formed from the U.V.F. The 36th (Ulster) Division was formed in Belfast in late 1914, was trained in various parts of Ulster, and was moved to France in October 1915. Twenty-nine thousand of the U.V.F. had volunteered for service.

Redmond, on the outbreak of war, had assured the government of his support and of that of the Irish Volunteers, offering repeatedly but vainly to join with the U.V.F. in defending the shores of Ireland, so that English troops might be withdrawn, and offering also to recruit the Irish Volunteers for service with the British army: 80,000 in fact volunteered. His volunteers were accepted but all his demands and requests were rebuffed: that Irish Volunteer units with their officers be taken into the expeditionary force; that there be an Irish division as there was an Ulster division. The volunteer movement indeed had split when Redmond made his commitment to the English cause at the beginning of the war, and the small minority led by Mac-Neill, Pearse, and others retained the original name of Irish Volunteers, while the great majority, who followed Redmond, and many of whom took up with the king's shilling the cause of gallant little *Catholic* Belgium (which is what the recruiting posters stressed in Munster, Leinster, and Connacht), took the name National Volunteers.

Pearse and his I.R.B. comrades, who broke with Redmond on this issue, did not feel that they owed any loyalty to England or that they should fight her wars. On the contrary they hoped that the great European war might provide an opportunity to strike against the colonial connection, and they planned accordingly. Connolly, with his tiny Citizen Army, was even more opposed to Irishmen fighting, not only in England's, but in any capitalist war, and he was bitterly disappointed to see Europe's socialist parties forgetting their principles when the drums beat and the banners waved, and hastening to wear the uniforms of Europe's various oppressors on both sides. He too was a nationalist of a kind, although he had made it clear that he was not interested in a mere change of flags but in attacking capitalism through colonialism. He too prepared to strike, and early in 1916 he worked out an agreement with the Volunteers to cooperate with them.

The plans for an uprising throughout the country in 1916 went badly awry – and even at best their hope of success depended on moral rather than military considerations. A cargo of arms from Germany, timed to arrive just before the rising, was captured and scuttled off the Cork coast. The secrecy with which a small group of leaders, concealing their intention from the figurehead, MacNeill, had laid their plans, operated against them, causing a muddle of orders and counter-orders, the postponement of the rising by a day, and a breakdown in communications. An effective force turned out only in Dublin, on Easter Monday, and even there it was far below strength; nevertheless the authorities were taken by surprise and the Volunteers and Citizen Army seized the centre of the city and held it with great courage for a bloody week against the British army – consisting in part of young recruits originally destined for France, who also fought with conspicuous courage. Eventually, after shelling and burning had reduced their strong-points, the insurgents surrendered, leaving central Dublin in ruins, many (military and civilian) dead, and Ireland changed. In the early days of May, morning after morning, the leaders of the rising were shot in Kilmainham jail, stunning with reiterated shock the minds of a population who had known these men, and who had seen over the years the long slow sour defeat of middle-class parliamentary agitation.

On 1 July the battle of the Somme opened, and the 36th (Ulster) Division was ordered out of their section of the British front at Thiepval Wood on the River Ancre to attack the German lines. They attacked with tremendous courage through terrible and continuous machine-gun fire, and drove a deep untenable salient into the German lines on the first day of battle, lost part of it by nightfall, and in two days of battle, having given an incredible display of courage and discipline, ended more or less where they had begun, in terms of ground gained. But their dead were heaped in thousands on the German wire and littered the ground that had been bitterly gained and bitterly lost: half of Ulster was in mourning.

These two bloody events drove Irishmen further apart than ever, for although the Catholic and nationalist Irish also, 200,000 of them, fought, and many died, at the Somme, at Gallipoli, at Passchendaele, and other places with names of terror in that appalling war, their sacrifice seemed, by the turn Irish history now took, irrelevant – barely a footnote in the developing myth by which the political tradition is animated:

> It was England bade our wild geese go
> That small nations might be free:
> Their lonely graves are by Suvla's wave
> Or the fringe of the Great North Sea;
> But had they died by Pearse's side
> Or fallen by Cathal Brugha
> Their graves we'd keep where the Fenians sleep
> With a shroud of the foggy dew.[32]

In Ulster, on the other hand, the Somme is more central in the Protestant political tradition, for, futile as the battle was, the Orangemen who fought in it displayed in the most convincing way that, however eccentric their 'loyalty' might seem at times, it was to them quite real, and they showed that in this they were, as Pearse had perceived, not ridiculous at all. Yet, even in Protestant Ulster, the Somme is truly central only to the tradition of the colonial ascendancy of the country houses; the European war was fought for no cause of the poor Protestants of Sandy Row or the Shankill Road, and their deaths too would have had more meaning for their people had they lost their lives defending the Ulster Hall against Asquith's troops in 1914.

Asquith himself, in the aftermath of the Dublin Easter rising, under pressure from America because of the executions, stopped General Maxwell, the military commander in Dublin, from shooting his prisoners, and announced to the house of commons on 11 May:

The government has come to the conclusion that the system under which Ireland has been governed has completely broken down. The only satisfactory alternative, in their judgment, is the creation, at the earliest possible moment, of an Irish Government responsible to the Irish people.[33]

He went to Ireland, returned, and told parliament that the government had asked Lloyd George to negotiate for 'agreement as to the way in which the Government of Ireland is for the future to be carried out', so that the home rule bill might be put into effect immediately, without waiting for the end of the war. The negotiations broke down at a stage when Redmond had accepted the temporary exclusion of six Ulster counties from the home rule provisions, and Carson the permanent exclusion of the same six. At the end of the year Asquith's government was replaced by the coalition under Lloyd George, in which Carson served as first lord of the admiralty, and the following year he cooperated to some extent with Lloyd George in the Irish Convention, purporting to be representative of the various bodies of opinion in Ireland, which was to work out a home rule settlement. The Convention, boycotted by Sinn Fein and by the groups which really by now represented opinion in most of the country, was irrelevant. It was, in any case, deadlocked, since the Ulster unionists held out for the permanent exclusion from home rule of all Ulster, although the unionists were still in a minority of one among the province's M.P.s. Since

83

a parliament for the excluded area was not in question at this stage, this narrow margin in the balance between unionist and anti-unionist M.P.s did not matter to the unionist cause.

At the beginning of 1918 Redmond died. He and his party had already by then lost their influence over the mass of the people, as by-elections clearly indicated. They had stood in the tradition, which stemmed from O'Connell's time and earlier, of political struggles which were essentially those of an emerging Catholic middle class to establish a position for itself within the colonial system. Their base was rural, and they had, like O'Connell's movements, drawn strength from the force of agrarian discontent. Parnell's skill in containing that discontent without diminishing its force, in the earlier part of his career, had made the party an instrument of power in the 1880s, but the destruction of Parnell by the church aided by a wing of the party had left the nationalists without any real force, even in parliament. Irish parliamentary nationalism from the death of Parnell until the war was little better than a form of sec- tarianism – especially in Ulster, where it was associated with the A.O.H. under the leadership of Joe Devlin. Now other forces were successfully competing, notably Griffith's Sinn Fein, which had joined with the Irish Volunteers. Griffith himself was in many ways a stereotype of the 'small man' of his time, in the urban sense. He was strongly opposed to the ascendancy, was in favour of the development of industry and of capitalism and violently opposed to trade unionism and the labour movement, as he showed clearly at the time of the 1913 lock-out in Dublin. His nationalism had little in common with that of the left wing of Fenianism which emerged in the I.R.B. and the Irish Volun- teers: it was a racialist, indeed, an imperalist, nationalism of a kind common enough in early twentieth-century Europe:

The right of the Irish to political independence never was, is not, and never can be dependent upon the admission of equal right in all other peoples. It is based on no theory of, and dependable in no wise for its existence or justification on the 'Rights of Man', it is independent of theories of government and doctrines of philanthropy and Universalism. He who holds Ireland a nation and all means lawful to restore her the full and free exercise of national liberties thereby no more commits himself to the theory that black equals white, that kingship is immoral, or that society has a duty to reform its enemies than he commits himself to the belief that sunshine is extractable from cucumbers.[34]

These ideas were for the moment overtaken, within the alliance now forming, by a militancy which was inspired by the 1916 rising, was provoked by what seemed to nationalists to be betrayal over home rule, and was brought to the point of critical decision by the conscription issue of early 1918.

The German offensive of 24 March broke through the allied lines at the junction of the French and British fronts and smashed through the British Fifth Army. The demand for more men was urgent; conscription had long been in operation in Britain; it was now proposed to raise the age limit from forty-two to fifty. Conscription had not been applied in Ireland for the obvious reasons that a large part of the population was not in sympathy with the war and that the force necessary to impose the conscription would be so great as not to justify the likely results. Now Lloyd George proposed to link conscription with an offer of immediate home rule. Carson, who had resigned from the War Cabinet in January but was privately consulted, approved of conscription but was strongly against linking the two matters. However, Lloyd George announced in parliament on 9 April that conscription was to be extended to Ireland, and that at the same time parliament would be invited to pass 'a measure of self-government' for Ireland.

The promise of this measure of self-government, while it was seen by the Ulster unionists as a new threat, was at this stage of no interest to southern nationalists, who had heard too many such promises. The conscription threat, on the other hand, they took very seriously, especially as it was rapidly passed into law. It drove all classes and groups in the population outside Protestant Ulster together in an extraordinary demonstration of solidarity against English rule, such as had not been seen on any previous issue, and it gave the new Sinn Fein, broader-based since 1917, the opportunity to take political leadership. For the parliamentary party, which since the outbreak of war had encouraged recruiting and supported the British war interest, now found itself obliged to oppose Lloyd George's conscription policy. For this belated opposition it received no credit. The Catholic bishops, meeting in Maynooth, issued a statement that the Conscription Act was 'an oppressive and inhuman law, which the Irish people had a right to resist by all the means that are consonant with the law of God'. In the face of this massive and solid resistance, the English did not attempt to apply the law. The 'measure of self-government' was also dropped, but Carson realized, when he was deserted by his old ally Bonar Law (who was in the government now), that the Tory alliance which had successfully combined force and subversion against home rule in 1914 was, like much else from the pre-war world, being consumed by the all-devouring war. New arrangements would be necessary.

The United States of America had been in the war since 1917, and their troops began to restore the situation in France in June 1918, rescuing the broken British and French armies and applying to the exhausted and war-weary Germans a new pressure which they could not resist. The war came to an end in November, and a general election was held immediately. In Great Britain there was a landslide victory for the coalition candidates who contested almost every constituency, and in Ireland there was a landslide for Sinn Fein, who swept the nationalists off the political map. Twenty-six unionists were also elected in Ireland, twenty-three of whom represented Ulster constituencies (two were returned by Trinity College, Dublin, and one by a Dublin constituency). These attended Westminster in the normal way. Many of the new Sinn Fein members were either avoiding arrest or in jail, for the new militancy in the country had already come into conflict with the English government, but those who were free to appear in public, instead of going to Westminster, assembled in Dublin in January 1919, proclaimed themselves the first *Dáil Éireann* (parliament of Ireland), and issued a statement of general aims, which is generally known as the Democratic Programme of the First Dail, and which begins:

We declare in the words of the Irish Republican Proclamation the right of the people of Ireland to the ownership of Ireland, and to the unfettered control of Irish destinies to be indefeasible, and in the language of our first President, Pádraig Mac Phiarais [i.e. Patrick Pearse], we declare that the Nation's sovereignty extends not only to all men and women of the Nation, but to all its material possessions, the Nation's soil and all its resources, all the wealth and all the wealth-producing processes within the Nation, and with him we affirm that all right to private property must be subordinated to the public right and welfare.

We declare that we desire our country to be ruled in accordance with the principles of Liberty, Equality and Justice for all, which alone can secure permanence of Government in the willing adhesion of the people. . . .[35]

The Dail established its own government, sworn to achieve an Irish republic, and it proceeded to organize passive resistance of various kinds to the colonial administration of the country. Its elected president was Éamon de Valera, who had commanded one of the insurgent units in 1916 and had been sentenced to death, and his deputy was Arthur Griffith. Michael Collins, of the I.R.B., organized the intelligence system which was to be one of the main weapons in the guerrilla warfare against the administration that developed over the next few years. Home rule, so far as most of Ireland was concerned, was a dead issue.

The Ulster unionists by this stage had broken with the southern unionists, whom they had shown themselves willing to abandon, and also with the English unionists, who in the course of the war had come round to the position of approving some form of home rule. Carson, who had refused office in Lloyd George's new coalition government, was, with his Ulster colleagues, in a somewhat isolated position as the Anglo-Irish struggle developed, with guerrilla warfare on one hand and on the other, military government, increasing repressive measures, and ultimately a policy of reprisals and burnings. The Ulster unionists remained formally opposed to any form of self-government for Ireland, but had long realized that some form of self-government was inevitable. They then demanded that the province of Ulster should continue to be governed as before from Westminster, whatever might happen in the rest of Ireland, but they had wavered on this demand when pressed, and it seemed clear that they would accept less than all of Ulster. Lloyd George now, at the end of 1919, made yet another proposal combining a form of Irish self-government with partition of the country. He produced an outline plan for the establishment of *two* parliaments in Ireland, something which had not appeared in any of the previous plans, and which had not formed a part of the Ulster unionist demands. Each parliament would have very limited powers, and provision was made for the later amalgamation of the two in a single government and a single parliament for the whole of Ireland. These proposals, which provided for the Dublin parliament even more limited powers than did the home rule bill which had been placed on the Statute Book in 1914, were of no interest at the time to the majority of the people of the country who had already elected the Dail, which was now, with difficulty (since most of its members, if not already in the hands of the authorities, were being sought by them), organizing resistance on behalf of the republic.

They formed, however, the basis of the bill which Lloyd George introduced in February 1920, and they *were* of interest to the northern unionists. The Ulster Unionist Council met on 6 March in Belfast to discuss what attitude they should take to the proposals. The provision in the bill of a parliament for the excluded northern area placed the unionists in a dilemma. The area proposed for exclusion in the bill was the six north-eastern counties, but the unionists' demand up to now had been for the exclusion of all nine counties of the historic province of Ulster, a demand which had caused them no qualms when the area was to be governed from Westminster, but which now raised delicate and difficult statistical and demographic questions. As Lord Cushendun puts it in his account of the conference:

To separate themselves from fellow loyalists in Monaghan, Cavan and Donegal, was hateful to every delegate from the other six counties, and it was heart-rending to be compelled to resist another moving appeal by so valued a friend as Lord Farnham. But the inexorable index of statistics demonstrated that, although Unionists were in a majority when geographical Ulster was considered as a unit, yet the distribution of population made it certain that a separate Parliament for the whole Province would have had a precarious existence, while its administration of purely Nationalist districts would mean unending conflict.

It was therefore decided that no proposal for extending the area should be made by the Ulster members.[36]

The Ulster unionists therefore, while not supporting it, did not oppose the bill, or challenge the reduction of the partitioned area to six counties (which included two where there were anti-unionist majorities). The Government of Ireland Act, 1920, received the royal assent and became British law on 22 December.

In the meantime, the Sinn Fein movement had developed into a fierce guerrilla war, which was being conducted in all four provinces. The para-military Royal Irish Constabulary, which, in their defended barracks throughout the country, had functioned as a combination of spies and prison-warders, were driven out of their barracks and into the towns, and the communications of the regular army were harassed. When special forces were recruited to conduct a campaign of repression and began burning towns and villages – culminating in the burning of the centre of the city of Cork – and were met with counter-attacks on centres of administration by the Volunteers (now increasingly known as the Irish Republican Army), a revolutionary situation developed in the country as the colonial system broke down and more and more classes of the community were driven into commitment to the cause of the republic. The government in England began to reverse its policy before the situation should be completely out of their control.

In May 1921 the elections were held for the two Irish parliaments under the provision of the Government of Ireland Act. Sinn Fein put up candidates, who were, however, pledged not to attend the new Dublin parliament, and most of these were duly elected. The Dublin parliament was summoned and was attended by four members, all representing Dublin University, the stronghold of unionism which Carson had represented for many years until, in 1918, he had changed to an Ulster constituency. These solemnly elected a speaker from among their number and adjourned indefinitely.

The other parliament, that in Belfast, showed a better muster. It assembled on 22 June, and was attended by the unionist members. It was opened by the king, George V, who made a speech which represented his personal intervention in Irish politics on the basis of discussions he had had in the preceding weeks with persons representing various interests in the country. He said:

> This is a great and critical occasion for the Six Counties, but not for the Six Counties alone, for everything which touches them touches Ireland, and everything which touches Ireland finds an echo in the remotest corner of the Empire. I appeal to all Irishmen to pause, to stretch out the hand of forbearance and conciliation, to forgive and forget, and to join in making for the land they love a new era of peace, contentment and goodwill.[37]

This was the signal for negotiations to begin to end the guerrilla war in Ireland and make a new settlement.

The Government of Ireland Act, 1920, was a dead letter, so far as the greater part of the country was concerned. One part of it, however, was already in effect; one part of the new Irish settlement had already been made: Ireland was partitioned; Ulster was partitioned. A settlement desired and welcomed by no party in Ireland had been imposed.

4   The Orange State

Then came the great War. Every institution, almost, in the world was strained. Great Empires have been overturned. The whole map of Europe has been changed. The position of countries has been violently altered. The modes of thought of men, the whole outlook on affairs, the grouping of parties, all have encountered violent and tremendous changes in the deluge of the world. But as the deluge subsides and the waters fall short we see the dreary steeples of Fermanagh and Tyrone emerging once again. The integrity of their quarrel is one of the few institutions that has been unaltered in the cataclysm which has swept the world.
Winston Churchill, 1922[38]

The Government of Ireland Act, 1920, established a separate parliament for the six counties of Antrim, Armagh, Derry, Down, Fermanagh, and Tyrone. This area, slightly less than a fifth of the island in extent, but with about a third of the population, was designated Northern Ireland in the act: to call it North-Eastern Ireland would be more accurate, but clumsy. The same act refers to the rest of the country as Southern Ireland, which is quite misleading. Indeed, one of the minor effects of partition was to create tiresome difficulties of nomenclature. It is virtually impossible to refer by name at once unequivocally and neutrally to either of the two states which were created in the country: the name chosen is in itself the expression of a shade of political opinion.

In the area selected for inclusion in Northern Ireland, there were about two unionist votes for each anti-unionist vote, but the distribution of these was very unbalanced. The great predominance of unionist votes was in the industrial area around

Belfast, with its high population density. Over most of the remaining part of Northern Ireland, including the thinly settled areas, anti-unionist votes would predominate locally, but there were large rural tracts (a good deal of Co. Derry, for example) where the predominance was unionist. Political allegiance remained closely linked to religious persuasion: in other words, the pattern of political opinion still followed closely the old patchwork of the two opposed cultures of plantation days. This patchwork was still reflected also in the economic distribution patterns: of the two communities thus distinguished by religious and political allegiance, the Catholic nationalists were by far the poorer. There was, however, especially in the industrial urban areas, a large working-class Protestant community, not now noticeably better off than their Catholic fellows.

The area clearly presented special problems which would daunt any government facing them for the first time. The people who now took over administration of the new statelet were, however, no newcomers to these problems, which, in the maintenance of the colonial establishment, they had long exploited. It has been remarked from time to time that there is irony in the fact that the first home rule to be applied in practice in Ireland was to be applied by those who had so tenaciously resisted the very idea. The irony is superficial. The real energy that fired the resistance to the breaking of the union did not come from the people of Ulster. Lord Randolph Churchill was not an Ulsterman; Carson was not an Ulsterman; Lord Milner was not an Ulsterman; Lord Roberts was not an Ulsterman; General Sir George Richardson was not an Ulsterman; General Hubert Gough was not an Ulsterman. The defiance of the English parliament that defeated home rule, brought the United Kingdom to the brink of civil war and Ireland beyond the brink, and partitioned Ireland was that of the officers and gentlemen of the English ruling class. At the end of the nineteenth century, and the beginning of the twentieth, the core of this class was still the landed aristocracy which on the whole traced its origins to the upheavals of the sixteenth and seventeenths centuries, and especially to the Williamite settlement of 1688. It had made its accommodations with the industrial and mercantile wealth which was the source of power in modern England and which it shared. The English unionists were prepared to go to considerable lengths to maintain the colonial union, but once they realized (as they did from the 1880s onward) that the small Irish Catholic middle class, using the Catholic masses of the people, could probably force a modification of the ascendancy settlement in Ireland, they looked for a base from which to counter-attack, to that part of Ireland where colonization had been most successful and where the greatest accumulation of wealth, through industrialization, had occurred. They 'played the Orange card', and worked to widen the division in the community which resulted from different religious and cultural traditions. Their sustained attack on the personal character of Parnell, which failed in the first attempt when the Piggott forgery was exposed but succeeded in the second when the O'Shea divorce action was procured, served the purpose of 'revealing' the home rule agitation as Catholic and clerically dominated, a bogey to frighten Ulster Protestantism. Their determination to hold a base in Ulster was shown not only in the character and extent of the revolt against parliament which they organized in 1914, but in their un-sentimental willingness to abandon southern, and indeed north-ern, unionists who were their collaborators in counties outside the six finally retained.

The reason why the boundary was drawn just where it was is plain from the reports of discussion in the Ulster Unionist Council and elsewhere – the decision itself, of course, was not made in Ulster but in London. It included two counties – Tyrone and Fermanagh – with nationalist majorities, so that it had not been drawn simply to include merely those counties which had unionist majorities, but was intended to include as large an area as possible while at the same time keeping within the total area a comfortable working majority for the union, a majority in fact of two to one. With this adequate voting strength, it would seem on the face of it that a government wishing to make the area viable as a political unit would proceed to conciliate and attempt to integrate the minority. The new unionist government proceeded to do the opposite: protesting their apprehensions of Catholic, nationalist, and republican threats, they showed by their actions and policies over the years that their real fear was of a union of the Protestant and the Catholic working classes. A nineteenth-century-style ruling caste, supported (at times uneasily and reluctantly) by an aggressive Protestant middle class, established, and maintained for half a century, power in Northern Ireland by a classic application of the principle of *divide et impera*.

The Government of Ireland Act was not expressly designed to create a permanent partition of Ireland. After its opening clause, which provided for the establishment of the two parliaments in the country, it went on to provide for the establishment of a Council of Ireland,

> With a view to the eventual establishment of a Parliament for the whole of Ireland, and to bringing about harmonious action between the parliaments and governments of Southern Ireland and Northern Ireland . . .[39]

and to give powers to the two parliaments to establish a parliament of Ireland. The legislative powers of the two parliaments were limited, and were broadly confined to internal matters. The act reserved absolutely legislative powers concerning the crown and its succession, war and peace, the armed forces, international relations, titles of honour, treason and citizenship questions, regulation of external trade, and some other matters relating to trade and communications, and it prohibited the making of laws which would discriminate for or against or interfere with any religious denomination. Police matters were reserved to the English parliament for a period of up to three years, and postal and related services 'until the date of Irish union'. In consequence of the reserved powers, which included fiscal as well as legislative powers, and which in fact gave a federal character to the form of union to be continued between England and Ireland under the act, provision was made in it for the continued representation of Irish constituencies in the Westminster parliament.

This act was already plainly inoperable in the greater part of Ireland at the time it was passed, and it never came into full effect in 'Southern Ireland'. It has, however, a double importance. It was the legislative instrument by which the partition of Ireland was accomplished, and it is the main part of the fundamental law, or constitution, of the anomalous subordinate state of Northern Ireland.

The king's speech at the opening of the Belfast parliament in 1921 in effect opened negotiations with the embattled Dail and I.R.A. A truce was shortly called to the fighting in the country, and there was a long uneasy lull before formal negotiations on new terms of settlement took place in London. In this lull the unity that had been welded among the people in the heat and stress of the fight rapidly fell apart again. The people who had, in ever-increasing numbers, actively or passively opposed the English presence in the country had in fact no common objective other than that of some kind of independence. The Democratic Programme of the First Dail, which had purported to set forth the objectives of the separatist movement in a revolutionary programme, was in fact no more than a form of words, and few of those who subscribed to it at the Dail meeting of January 1919 had regarded it as a serious policy. Its purpose was to win the assent of the labour movement to Sinn Fein and to the Sinn Fein Dail. Even so, in its drafting stage (where the main work was done by Thomas Johnson, leader of the Labour party and successor to Connolly, who had been shot after the 1916 rising) the Democratic Programme had caused serious misgivings and had been extensively altered, Collins being one of the chief objectors to its socialist content. Sinn Fein itself, in its expanded form as a national movement after 1917, had grafted on to Griffith's original ideas more revolutionary ones which were in many ways incompatible with them. Splits and fissures began to appear in the revolutionary movement even before a small group of negotiators, led by Griffith and Collins, went to

London in December to work out, under threat from Lloyd George of 'immediate and terrible war', terms of agreement with London. When, given an ultimatum, they signed terms and brought them home, all sections of the republican movement were disappointed with what had been achieved, but the disappointment took effect in different forms. The president of the 'republic' of 1919–21, Mr de Valera, had shown a shrewd enough politician's instinct in not going to London himself: any terms that could be obtained from the English were certain to be less by far than was demanded, and by holding aloof he reserved his position. In the Dail debate on the terms of agreement, he voted against ratification, found himself in a minority (by a narrow margin), and ultimately, after a period of embittered and complex struggle, found himself following the lead of left-wing republicans in opposing by force the new government, headed by Griffith, that established itself in Dublin, with English backing, under the terms of agreement.

One of the most interesting features of the political struggle within the Sinn Fein movement, which led in mid-1922 to the outbreak of civil war after the English had withdrawn their troops, is that the issue of partition was hardly raised. The debate turned on the oath of allegiance to the king of England, which was required under the terms of agreement, and it was essentially a struggle between those who were content with 'home rule' – in other words a position for the Catholic middle class in what remained basically a colonial situation – and those who wished to break the colonial connexion. All eyes were so fixed on the immediate prospect of some form of power in Dublin that the actual taking over of power by the unionists in Belfast was hardly observed. Only Collins seems to have been prepared to take forceful action in the north (although he had signed the articles of agreement and was at the time a member of the government that had ratified them) but Collins was killed early in the civil war.

The 'Articles of Agreement for a Treaty between Great Britain and Ireland' signed in London on 6 December 1921 related to the whole of Ireland and, subject to a certain condition, they superseded the Government of Ireland Act, 1920. The condition was that for a month after the passing of the act of parliament for ratifying the articles, they should not apply in Northern Ireland, and that within that month the parliament of Northern Ireland might present an address to the crown the effect of which would be that in the six counties the Government of Ireland Act would continue to have effect, while the treaty articles would apply only in the remaining twenty-six counties. In other words, Northern Ireland might opt out, which it promptly did. The rest of Ireland was given commonwealth status under the crown, as the 'Irish Free State', whose position 'in relation to the Imperial Parliament and Government and otherwise shall be that of the Dominion of Canada. . . .' England retained naval and military bases under the treaty articles at Berehaven, Queenstown (now Cobh), Belfast Lough, and Lough Swilly.

The civil war was fought out in the year from mid-1922 to mid-1923. The new Free State government in Dublin repressed the republicans ruthlessly, shooting large numbers of its leading opponents out of hand. While the war was still going on, the new government negotiated with representatives of the southern unionists, that is the Protestant ascendancy which had held sway in Ireland until now, in a strenuous effort to reassure them as to their own respectability now that the English had left. Rural revolutionary movements – the setting up of soviets in some areas, the burning out of country houses, and the taking over of estates by the local tenants – were effectively checked within a few years; the left wing of the republican movement was broken, chiefly by the shooting of prisoners; every effort was made to safeguard property. Institutions of the guerrilla period, such as the Sinn Fein courts, which had functioned as underground rivals of the English courts (sometimes effectively) and the Sinn Fein police, were dismantled, and were where possible replaced by restoring what had preceded them. Most of the apparatus of colonial administration was restored, although some parts of it, such as the Royal Irish Constabulary, must, because of the odium in which they had been held, be swept

97

away. A new, unarmed, police force was established – a daring but successful move in time of civil war. In general, the new government made every effort to demonstrate that it was *not* revolutionary, and in this it was on the whole successful. By the middle 1920s, in social terms, counter-revolution was triumphant in Ireland north and south.

In the north the setting up of the new state was accompanied by a mounting crescendo of sectarian violence which rivalled the outbreak of 1886 in Belfast. There had been several outbreaks of rioting in the interval, notably in 1898, in which the Catholics of Belfast were the chief victims. In 1912 there had been a sporadic rioting, beginning at the end of June when a procession of the Ancient Order of Hibernians attacked a Protestant Sunday-School outing. In 1920, with the guerrilla war throughout Ireland at its height, the sectarian violence took the form chiefly of a sustained attack on the Catholic population, largely by armed members of the U.V.F. The situation was already serious when the government (that is the English government, for the partition had not yet taken place) opened recruiting on 1 November 1920 for the Ulster Special Constabulary. Three classes of the Constabulary were established, and distinguished as A, B, and C. Class A was for those willing to do full-time duty and to be posted anywhere within Northern Ireland (anticipating the partition, which did not become law until November); Class B was for those willing to do part-time duty in their own locality; and Class C was for those willing to go on reserve which would be called up only in case of grave emergency. Recruitment to those forces came mainly from Orangemen, who were, many of them, members of the U.V.F., and they consisted largely of the same people who had been burning out Catholic homes and driving the population on to the streets. Not unnaturally the creation of such a police force added to the violence, which took on the character of a full-scale pogrom against the Catholics, especially in Belfast. The special constabulary were armed (by the English government at this stage) and were in effect used as an instrument of terror to prepare the way for the new state by using what were by now in north-east Ireland the traditional methods of sectarian violence, but this time with the difference that the perpetrators were in uniform. The I.R.A., at the height of its activity against the crown forces and the Black and Tans, retaliated, and what amounted to a separate, and savage, civil war was fought in the north.

When the election of May 1921 was held under the Government of Ireland Act, the anti-unionists in the six counties, as in the other twenty-six, contested it, but with the same understanding – that they would not recognize the new Belfast parliament and that they would not take their seats in it. This (although they later modified their stand when a twenty-six-county parliament was in fact set up in Dublin) set the line of deep division for the new state, which began its existence with a very large proportion of its population refusing to recognize its right to do so. It added to the violence, to the effort on the one hand to bludgeon the people into submission to the new Ulster ascendancy and on the other hand to the reprisals carried out by the armed nationalists. The special constabulary in their first two years of existence earned a reputation which they never afterwards lost. In June 1921 they entered a house near Newry, beat up its elderly owner and killed his two sons. In March 1922 'uniformed men', almost certainly specials, murdered five members of a single family (the McMahons) in Belfast. Almost 300 people were killed before the bloodshed ended, 232 of these deaths being in the year 1922. They included two Unionist M.P.s. A boycott on goods produced in the north had been widely enforced by the I.R.A. since 1920, and the warfare in the north, seen by the I.R.A. as defensive and as arising from the onslaught on Catholic areas in 1920, was seen by many Ulster Protestants as offensive, an attempt to destroy the new six-county state.

The Royal Irish Constabulary was being phased out at this time, and indeed its numbers had greatly decreased since shortly after the outbreak of guerrilla warfare as the result of resignations. It was disbanded in 1922. The Minister of Home Affairs in the new government, Sir Dawson Bates, had set up a committee of inquiry which recommended the establishment of a new police force, to be organized under a single command for the whole of Northern Ireland – not on a local basis as in England – with a strength of up to 3,000, one third of whom should be Roman Catholics. The force, the Royal Ulster Constabulary, was established on 1 June 1922, and, like its predecessor the R.I.C., it was an armed force.

The powers of these para-military police forces were greatly enlarged by the Civil Authorities (Special Powers) Act, also passed in 1922, under which the Minister of Home Affairs received authority, by making regulations, to 'take all such steps and issue all such orders as may be necessary for preserving the peace'. Regulations were issued under this act enabling the police to arrest people without a warrant on 'suspicion of acting, having acted, or being about to act' in a manner contrary to the peace, and to hold them indefinitely without charge. They might also search persons, premises, or vehicles anywhere without a warrant, close roads, paths, or bridges without warrant or warning, and seize property. These regulations were made in time of civil war, but the act was renewed annually until 1933, when a similar, but permanent, act replaced it.

The head of the first government of Northern Ireland was Sir James Craig, who had led, with Carson, the rebellion against home rule. Where Carson, no Ulsterman, and his English allies had used Ulster to try to save the union, Craig used the union to save Ulster – that is, to hold for his creed and class as much of Ulster as he could. He was faced in these early years with the clauses of the Anglo-Irish treaty articles which had permitted Northern Ireland to opt out of the Irish Free State by presenting an address to the crown, but which went on:

Provided that if such an address is so presented a Commission consisting of three persons, one to be appointed by the Government of the Irish Free State, one to be appointed by the Government of Northern Ireland and one who shall be Chairman to be appointed by the British Government, shall determine in accordance with the wishes of the inhabitants, so far as may be compatible with economic and geographic conditions, the boundaries between Northern

Ireland and the rest of Ireland, and for the purposes of the Government of Ireland Act, 1920, and of this instrument, the boundary of Northern Ireland shall be such as may be determined by such Commission.[40]

The policy of the Unionist government in its first few years, then, was to ensure that they yielded nothing as a result of the deliberations of this commission. They did this at first simply by refusing to appoint their representative. The Irish delegates who signed the treaty articles in London appear to have been led to believe that the directions given to the commission would cause them to restore to the Free State the extensive nationalist areas outside the dense concentration of unionist voters around Belfast; and they seem to have been confident that two counties, or more, would be transferred to the jurisdiction of Dublin, leaving Belfast with an area too small to be viable. The qualifications to 'the wishes of the inhabitants' in the articles themselves give no such clear direction, but Craig in any case, by refusing to appoint a representative, reserved his position and avoided being a party to any ruling which might deprive Northern Ireland of territory.

In 1924 the British government, after the treaty articles had been suitably amended, appointed the Northern Ireland representative – J. R. Fisher, a Belfast unionist – and the Dublin government appointed Eoin MacNeill. The chairman was Justice Feetham of South Africa. The commission conducted its work in private but in November 1925 the *Morning Post* published a map showing minor modifications of the boundary and the transfer of one large area of Donegal to Northern Ireland. At this MacNeill resigned, and shortly afterwards William Cosgrave, President of the Executive Council of the Irish Free State, conferred in London with Craig and with the English government, and on 3 December a new agreement was signed, by which the powers of the boundary commission were withdrawn and the border remained unchanged. The three parties concerned signed the agreement of 1925. The northern administration could, and did, now claim that Dublin had given *de jure* recognition to the border.

A kind of fitful peace had come to Northern Ireland by the end of 1923, but it was due largely to exhaustion, and the area remained bitterly divided. Belfast was under curfew for four and a half years, until Christmas 1924. It had enjoyed a period of some prosperity just before the war; but its people had endured, as well as civil war, the hardships of a major strike, starting in the shipbuilding and engineering industry and spreading as other workers came out in sympathy, in early 1919. Now, starting with the severe and widespread slump of 1921, the city, and Northern Ireland as a whole, faced prolonged and almost unremitting depression. The area had free trade with Great Britain, and found there a market for its agricultural produce, but the newly erected border had severe effects on some towns and areas, notably the city of Derry, on the west side of the Foyle, which lost its natural hinterland. In the east, the main industries were shipbuilding and a related group of engineering industries, and the linen and clothing industries. The industries were over-specialized, and gave unbalanced employment. They also depended heavily on export markets, which they failed to find in sufficient numbers in the 1920s and 1930s. Unemployment climbed from 18 per cent (of insured workers) in 1923 to about 25 per cent within a few years, and although in the 'boom' of the late 1920s (when the declining linen industry enjoyed a brief revival) it fell to 15 per cent, it rose again to an *average* of over 25 per cent throughout the 1930s. In the shirtmaking city of Derry, which has remained economically depressed (apart from some prosperity in the later years of the Second World War) since the foundation of Northern Ireland, there were virtually no jobs for men, and it has long been the tradition that the women go out to work and the men remain idle.

Other social ills, after a century of sectarian strife and exploitation of sectarianism, were grave. The new government in 1922 set up a committee, the Lynn committee (with which Catholics refused to collaborate), to examine the educational position. It found that at least 12,000 children of school-going age in Belfast had no school places, while many of the school places that did exist were in unsanitary or otherwise unsuitable schools. The committee recommended the establishment of a system of primary education which would perhaps not have been in strict conformity with the section of the Government of Ireland Act which prohibits the parliament of Northern Ireland from making

a law so as either directly or indirectly to establish or endow any religion, or prohibit or restrict the free exercise thereof, or give a preference, privilege, or advantage, or impose any disability or disadvantage, on account of religious belief ... or affect prejudicially the right of any child to attend a school receiving public money without attending the religious instruction at that school. ...[41]

While it found that there were too many small denominational schools, it recommended that the existing system of religious instruction in schools should continue. The Education Act of 1923 did not follow this recommendation. It made provision for three categories of primary school: those wholly maintained by local authorities; 'four-and-two-committee' schools (which were voluntary schools run by committees with two local authority representatives and four representatives of the body providing the school); and other voluntary schools. Where full costs were borne from public funds, the education authority was not to provide any religious instruction, and the religious denomination of the teacher was not to be taken into account in making an appointment. Religious instruction might be given by ministers of religion and other persons for half an hour a day where parents wished it, but any child might be excused from attending this. The Minister of Education, Lord Londonderry, explained that the object of these provisions was to encourage mixed education, of Protestants and Catholics together. A campaign against the provisions was mounted by the three principal Protestant churches through a United Education Committee, and by a committee of the Grand Orange Lodge of Ireland. The Education Act was seen as an attack on the Bible. At a conference of the United Education Committee in March 1925, Mrs McGregor Greer declared:

It [the school question] is one that is too sacred for any heat to be shown, and if we desire peace and harmony in our Province how better bring that about than by teaching the Bible?[42]

Craig then consulted with the secretaries of the two committees and overruled the Minister of Education. A new act was passed, and Protestant (but not Catholic) schools began to be transferred in some numbers to local authority control, to qualify for full salary and maintenance grants. Further pressure continued until in another education act in 1930 it was laid down that where the parents of not less than ten children made application it should be the duty of the education authority to provide Bible instruction in a school, and in transferred or provided schools it would be the duty of teachers, if required to do so, to give instruction in the Bible. To meet Catholic objections that state schools were now providing Protestant teaching, provision was made in 1930 for 50-per-cent grants for capital expenses in approved non-transferred schools (later raised to 65-per-cent). Thus, after an initial attempt by an education minister who disliked sectarianism, segregated education, undoubtedly one of the principal ways in which the divisions in the community are perpetuated, was reinforced in the education system of Northern Ireland. And the segregation itself, if not its mode of application, was to the satisfaction of all religious denominations.

The influence which operated very effectively on the Northern Ireland government in this matter of Bible instruction in state primary schools was that of the three main Protestant denominations, together with the Orange institute; and the operation of this influence has been characteristic of the new statelet since its inception. Treading somewhat carefully and warily at first, adhering closely to the provisions in the Government of Ireland Act which had been inserted to provide some scrap of protection for the Catholics who were being abandoned to an Orange government, the unionist rulers of northeast Ulster, gradually feeling more secure, began to realize the usefulness of inhibiting a similar feeling of security in their followers. Extremist sectarians, impatient at the caution with which the government felt its way into a position of strength, taunted it with displaying weakness. In 1931 the Ulster Protestant League was founded, to urge all good Protestants not to employ Catholics, not to work with them, not to deal with them, and to accuse the government of softness in its dealings with what was regarded as the enemy within. This agitation, in depression-stricken Belfast, where a large part of the population was on the verge of starvation, was designed, with unemployment running at over 30 per cent, and the competition for jobs almost literally a matter of life and death, to embitter still further the bitter divisions of the city and the province. Yet, at first, hunger seemed to drive the army of unemployed together, not apart. A march of the unemployed on parliament had been banned in 1925, successfully. In 1932, a hunger march of the unemployed was again banned, but crowds gathered in the working-class areas of central Belfast. Police baton-charged the unemployed workers on the Falls Road, in the Catholic area, and then opened fire, over their heads. The Protestant unemployed of the Shankill Road rioted in support of their Catholic fellows, and yet again Belfast saw wrecking, burning, and killing: two men died of wounds. But it had not been a sectarian riot.

From this point on the government itself began to join in sectarian rabble-rousing. Craig, now Lord Craigavon, and some of his fellow ministers in government began to outdo the Ulster Protestant League in their statements. In 1932, Craigavon said: 'Ours is a Protestant government and I am an Orangeman.' In 1934 he said:

I have always said I am an Orangeman first and a politician and member of this parliament afterwards . . . all I boast is that we are a Protestant parliament and a Protestant state.[43]

Sir Basil Brooke, who was Minister of Agriculture from 1933 until 1941 and later prime minister, said on 13 July 1933:

There are a great number of Protestants and Orangemen who employ Roman Catholics. I feel I can speak freely on this subject as I have not a Roman Catholic about my own place. . , . I would

105

appeal to Loyalists, therefore, wherever possible, to employ good Protestant lads and lassies.[44]

Referring back to this statement in March 1934, he said:

> Thinking out the whole question carefully ... I recommend those people who are loyalists not to employ Roman Catholics, ninety-nine per cent of whom are disloyal. ... I want you to remember one point in regard to the employment of people who are disloyal. There are often difficulties in the way, but usually there are plenty of good men and women available and the employers don't bother to employ them. You are disfranchising yourselves in that way. You people who are employers have the ball at your feet. If you don't act properly now, before we know where we are we shall find ourselves in the minority instead of the majority.[45]

In the hungry 1930s such instigations of employers, coming from members of the government, were a potent weapon of oppression, and the incitement of sectarian fears was a proven weapon of division to counteract the dangerous tendency towards solidarity among the urban workers. For the real potential danger to the permanent Tory establishment in Northern Ireland lay not in the Catholics, who, although most of them were opposed to the separate existence as a state of the six counties, were in a minority planned for safety by those who framed the constitution, but in the Protestant workers. These *must* be held to unionism if the establishment was to survive, and the effective way of doing this was to keep them constantly reminded of the dangers of Catholic domination should the Free State take over Northern Ireland. At times when other matters – such as unemployment and hunger – tended to distract the Protestant workers from this danger, their fears and suspicions of Roman Catholicism were roused by inflammatory speeches.

The speeches were all too successful. The resentment and bitterness of the unemployed Protestant workers was turned, not against the social and economic system which exploited them, but against their 'disloyal' Catholic fellow workers in outbreaks of violence which were sporadic until 1935, when tension built up in Belfast as the day of assertion of Protestant

dominance, 12 July, approached. The Minister of Home
Affairs, Sir Dawson Bates, banned parades and demonstrations
but then yielded to protests and pressure from the Orange order
and withdrew the ban. The parades sparked off three weeks of
burning, wrecking, and killing in one of Belfast's worst outbreaks of sectarian rioting. This time the conflict was one-sided.
The Catholics in their ghettos, dispirited by want and the long
years of economic depression, not yet recovered from the terrible days of 1920–22, were the victims. Their bishop, Most
Rev. Dr Mageean, who organized efforts to house those who
had been deprived of their homes and to provide other kinds of
relief, made strenuous, and on the whole successful, endeavours
to persuade his people not to retaliate or attempt reprisals.
Twelve people were killed, and the city coroner,
T. E. Alexander, in reporting his finding that the cause of death
was gunshot wounds in each case, gave his view that
inflammatory and provocative speeches from 'so-called leaders
of public opinion' were responsible.

The Government of Ireland Act, 1920, provided for elections
to the two houses of commons, in Dublin and Belfast, by the
system of election which had been introduced experimentally in
Ireland after 1918, but the Act allowed the system to be
changed after three years. The system was that of proportional
representation by means of the single tranferable vote, which
was also embodied in the constitution of the Irish Free State
and continues to be the voting system in the Republic of Ireland. Mainly in the interests of 'stable' government (that is, an
electoral system which gives an extra advantage in representation to the majority party) Craig in 1929 abolished the system
and restored the 'straight vote' on the English pattern. In advocating the change he said:

What I hold is, if the Ulster people are ever going – and I pray
they may not – into a Dublin Parliament, they should understand
they are voting into a Dublin Parliament, and not be led by any
trick of a complicated electoral system, such as Proportional Representation.[46]

The change was only one of a number of devices employed in

the electoral machinery to reinforce and maintain the control of
the six counties by the Unionists. There were in fact three separate main electoral systems open to control. Under the federal
arrangement made in the Government of Ireland Act, Northern
Ireland returned twelve M.P.s to Westminster. These were
elected in the ordinary way at British general elections and at
by-elections, and the franchise for the Westminster members
was (and still is) identical with the rest of the United Kingdom.
The United Kingdom Boundary Commission was responsible
for review of the constituency boundaries. Apart from the reserved powers specified in the Government of Ireland Act, the
Act also clearly spelled out the supremacy in all matters of the
Westminster parliament:

> Notwithstanding the establishment of the Parliaments of South-
> ern and Northern Ireland, or the Parliament of Ireland, or anything
> contained in this Act, the supreme authority of the Parliament of
> the United Kingdom shall remain unaffected and undiminished over
> all persons, matters, and things in Ireland and every part
> thereof.[47]

In practice, however, Westminster had not exercised these
rights, and had not legislated on specifically Northern Irish
matters, while the Northern Ireland parliament (established in
due course in a grandiose new building at Stormont, outside
Belfast) has legislated on matters within the competence of
Westminster.

The parliament established in Northern Ireland itself consisted of a house of commons of fifty-two members and a
senate of twenty-six members. The franchise for elections to the
Northern Ireland house of commons was somewhat different
from that for the Westminster house, since it allowed plural
voting. There was a business vote which could be exercised, in
addition to the ordinary vote, by a man who occupied business
premises in a constituency to the value of £10 or more per
annum. There was also a graduate vote for four seats for the
Queen's University of Belfast.

The Stormont electoral system allowed for manipulation in

several ways, and the business premises vote in itself gave a bonus of votes to unionism, since the business and professional class in the community was predominantly not only Protestant but reliably unionist. The most obvious opportunity for manipulating the electoral system here was in the drafting of constituency boundaries through the practice of gerrymandering. It was in local government electoral systems, however, with their special importance for schools, housing, and other matters that directly and continuously affected the lives of the people, that opportunities for manipulation through property qualifications, plural votes, and gerrymandering were fully and seriously exploited. The combination of discrimination in employment, manipulation of electoral systems, and further manipulation of the resources of local government to create segregation and what amounted to ghetto conditions was used in the 1930s both to perpetuate and to reinforce the equivalent of a caste system. These methods were also used to operate a system of population control which would keep the faster-breeding Catholics at a fairly steady proportion of the whole population by exerting selective pressures on them towards emigration.

In the south, in the 1920s and 1930s, the violence which had accompanied the establishment of the new state gradually diminished. The Dublin government, which had been successful in the civil war in defeating revolution, faced a crisis within its own ranks immediately afterwards, centring on a mutiny in the army, after which it swung further to the right in its political and social policies. The defeated republicans also split on ideological issues, and their right wing, led by Éamon de Valera, formed a new political party, *Fianna Fáil*, and prepared to enter the Dail. The basic organization had been thoroughly done, through the sections of the I.R.A. that had opposed the treaty and through the underground network of the revolutionary years, before the new party was formally inaugurated, and it was immediately able to enter parliamentary politics with a firm basis of rural radical support. In 1927 Mr de Valera and his followers swallowed the oath of allegiance with their eyes metaphorically shut and entered the Dail as the main opposition party, and in 1932, with the aid of the Labour party, they were able to form a government. Fianna Fail by this stage was not a revolutionary party, although it looked it to the middle-class and conservative Catholics of the government which had held office under Cosgrave since 1922 – so much so that there was some doubt at the time if the Free State army would allow them to take office at all. Fianna Fail was essentially populist: it supported and was supported by the small farmers and small business people, and it also cultivated with considerable success the working-class vote. It opposed and repudiated the treaty settlement of 1921 with England, and proceeded by various means to dismantle it. Of these methods, its refusal to pay the land annuities – instalments by which, under terms of the final financial agreement with England in the 1920s, Irish farmers, through the Free State government, repaid to the British government the capital cost of buying out the landlords – brought it its greatest difficulties, for it led to a tariff war between the two countries which bore heavily on the Irish farmers.

The policies of Fianna Fail – who had fought their elections with the slogan 'On to the republic!' – were not, it emerged when they came to put them into action, revolutionary, or even republican. They were the policies of Griffith: self-sufficiency, capitalism tempered by a particularist nationalism, a dismantling of the emblems of subjection but a willingness, scarcely less than that of their predecessors in government, to be involved in reality in the colonial system; radical conservatism. The restoration of the unity of Ireland was a much declared object of policy, but no active measures were taken towards accomplishing it: most energy was taken up with legalistic concern with the forms of the Free State's connection with England, with the creation of conditions in Ireland for private capitalism, and with following their predecessors' lead in establishing state-capitalist enterprises. Fianna Fail retained the broad base of rural and working-class support that has always been essential to effective national movements in Ireland, and it also succeeded in coping with a blue-shirted fascist organization which underwent several changes of name but was associated with the right wing of the former government group (represented today, although only in a very general way, by the Fine Gael party). Fianna Fail defeated the blueshirts (who attempted a mass march to the Dail by contingents from all over the country) by recruiting large numbers of former I.R.A. members into the army, and also by relying tacitly for the moment on the still large I.R.A. force that remained independent of the Free State army, and that had not followed Fianna Fail's break from the old Sinn Fein republican movement.

In 1937, as part of the policy of repudiating the settlement of 1921 and the settlement of 1925, the Dublin government put before the people a draft new constitution, which was passed in a referendum by a small majority of the voters of the twenty-six counties of the Free State. This document, in terms of the island as a whole, was divisive. It was drafted in consultation with Roman Catholic leaders, and while it falls short of what the church would regard as fully acceptable, it does none the less embody Catholic views on church–state relations to some extent. It also falls far short of enacting the 'rights of man' in the country, and indeed its provisions for fundamental human rights are (like many of its other provisions) so qualified as to give somewhat doubtful protection. Article 2 of the constitution of 1937 reads:

The national territory consists of the whole island of Ireland, its islands and the territorial seas ...

and constitutes in effect a repudiation of the agreement signed in 1925, a repudiation reinforced by article 3:

Pending the re-integration of the national territory, and *without prejudice to the right of the Parliament and Government established by this Constitution to exercise jurisdiction over the whole of that territory*, the laws enacted by that Parliament shall have the like area and extent of application as the laws of Saorstat Éireann (the Irish Free State) and the like extra-territorial effect.[48]

The fourth article declared that the name of the state is 'Éire, or in the English language, *Ireland*'. This is a translation of the

Irish text of the constitution, which is the primary text, and 'Éire' is simply the Irish word for 'Ireland'. The article, naming the state 'Ireland', created a difficulty in referring to the *de facto* twenty-six-county state, and the practice was immediately adopted in Northern Ireland and in England of referring to the twenty-six counties as 'Eire'.

Among other articles in the constitution which were pointed out at the time, or have been since, as indicating that indeed 'home rule was Rome rule' was article 44.1.2°:

> The State recognizes the special position of the Holy Catholic Apostolic and Roman Church as the guardian of the Faith professed by the great majority of the citizens.

This article does, however, go on:

> 44.1.3°. The State also recognizes the Church of Ireland, the Presbyterian Church in Ireland, the Methodist Church in Ireland, the Religious Society of Friends in Ireland, as well as the Jewish Congregations and the other religious denominations existing in Ireland at the date of the coming into operation of this Constitution.

Article 41 deals with the family:

> 41.2.2°. The State shall, therefore, endeavour to ensure that mothers shall not be obliged by economic necessity to engage in labour to the neglect of their duties in the home.
> 41.3.2°. No law shall be enacted providing for the grant of a dissolution of marriage.
> 41.3.3°. No person whose marriage has been dissolved under the civil law of any other State but is a subsisting valid marriage under the law for the time being in force within the jurisdiction of the Government and Parliament established by this Constitution shall be capable of contracting a valid marriage within that jurisdiction during the lifetime of the other party to the marriage so dissolved.[48]

The first president elected under the constitution was, however, a Protestant, Douglas Hyde, who had been one of the founders of the Gaelic League.

The twenty-six-county state was, after the enactment of this constitution, in a curious and ill-defined relationship to the

United Kingdom and the Commonwealth, and the position was not clarified until 1949.

In 1938 the 'economic war' between Ireland and England came to an end when Chamberlain and Mr de Valera concluded an agreement by which the annuities question was settled on payment of a lump sum of £10 million by Ireland, and the army and navy bases at Irish ports which were reserved by England in the articles of agreement of 1921 were handed over to the Irish army. Thus, when war broke out in 1939, and the Irish government declared its neutrality, England was denied the bases on the south and south-west coasts of Ireland which would undoubtedly have been of great advantage in the war, especially when the battle of the Atlantic was being fought – although their use would probably have involved Ireland in the war. This caused considerable resentment in England, and Churchill in particular was so resentful that he devoted part of his victory speech in 1945 to an attack on Irish neutrality. In 1940, indeed, he had offered – in studiously vague terms – Irish reunification to Mr de Valera in return for participation in the war.

To Northern Ireland the war brought a prosperity it had not known since the state came into being as a separate entity. Wartime industries developed, mainly in the area around Belfast. Derry became a major naval base, one of the nerve-centres of the Atlantic battle. Thousands of troops thronged into Northern Ireland for training, and there was a good deal more movement across the border than before the war, as workers came from the south to the wartime factories and plants, and as people travelled south for short periods to escape the war and to obtain in Dundalk, Dublin, or other centres, foods and other commodities in short supply in the United Kingdom. Craigavon, who was prime minister when the war began, but who died in 1940, suggested that conscription be applied in Northern Ireland, but the London government did not comply, and Northern Ireland's involvement in the war in this respect was not excessively large.

Mr de Valera several times asserted the claim written into

his constitution to the right of his government to concern itself with affairs in Northern Ireland. When Belfast was subjected to a severe incendiary air-raid on the night of 15 April 1941, he sent fire-brigades from Dublin and other centres in the twenty-six counties across the border. Again, in 1942, when American troops arrived in Northern Ireland to begin training for campaigns in Africa and Europe, he protested formally to the United States for sending troops into Irish national territory uninvited by the Dublin government and provoked a predictable reply from the new Northern Ireland prime minister, Andrews. These, however, were mere assertions of old and familiar attitudes.

It was in the years after the war that some changes, minor at first, began, both within Northern Ireland itself, and in the relationship between Dublin, London and Belfast. The situation in terms of population balance and firm Unionist control was restored immediately the war ended in the north. Unlike many of the Irish workers who went to the war-industries in England, the workers from the south who had gone north for war-work were not expelled from the territory. Their position had been made clear from the outset: they might not stay on and have votes.

In the south (where, unlike Northern Ireland, changes of government do from time to time take place) Fianna Fail, after sixteen years in office, was replaced in 1948 by a coalition government under John A. Costello, of Fine Gael. The government included a new party, Clann na Poblachta, which drew its support from that considerable body of opinion in the country which deprecated Fianna Fail's failure, in the words of their own old slogan, to press 'on to the republic'. Fine Gael was, for some years up to this, the declared 'commonwealth party', and as such had been doing badly until it was saved, possibly from extinction, by the 1948 coalition. Now it, or its leader, made the sudden decision to outdo Fianna Fail, and at the same time clarify Ireland's external relations by declaring a republic. This produced reactions from Northern Ireland, and from the British government, and yet another act of parliament was passed at Westminster to define England's relations with Ireland, which, while it contained no change of substance in the existing position, did give additional guarantees to Stormont, so that the Ireland Act, 1949, is in effect part of the constitution of Northern Ireland. The Westminster act, taking note of the (Irish) Republic of Ireland Act, 1948, reads in part as follows:

1 (1) It is hereby recognized and declared that the part of Ireland heretofore known as Eire ceased, as from the eighteenth day of April, nineteen hundred and forty-nine, to be part of His Majesty's dominions.

   (2) It is hereby declared that Northern Ireland remains part of His Majesty's dominions and of the United Kingdom and it is hereby affirmed that in no event will Northern Ireland or any part thereof cease to be part of His Majesty's dominions and of the United Kingdom without the consent of the Parliament of Northern Ireland.

   (3) The part of Ireland referred to in subsection (1) of this section is hereafter in this Act referred to, and may in any Act, enactment or instrument passed or made after the passing of this Act be referred to, by the name attributed thereto by the law thereof, that is to say, as the Republic of Ireland.

2 (1) It is hereby declared that, notwithstanding that the Republic of Ireland is not part of His Majesty's dominions, the Republic of Ireland is not a foreign country for the purposes of any law in force in any part of the United Kingdom or in any colony, protectorate or United Kingdom trust territory ...[49]

The Republic of Ireland Act has sometimes been seen as a further stage in the drift apart of the two parts of Ireland. In a very limited sense it was: it made clearer, and therefore perhaps reinforced, the legalistic distinctions between the two which partition had brought about. But the word 'republic' had by now, in Irish usage, been deprived of much of its original force and meaning: as used in these acts it meant little more than 'anti-union', and Mr Costello, the prime minister whose name is associated with the Irish act, stood very much in the tradition of Redmond's parliamentary party which the old republicanism had overthrown. In Northern Ireland itself the old intransigently separatist movement – the 'republican movement' –

survived, as it still did in the south, but greatly diminished.

The opposition to unionism in Northern Ireland had failed down the years to take coherent parliamentary form. This was because normal parliamentary democracy could not function in a state where the citizens were divided, in the proportion of two to one, on the right of the state itself to exist, and where the same division, involving the same two main groups, affected religion, education, employment, housing, wealth and property, history, culture, and social life. A change of government was theoretically possible under the constitution but was not practically possible in a situation where every general election was a plebiscite, and where the ruling party had always taken the view expressed by the prime minister J. M. Andrews: 'a Unionist government must always be in power in Northern Ireland.'

The extreme activist wing of the non-parliamentary separatist movement was the I.R.A. Its tradition came, somewhat deviously, from the Fenians by way of the Irish Volunteers who, in the guerrilla war against the Black and Tans, became known as the Irish Republican Army. This army divided, on the issue of the treaty articles in 1922. Part of it became absorbed into the Irish Free State army; another part, continuing to call itself the I.R.A., fought the Free State army in the civil war of 1922–3. In 1925, it broke with Mr de Valera when he made the first moves towards entering the Free State Dail. Having made the break the I.R.A. moved further to the left, but although one of the Army Council members, Peadar O'Donnell, involved himself in Co. Donegal in the renewed agrarian struggle, the organization as a whole did not follow, and further divisions occurred. An effort in the 1930s to link the I.R.A., still relatively strong in numbers, with the Labour movement, failed. In 1936 the I.R.A. was declared an unlawful organization by the Fianna Fail government, and later its chief of staff was sentenced by military tribunal to three years' penal servitude for membership of it. The organization had been following an uncertain course between committing itself to a socialist ideology in which imperialism was seen as essentially 'the highest form of capitalism' and committing itself to the limited objective of ending partition.

The 1938 agreement with England negotiated by Mr de Valera brought the partition issue to the fore again, because the matter had been discussed at the talks and Mr de Valera made a number of speeches about it afterwards. In an interview which he gave to the *Evening Standard* (London), published on 17 October 1938, he made a new proposal to Stormont:

Taking into account the prevailing sentiment of the present majority of the Six Counties and bearing in mind also the sentiment of the minority there and the majority in the whole island, here is what I propose. If I could have my own way, I would have immediately a single All-Ireland Parliament, elected on a system of proportional representation so as to be fair to minorities – this might entail a different form of executive. But what I propose, in the existing situation, is not that. I would say to Belfast: 'Keep all your present powers. We ask only one thing of you. We think the area you control is not the area which in justice you could claim, even for a local parliament, but we make the concession if you guarantee fair play for the minority and consent to the transfer to an all-Ireland Parliament of the powers now reserved to the Parliament at Westminster.

I want to make it it as easy as possible for Northern Ireland to join us, because it is my fixed belief that, once we are working together and prejudices eliminated, the North would speedily find it more economical and satisfactory to surrender their local parliament altogether and come into a single All-Ireland Parliament.

To which Lord Craigavon replied: 'I can only reiterate the old battle-cry of Northern Ireland – "No Surrender!" '[50]

Shortly after this exchange, in late November, some activity began on the border. On the night of 28 November an explosion destroyed a cottage near Castlefin, in Co. Donegal, killing three men, and the following night a number of customs huts were destroyed simultaneously by fire along the border. On 15 January 1939 the I.R.A. issued a statement which was posted up about the country as a proclamation. It called upon England

... to withdraw her armed forces, her civilian officials and institutions, and representatives of all kinds from every part of Ireland as an essential preliminary to arrangements for peace and friendship between the two countries; and we call upon the people of all Ireland, at home and in exile, to assist us in the effort we are about to make, in God's name, to compel that evacuation and to enthrone the Republic of Ireland.[51]

An ultimatum was delivered to the English Foreign Secretary, demanding the immediate withdrawal of British troops from Northern Ireland – within four days. The campaign which followed the lapse of this ultimatum consisted of sporadic sabotage and bombing in England. The bombs were placed in suitcases, parcels, or post-boxes and left to explode; seven people were killed and 137 injured. As a result of the opening of this campaign the Dublin government passed two acts, the Treason Act, which became law on 30 May 1939, and the Offences Against the State Act (similar in intent to the Special Powers Act in Northern Ireland), which became law on 14 June 1939. In Westminster a Prevention of Violence (Temporary Provisions) Act became law on 28 July 1939. The campaign in England ended with 1939, and during the war the I.R.A. formed an ineffective alliance with Nazi Germany. Large numbers of the republicans or suspected republicans were interned in Northern Ireland, as were considerable numbers in the south, where some were also executed.

After the war the activity of the I.R.A. and other republican groups in relation to Northern Ireland did not begin to revive until 1950. There were armed raids in 1954 and 1955, and then in 1956, on 12 December, a new campaign was proclaimed in a statement issued by the Army Council of the I.R.A.:

Resistance to British rule in occupied Ireland has now entered a decisive stage. Early today, Northern units of the Irish Republican Army attacked key British occupation installations.

Spearheaded by volunteers of the Irish Republican Army, our people in the Six Counties have carried the fight to the enemy. They are the direct victims of British Imperialism and they are also the backbone of the national revolutionary resurgence. . . .

We call on Irish men in the British Armed Forces to stand by the motherland and refuse to bear arms against their own countrymen.

We call on members of the R.U.C. and B Special Constabulary to cease being tools of British Imperialism and either stand on one side or join us in the fight against tyranny. . . .

The foe will use his considerable resources to divide us by fanning the fires of bigotry and sectarianism – twin enemies of Irish Republicanism. Let us be on our guard, a free Ireland cannot tolerate the one or the other. . . .[52]

The I.R.A. were not alone in this new campaign, which was directed mainly against border areas in Northern Ireland. A group known as Saor Uladh (Free Ulster) had been founded in 1953, as a political association which, since it believed in the use of force, had a military arm. Its founder, Liam Kelly, of Pomeroy, Co. Tyrone, was a senator in both Stormont and Dublin. Another group, a breakaway from the I.R.A., had carried out a successful arms raid on Armagh military barracks in 1954, and the I.R.A. itself had carried off a quantity of arms in a well planned raid on Arborfield barracks (in England) in 1955. But the main border campaigns opened in 1956 and continued with some vigour until 1959. The I.R.A. declared the campaign at an end in a statement of February 1962, stating, however, that its organization was intact and could be called into action again.

The raids of the 1950s, unlike those of 1939, avoided attacking civilians, and also police or army personnel in the Republic. They were mainly made across the border and directed at various installations – bridges, police barracks, customs posts, and the like – and they had a limited success in reviving the border issue in the Republic, and winning some sympathy for the I.R.A. Sinn Fein, the political wing of the republican movement, put up candidates in the 1955 elections in Northern Ireland and won over 150,000 votes. Two Sinn Fein candidates were elected to Westminster that year, but neither could take his seat: they had both been captured after an I.R.A. raid for arms on Omagh military barracks and were, as convicted felons, ineligible to sit in the English parliament. One of the two, Thomas Mitchell, had been elected from the constituency of Mid-Ulster, which fourteen years later was to return Bernadette Devlin to Westminster.

The Northern Ireland government handled the border campaign coolly The damage done to bridges and other installations was not very heavy; the loss of life over a period of years was relatively small – and included a number of republican lives. The campaign indeed helped to strengthen unionism and the colonial connection: it was small-scale, dispersed, and a mere violent reiteration of an argument which Ulster unionism had long since learned to rebut with ease. While the campaign roused a certain amount of sympathy in the Republic and among the minority in Northern Ireland for the aims of the republicans – as was seen in the funeral of Sean South of Garryowen, killed with Fergal O'Hanlon in a raid on Brookeborough police barracks on 1 January 1957 – it could also lose it, as when Sergeant Ovens of the R.U.C. was killed by a bomb in a booby-trapped farmhouse in August 1957. The main effect of the unsuccessful campaign was to strengthen unionism, by renewing, at a time when it might have begun to fade, the Ulster Protestant sense of being an embattled community, under siege from the forces of evil.

In the meantime, the main argument which had been used by unionists since the 1880s in their campaigns against Dublin rule was reinforced by a political episode in the south. Mr Costello's coalition government, which had come into office in Dublin in 1948, was made up of all parties in the Dail other than Fianna Fail – Fine Gael, deriving essentially from the party that had formed the first Free State government; Clann na Poblachta, the new party derived from a section of the republican movement who had decided, like Mr de Valera in 1926, to take a parliamentary line; the Labour party, a pale shadow of that founded by James Connolly; and an even paler shadow, the National Labour party (which had swarmed off from the parent Labour party hive a few years earlier after the expert application of some Red smoke by Fianna Fail); and a farmers' party. The Minister for Health, Dr Noel Browne, was a member of the Clann na Poblachta party, and the leader of the party, Mr Sean MacBride, was Minister for External Affairs.

In 1950 Dr Browne had in hand a scheme for a Mother and

Child Health Service, which would eliminate the means test in the existing Public Assistance system and was intended to provide a full state medical service in respect of maternity and related matters for all sections of the community. The scheme met with resistance in several quarters, including the Irish Medical Association, which, like most professional organizations of its kind in the free-enterprise world, was generally opposed to the intervention of the state in its affairs. On 10 October 1950, the bishop of Ferns, Most Rev. Dr James Staunton, in his capacity as secretary to the Catholic Hierarchy, wrote to the Taoiseach (prime minister) to advance episcopal objections to the scheme, on the grounds that:

... In their [i.e. the bishops'] opinion the powers taken by the State in the proposed Mother and Child Health Service are in direct opposition to the rights of the family and of the individual and are liable to very great abuse. Their character is such that no assurance that they would be used in moderation could justify their enactment. If adopted in law they would constitute a ready-made instrument for future totalitarian aggression.

The right to provide for the health of children belongs to parents, not to the State. The State has the right to intervene only in a subsidiary capacity, to supplement, not to supplant. . . .

It is not sound social policy to impose a state medical service on the whole community on the pretext of relieving the necessitous 10% from the so-called indignity of the means test. . . .

Education in regard to motherhood includes instruction in regard to sex relations, chastity and marriage. The State has no competence to give instruction in such matters. We regard with the greatest apprehension the proposal to give to local medical officers the right to tell Catholic girls and women how they should behave in regard to this sphere of conduct at once so delicate and sacred. . . .

The elimination of private medical practitioners by a State-paid service has not been shown to be necessary or even advantageous to the patient, the public in general or the medical profession. . . .

The Bishops are most favourable to measures which would benefit public health, but they consider that instead of imposing a costly bureaucratic scheme of nationalized medical services the State might well consider the advisability of providing the maternity hospitals and other institutional facilities which are at present lacking and should give adequate maternity benefits and taxation relief for large families. . . .[53]

In March 1951 the archbishop of Dublin, Most Rev. Dr J. C. McQuaid, acting on behalf of the bishops, reopened the correspondence with the government on receiving a pamphlet outlining the proposed scheme, which did not meet the objections of the bishops. There ensued a division within the government. On 15 March the Taoiseach wrote to the Minister of Health:

. . . I understand that you have not replied to His Grace's letter. I am afraid you do not appear to realize the serious implications of the views expressed in that letter, since you have, by advertisement and otherwise, continued to publicize the scheme to which objections have been taken. Such action might well seem to be defiance of the Hierarchy. . . .

I have no doubt that all my colleagues and, in particular, yourself would not be party to any proposals affecting moral questions which would or might come into conflict with the definite teaching of the Catholic Church. Having regard to the views expressed in the letters received from the Hierarchy, I feel that you should take steps at once to consult Their Lordships so as to remove any grounds for objection on their part to the Mother and Child Service and to find a mutually satisfactory solution of the difficulties which have arisen. . . .[54]

Dr Browne defended his position in continued correspondence, all of which at this stage was private. He expressed his willingness to amend the scheme to see that it contained nothing 'contrary to Catholic moral teaching' but not to amend it in respect of other objections. It emerged, as the correspondence continued, that the bishops were satisfied with the Minister's assurance regarding the scheme itself in respect of the sex-education question, but that they were not satisfied with the principle in relation to this embodied in the (Fianna Fail) Health Act, 1947, under which the scheme was to be operated. Dr Browne had indicated his willingness to amend the act, but the bishops put forward objections to the actual scheme under a number of other headings, some of which would seem to be somewhat remote from faith and morals:

Secondly – In this particular Scheme, the State arrogates to itself a function and control, on a nation-wide basis, in respect of health services, which properly ought to be and actually can be efficiently secured, for the vast majority of the citizens, by individual initiative and by lawful associations. . . .

Fourthly – To implement this particular Scheme, the State must levy a heavy tax on the whole community, by direct or indirect methods, independently of the necessity or desire of the citizens to use the facilities provided. . . .

Sixthly – This particular Scheme, when enacted on a nation-wide basis, must succeed in damaging gravely the self-reliance of parents whose family-wage or income would allow them duly to provide of themselves medical treatment for their dependants. . . .[55]

Refusing to give way, Dr Browne was asked by the leader of his party, Mr MacBride, to resign. He published the full correspondence.

Not unnaturally, this case was seized on by Northern unionists as a clear demonstration of the power of the Roman Catholic church in the Republic. The publication of the correspondence, however, came as a shock to many people in the Republic itself, not because the bishops should have views and influence on the matter in question, but because it was revealed that this influence could be used, powerfully, to operate in private on the government. In the debate on the matter in the Dail, some statements were made – such as Captain Peadar Cowan's that

The most disquieting feature of this sorry business is the revelation that the real government of the country may not, in fact, be exercised by the elected representatives of the people as we believe it was, but by the Bishops, meeting secretly and enforcing their rule by means of private interviews with Ministers and by documents of a secret and confidential nature sent by them to Ministers and to the Head of the alleged Government of the State – [56]

which were used to demonstrate that Rome rule was practised south of the border. However, the Costello government fell shortly after this episode and largely because of it, and Fianna Fail returned to office.

Mr de Valera, when out of office in the period 1948–51, had found leisure to take an active interest again in the partition question, and had conducted a vigorous campaign of agitation, which included a visit to the United States of America and another to Australia, making speeches and encouraging local Irish-exile groups. The Dublin government, not to be outdone, joined in the agitation. Its head, Mr Costello, went to Canada, and it was while he was there that he announced his government's intention of declaring a republic. The Minister for External Affairs travelled widely, speaking on partition and raising it as an issue wherever he could, to the satisfaction, no doubt, of sentimentalists of Irish blood and nationalist tradition. A national committee, the Mansion House Committee, was formed, to raise funds to co-ordinate the anti-partition campaigns, meet the expenses of anti-partition candidates in Northern Ireland, and print large quantities of (usually) green-white-and-orange-coloured propagandist literature on the subject. The chief effect of the campaign was to stimulate the Stormont prime minister, Sir Basil Brooke, into a speaking tour in opposition to it, and perhaps to rouse Mr Costello to his declaration of the republic, which in turn brought the Ireland Act with its English guarantee to Northern Ireland. After Mr de Valera's return to office in 1951, the whole sound and fury died down. History as tragedy had duly been repeated by history as farce, and after the Mansion House Committee campaign, partition has ceased to be an issue of practical inter-governmental politics in Ireland, but has taken its place with the Irish language and other once-burning questions as a subject merely for certain ritual and formalistic observances.

In spite of the I.R.A. campaign on the border in the later 1950s, this period from 1945 to about 1956 marked the beginnings of changes in Britain, and in the outside world, which in due course began to have some effect on Ireland, north and south. Changes of a kind came within the country too. In Dublin, in 1959, Mr de Valera retired from politics, becoming president of Ireland and giving way to Mr Sean Lemass as Leader of Fianna Fail and Taoiseach. In Northern Ireland, in 1963, Captain Terence O'Neill succeeded Viscount Brookeborough as prime minister.

5   Freedom, Religion and Laws

It is frightfully hard to explain to Protestants that if you give Roman Catholics a good job and a good house, they will live like Protestants, because they will see neighbours with cars and television sets.

They will refuse to have eighteen children, but if a Roman Catholic is jobless, and lives in the most ghastly hovel, he will rear eighteen children on National Assistance.

If you treat Roman Catholics with due consideration and kindness, they will live like Protestants in spite of the authoritative nature of their Church. *Captain Terence O'Neill, May 1969*[57]

The economic depression which added to the troubles of the people of Northern Ireland from the foundation of the state lasted until the Second World War, which brought about considerable change. Powers assumed by the Unionist government in 1932, and extended in 1937, to assist new industries had little effect until the demands of war began to be felt. In 1937, a new, war, industry was established in Belfast when the manufacture of aircraft began in the factory of Short Bros. and Harland, near the shipyards. When the war began, employment rose rapidly as building and construction, shipbuilding, engineering, and aircraft manufacture expanded, as did the textile industry to meet an increased wartime demand, partly for military clothing. The pressing need in the United Kingdom for food which did not take up shipping space created a demand for the products of agriculture, which had also been depressed before the war.

Unemployment dropped in the war years to about 5 per cent. After the war it gradually became clear that the structure of

Ulster industry, and with it the structure of power in Northern Ireland, was changing, as the late nineteenth-century style of capitalist enterprise, with a few great family firms closely integrated into the Tory establishment, gave way to the advanced capitalist 'managerial' style of international enterprise. Diversification of industry had begun with the war demands, and was maintained, and Northern Ireland as a whole did not relapse into the depressed condition of the inter-war years, although some parts of it did. Again gradually, the tendency which has been common in the advanced capitalism of the western world in general manifested itself in Northern Ireland – the tendency for industry and population to shift into great agglomerations and conurbations, draining economic and social life slowly from peripheral areas. This trend showed itself in Ireland as a whole as a move towards the coast which faces Britain and Europe – the east. In Northern Ireland a measure of prosperity continued after the war in the area around Belfast, and east of the Bann in general. It was not maintained to anything like the same extent west of the Bann, and Derry, the second city of the province, relapsed into depression and a condition of high unemployment, especially for men. Since the area east of the Bann was also the predominantly Protestant and Unionist area, these economic trends tended to reinforce the political and social divisions of the state.

The numbers employed on the land, in shipbuilding and in the linen industry steadily declined. The Unionist government, progressively influenced by the new-style economy and also by the need to keep in line to some extent with England (formalized in what is known as the 'step-by-step policy'), repealed its ineffective legislation of 1932 and 1937, and enacted new laws: the Industries Development Act, 1945, the Capital Grants to Industries Act, 1954–62, the Industries Development Act, 1966. Those acts provided grants, loans, and other financial subventions to new industry and gave powers to the government to acquire land and erect industrial buildings. The new diversification showed itself in the establishment of at least one major industry on a large scale in the area – man-made fibres –

and a number of smaller industries, including the manufacture of computers, telephone exchange equipment, car components, and processed and manufactured products based on agriculture. These post-war industries had provided, by 1968, employment for about 60,000 people – not enough to counterbalance the reduction of employment on the land (by about the same amount in the same period) as well as the considerable reduction in the numbers employed in shipbuilding and other traditional industries. Lack of diversification had exposed industry in Northern Ireland to the full effects of world depression. It is doubtful, however, if the new diversification offered protection against a further slump, for most of the new industries were local and peripheral ventures by great international complexes. And the post-war development suffered from the weakness of planning by inducement, and failed to solve the area's chronic unemployment problem. In 1966 the average unemployment of insured persons in Northern Ireland was 6.1 per cent, as compared with 1.5 per cent in the rest of the United Kingdom. This figure is a great improvement on the extremely high figures of the 1930s, but it is an average, which masks the considerable imbalance in unemployment within the area, between east and west, between Protestant and Catholic.

The 'step-by-step' policy was forced on the Unionist government by the logic of their political position as much as by the circumstances of their relationship with England. Unionists had strongly opposed home rule, when that rule was to be exercised from Dublin, but having been given a limited home rule themselves they proceeded, with the acquiescence of English governments (which, up to the war, had been mainly Conservative), to extend those limits in practice. The prerogatives of the Westminster parliament not being exercised, the idea of 'development' of the Northern Ireland constitution was fostered by the Unionists, and the rule 'United Kingdom matters for Westminster, Northern Ireland matters for Stormont' came to be regarded by them as part of that constitution. However, unlike the United Kingdom, Northern Ireland, in so far as it exists as a separate political entity, has a written constitution, in the form of the Government of Ireland Act, 1920, and the Ireland Act, 1949, and the established practice that, for example, internal Northern Ireland affairs should not be debated at Westminster remained no more than a convention. Devolution itself, however, would be in danger if Northern Ireland were seen to be too much out of line with the neighbouring island, and the 'step-by-step' policy was designed to avoid this. The post-war Labour government in England and the creation of the welfare state put some strain on the arrangement. The Stormont government, unchanged and unchanging, remained Unionist and Tory: its representatives in Westminster opposed the Labour government's welfare legislation. Yet the step-by-step principle required that in Northern Ireland the same party should advocate and put forward the same proposals as they opposed in Westminster. The whole structure of society and politics in England had been much more changed by and through the war than had anything in the Northern Ireland situation: the Unionists, if they were to continue the step-by-step policy, now that Labour was in power in England, must reflect these changes. They did so.

The effects of the extension of welfare state policies to Northern Ireland were complex, and indeed have not yet fully worked themselves out. An arrangement was made whereby the system of national insurance would be the same, in terms of contributions and benefits, as in the rest of the United Kingdom: a separate Northern Ireland fund was adjusted to the British funds, and legislation was enacted by which payments were made from the central government into the exchequer of Northern Ireland to subsidize from Great Britain payments for pensions and allowances equal to those in England. No religious discrimination could be made in the welfare state services, since these must be run on the same lines as in England. An immediate effect therefore was to ease the burden on the Catholic population of Northern Ireland of the already existing economic and social discrimination. The unemployment rate among Catholics as compared with the unemployment rate for the area as a whole has, for example, tended to be about twice as high.

This has always placed a selective pressure on Catholics to emigrate, and has kept the Catholic proportion of the population in Northern Ireland more or less stable in spite of their considerably higher birth rate. Now, with relatively high unemployment and health benefits, the pressure towards emigration was lessened.

The higher Catholic birth rate has been, since the foundation of Northern Ireland as a separate state, a constant subject of Unionist warnings to the Protestant population. The fear of being out-bred has ever been present, and the Unionists have been able to call on the Protestant employers and workers alike to exert economic pressure to drive Catholics out of the area. This undoubtedly is one of the chief functions served by the recurring sectarian riots and pogroms in Belfast: driving Catholics out, whenever the pressure of their numbers was felt, has been a feature of these. The extent of the danger which has been, and still is, apprehended by the Protestant population to their 'ascendancy' in this respect is shown by the fact that at any given moment the number of Catholic children of school-going age is nearly half that of the total of such children (and in 1969, according to Captain O'Neill, the proportion of Catholic children was 51 per cent). It is only by the operation of selective pressures, mainly economic, that the proportion of Catholics in the population as a whole has been kept relatively stable. Since the war, it has shown a tendency to rise slowly, as follows:

1911	34.4%
1926	33.5%
1937	33.5%
1951	34.4%
1961	34.9%

This aspect of the welfare state undoubtedly caused concern to the Unionists, and in 1956 they attempted to depart from the step-by-step policy, precisely on the question of large families. The Westminster government in that year increased family allowances and in the process introduced a differentiation between the second child and subsequent children, by which a larger allowance was paid for each child after the second. The Northern Ireland government in introducing parallel legislation modified the increase so that the differentiation would operate in the opposite way, larger allowances being made for the second and third children than for subsequent children. Catholics pointed out that this departure from the Westminster government's formula was discriminatory, and many Unionists pointed out that it was a dangerous departure from the step-by-step policy. The Presbyterian General Assembly in June, in a resolution, supported the Catholic complaint that the proposal could be interpreted as 'an intentional and political discrimination against them' and called on the government to fall into line with the English scheme. The government gave way, and preserved the step-by-step principle.

The welfare state, however, if it embodied principles contrary to those of the Unionists who controlled Northern Ireland, and if it did have, for them, some dangers, also helped to consolidate the position of Northern Ireland as a separate state in relation to the rest of Ireland. In the 1950s and early 1960s the Republic lagged far behind Northern Ireland in the social services and benefits it could provide. Nationalists in the north, who remained opposed to the maintenance of the partition of Ireland, must nevertheless now think twice before they would make any move which might bring them into the social and political system of the Republic, and so deprive them of the health, education, and welfare services they became accustomed to in the post-war period. The Unionists soon began using as an argument in favour of Northern Ireland – as against the Republic – the social legislation of their Labour opponents in England. The whole experience of living through a few years of Westminster Labour government was, however, a new one for them, and it tempered, even more than had the taste of political power they received in 1920, their enthusiasm for a union under the English *parliament*. Like their forerunners under Carson and Craig, Unionists were, in their own way, home rulers. Not until the Attlee government gave way to Churchill's was the step-by-step policy relatively free from strain.

Of all the provisions of the welfare state, the most significant for the political situation in Northern Ireland was probably the provision for reasonably ready access to higher education made under the Education Acts. In the very nature of the case, however, there is a time-lag in the appearance of the effects of improved educational facilities, but by the late 1950s that large section of the community in Northern Ireland which had been excluded from the benefits of further education, and which included a very high proportion of the Catholic population, was beginning to pass through university.

The Queen's University of Belfast was founded in 1845, as one of three Queen's Colleges (the others were at Cork and Galway), under an act of parliament by which the colleges were required to be non-sectarian (for which they were opposed by the Roman Catholic bishops). Under the Irish Universities Act, 1908, the college became a separate university, the other two becoming colleges of the new National University of Ireland. At this time the Belfast university was attended mainly by Presbyterians, since Church of Ireland students tended still to go to the old ascendancy university in Dublin, to Trinity College. Belfast had about 5 per cent of Catholic students. The establishment in 1909 of a department in scholastic philosophy, the recognition of the (Catholic) Mater Misericordiae hospital in Belfast as a teaching hospital, and the appointment of a professor of Celtic, all encouraged a larger Catholic attendance, and the proportion rose to about 22 per cent by 1960. The significant change which began to be apparent about that date, however, was that Catholics, as well as Protestants, of the lower middle and working classes, through the new system of grants and allowances, now began to find it possible to obtain higher education.

Social and economic change, much of it beyond the control of the group of people who had ruled Northern Ireland since 1920, placed strains on the Unionist party itself. By the nature of the situation – which demanded permanent one-party rule – the Unionist party as a whole had within it at all times disparate elements. It was a coalition of interests which were fully united

131

only in their determination never to let the Catholics take over – the determination still, after three centuries, of colonial settlers to resist native rule at all costs. Since Northern Ireland was not an independent state, this aim had to be pursued with some circumspection, through a political machine that would regularly and efficiently deliver a solid Unionist vote, and through a measure of intimidation and discrimination that would be sufficient to keep the large minority cowed and in subjection without arousing the undue interest of the outside world – especially the parliament of Westminster. The Unionist party machinery was perfected by building up the Orange institute and integrating it fully into the party and into the state – a secret religious brotherhood which enabled an almost totalitarian system to be perfected within the forms of a parliamentary democracy.

For it is important to note that, although it held regular elections, and even returned members to Westminster, Northern Ireland was not until the 1960s a parliamentary democracy in any normal sense of the term, since the electorate had never the opportunity to choose between normal political issues or normal political persons. The issue put at every election was that of the continuance or dissolution of the state, and the full apparatus of the permanently ruling party operated through the Orange institute, to which all Unionist members of parliament as a rule belonged, and through the religious persuasions of the majority, to ensure that no other issue should intrude. It could not be otherwise, for the six counties of north-east Ireland are not and were not and could not be – unless a revolutionary change of heart were to occur on one side or the other – viable as a democratic state. The minority opposed to the very fundamentals of the constitution was, and is, too large. The division is too deep.

It was important for the continuance of Unionist rule in Northern Ireland that it should be virtually totalitarian, in that control should extend to every aspect of political and social life: it was equally important that this control, although total, should be exercised with some moderation. This was not only because England had to be considered, but because the great majority of those who voted for and otherwise supported the Unionist government believed or professed to believe in parliamentary democracy. It was important, and has always been a main object of the Unionist policy of control, to keep the labour movement in the industrialized north-east from breaking away, and for this it was necessary to mask Tory policies and show them in another guise: Protestantism.

For more than forty years a delicate balance was maintained within the party between religious fanatics who took seriously the drumming in of the party's and the state's Protestant character, and 'progressive' Unionists and others on the other hand, who took too much to heart the protestations of democracy, some of them to the extent that they believed the liberties and laws of the Williamite constitution might be extended to other than Protestants.

The balance became increasingly difficult to maintain. The abolition of proportional representation in the 1920s had helped to cope with the danger of splinter groups and parties. In the war years, a change from the overt state Protestantism of the 1930s became necessary, and there was a purge of those, led by the prime minister, J. M. Andrews, who had failed to modify their demeanour on this matter, in favour of those, led by the new prime minister, Viscount Brookeborough, who were willing to accommodate the tone of their pronouncements to the changing times. In the 1960s, when Ireland north and south was opening to investment from foreign capital, when both parts of the country were involved in and expecting to be affected by the prolonged haggling with the European Economic Community, when 'Welfare' was an established fact of political life, and the beginnings of the consumer culture usually referred to as affluent were blurring the sharpness of old cultural distinctions through the mass-communications media, a further change became necessary, both for the party's 'public relations' and for its internal regrouping. When Viscount Brookeborough, a Unionist of the old school, retired, he was replaced in 1963 by Captain Terence O'Neill.

Captain O'Neill, a descendant of the Chichester family which had been among the rulers of the colonial settlement in Northern Ireland since the seventeenth century (just as his predecessor, Viscount Brookeborough, was descended from another seventeenth-century colonial landlord family), presented nonetheless an image different from the stern and dour representation of Cromwellian Protestantism that had been part of his predecessors' stock in trade as politicians. His coming to office was accompanied by a change in the manner of Ulster unionism. It coincided with other changes. In 1963 Pope John XXIII died, but not before he had convened the second Vatican Council and caused an upheaval within the Roman Catholic church and a reorientation of its rigid institutional framework. The new efforts of the Roman Catholic church to enter into 'dialogue' with other Christian churches were to have repercussions in Northern Ireland.

Changes of significance for Northern Ireland were also happening in the Republic in the early 1960s, many of which had their origins in the preceding decade. The Republic had emerged from the isolation of neutrality in a warring world with much the same policies and problems as it had in the prewar period – still protectionist, under-industrialized, impoverished, and, as a community, dispirited by chronic emigration. Mr de Valera's government, from 1932 onwards, had tried, while dismantling the 1921 treaty agreement and developing a policy of economic self-sufficiency, not to break away completely from the English system. Mr de Valera himself had frequently indicated his interest in preserving the cultural tradition of the old Gaelic nation; at the same time he adhered to some elements of the republican tradition – especially in so far as it recognized 'the common name of Irishman' as one to be valued among differing traditions and creeds; at the same time he accepted the colonial economic system in many of its aspects. His policy began to break down even before the war; the war years themselves, when many thousands of citizens flocked into the factories of wartime England, and many thousands more into England's armed forces, saw it begin to collapse. Massive emigration became the main feature of the period immediately after the war, rising to a point in the 1950s where it was approaching (in proportion to the smaller population) the scale of the post-famine years. The Fianna Fail minister who for much of this period was responsible for economic matters in one way or another, Mr Sean Lemass, had endeavoured to encourage the development of small-scale industry through protectionist policies. This failed to cope with the problem of under-employment, since the number of jobs created in new industries was matched by the decrease in numbers employed on the land.

It was when Mr de Valera was out of office, in 1950, that the first serious steps were taken towards economic co-operation between the two governments in the island, with a joint scheme for drainage of the Erne basin, and for an Erne hydroelectric station. Then in 1951 the two governments took over jointly the Great Northern Railway, which linked Dublin with Northern Ireland, and in 1952 the two governments jointly took over the Foyle fisheries and set up an administrative commission. The second inter-party government, which took office in Dublin in 1954, again under Mr Costello, initiated developments that were to be of great importance to the Republic and, in time, to bring about a change in the relationship between the Republic and Northern Ireland. This initiative consisted in offering inducements – mainly in the form of grants to attract foreign industrial development but also involving some tax exemptions to promote export industries. This was a year of economic crisis, with emigration approaching its peak of 60,000 in a year and unemployment rising towards a figure of 90,000. In 1957 the government went out of office and Mr de Valera returned, until his retirement from party politics in 1959. Under Mr Lemass's administration, the initiative of 1956 was followed through. He began, in fact, the delicate task of turning Fianna Fail policy in a wholly new direction, while at the same time retaining the traditional vote which the party, through its extremely efficient machine, had held since 1932.

In 1958 the government published a detailed paper entitled *Economic Development,* and broke precedent by naming the Secretary of the Department of Finance (head of the Irish

Civil Service), Mr T. K. Whitaker, as its author. The paper emphasized the need for productive capital investment, in a detailed analysis. Its first appendix was a memorandum for the government, dated 16 December 1957, which consisted of a minute from Mr Whitaker to the Minister for Finance, in which the secretary refers to

... the desirability of attempting to work out an integrated programme of national development for the next five or ten years, which I believe will be critical years for the country's survival as an economic entity.

I have not a 'Plan' in mind. There would be little sense in trying to establish any rigid pattern of development for a small country so exposed to the perpetual flux of world economic forces....

What is urgently necessary is *not* to know that more resources should be devoted to productive rather than non-productive purposes but rather to know what are the productive purposes to which resources should be applied and what unproductive, or relatively unproductive, activities can, with the minimum social disadvantage, be curtailed to set free resources for productive development....

... a slowing down in housing and other forms of social investment must be faced from now on because of the virtual satisfaction of needs over wide areas – and it is necessary to find productive investments which will prevent the unemployment problem from becoming very serious....

While I deprecate planning in any rigid sense, I am convinced of the psychological value of setting up targets of national endeavour, provided they are reasonable and mutually consistent. ...[58]

The government then announced its first programme for economic expansion, beginning at the end of 1958, and in 1964 Mr Lemass's government introduced the second programme, which was intended to cover the period to 1970.

It was partly because these programmes of free-enterprise planning, which aimed at attracting foreign investment and developing the economy (and, inevitably, the society) on capitalist lines, brought the Republic into line with Northern Ireland that relations between Dublin and Stormont began to change. Mr Lemass's government, in escaping from the dilemma of Ireland's economic and social stagnation and decay and consequent demoralization, by abandoning the old economic policies which Fianna Fail had largely inherited from Griffith's Sinn Fein, had also, inevitably, jettisoned much of the party's old political and cultural ideology – although this was not made explicit. As the changeover of generations took place, within the leadership of Fianna Fail, as within the leadership of the Ulster Unionists, as one veteran after another of the struggles over home rule, the republic, and partition left the scene, the new leaders looked at one another and realized that they had a good deal in common.

Mr Lemass himself was a veteran of the guerrilla war, but he presided over the change to the new policies. The policies stimulated or coincided with developments in the economy. The party, while contriving to retain its hold on the small farmers and the rural workers, began to attract much more middle-class and business support. There were many signs of ideological change. In 1958 Mr Donal Barrington read a paper to the Printers' Co-operative Society in Dublin (later published as a pamphlet, *Uniting Ireland*) in which he attacked the whole concept of the Mansion House Committee and the anti-partition campaign which Mr de Valera had inaugurated ten years previously, and said:

Our task is simply, by withdrawing the threat of external coercion, to permit Northern politics to evolve in a normal and peaceful way.

Once we have taken the steps outlined earlier in this paper to reduce tension between North and South and to create the conditions in which a unity of wills can grow, then we should say no more in public on the subject of Partition than is necessary, but should let commonsense and goodwill do their work. It would be a good thing if every man who contemplates speaking on Partition in public should ask himself the question – 'Will my speech really help to unite Ireland?' We should, however, keep ourselves well informed on the problems of the North for knowledge will help to protect us against mistakes of policy such as we made in the past.[59]

Mr Barrington was adopted by the Fianna Fail party as a candidate for the Irish senate in the election of 1961. The policy he suggested was, in effect, put into operation by Mr Lemass's government.

In 1963, in a speech which made explicit the new outlook of the Dublin government, Mr Lemass said:

We recognize that the Government and Parliament there [in Northern Ireland] exist with the support of the majority of the people of the Six County area – artificial though that area is. We see it functioning within its powers and we are prepared to stand over the proposal that they should continue to function within those powers, within an all-Ireland constitution for so long as it is desired to have them. Recognition of the realities of the situation has never been a difficulty with us. . . .

The solution of the problem of partition is one to be found in Ireland by Irishmen. . . .[60]

At the beginning of 1965, Mr Lemass paid an unannounced visit to Stormont, where he conferred with Captain O'Neill, and shortly afterwards Captain O'Neill returned the visit in Dublin. It was announced that these direct contacts, the first between the heads of the two governments since the foundation of the separate states, would continue, and that similar direct contacts in Dublin and Stormont would be made by ministers of the two governments to discuss matters of common concern. Northern Ireland obtained a number of concessions in trade and related matters from the Republic as a result of these continuing talks. The Republic received little that was concrete in return, but the government clearly was satisfied that the ice had been broken and that it did not have to continue maintaining a posture of injured righteousness on the partition question either to Stormont or to Westminster. Ireland, like the United Kingdom, had its application in to join the European Economic Community, and at the end of 1965 the Fianna Fail government negotiated a Free Trade Agreement with England, to come into effect in 1966 and, over a period of ten years, to dismantle the tariff barriers between the two countries and, in economic terms, restore the union. By the late 1960s, some of the Republic's problems had been solved, in the short term at least. Emigration had been stabilized at a fairly low level, and 'affluence' had produced a good deal of conspicuous consumption. The country-side, especially in the west, was being steadily depopulated into the towns, especially in the east. Tourism was a major industry. There was a great deal of foreign capital investment, and a good deal of government money spent in enticing it – some of it on distinctly off-white elephants. There was a building boom, in office-blocks. There was a widening gap between rich and poor. There were more rich men in politics than there had been in the idealistic 1920s and 1930s. For the sore thumb of partition, which Irish spokesmen had displayed around the world fifteen years or so before, Mr Lemass had borrowed Captain O'Neill's velvet glove. There were indications and more than hints from government spokesmen that, although Ireland had been neutral in the Second World War, unlike Switzerland she had no set policy of neutrality, but was willing to claim her place in what was still, down to about 1966, widely referred to as the free world. Mr Lemass had a well-deserved reputation as a prag-matist: he had a keen eye for a good mess of pottage. Among the other pragmatisms of the middle 1960s, it was made plain by the Dublin government that it was not prepared any further to sponsor the minority in Northern Ireland in the airing of their grievances, and Fianna Fail's faithful allies in Northern Ire-land, the Nationalist party, led by Mr McAteer, abandoned their stand of many years in Stormont and accepted the style of Her Majesty's Loyal Opposition.

The new entente of Fianna Fail and the Ulster Unionist party withstood its first strain when, in 1966, the fiftieth anniversary of the Easter rising of 1916 came to be celebrated. Captain O'Neill, in spite of protests from the Unionist right, permitted well-mannered commemorations in Northern Ireland. The Dublin government, with pomp, ceremony, and an air of finality, buried the republican dead.

The structure of the state and of politics in Northern Ireland was such that parliamentary opposition was frustrated – all the more so since the main opposition group was opposed not merely to the government but to the constitution. Opposition M.P.s could make some efforts to look after their constituents, and the opposition could gain control of a local authority here and there, but they could exert no effective pressure or check on a government which was confident of being permanently in office. Through the half-century since the beginning of the state, the main opposition party had been the Nationalist party. The northern wing of the old Irish Parliamentary days before the First World War had a character of its own, under the leadership of Joe Devlin, largely because of its association with the sectarian Ancient Order of Hibernians. The party was strongly clericalist in character. In 1918, when Sinn Fein was everywhere through the country making inroads into the anti-union vote, it was plain, from one or two by-elections, that the Nationalists in the north still held a strong position, which they were not disposed to yield to Sinn Fein. When the general election of that year came about, the Catholic bishops of the north suggested that the Ulster constituencies be divided by agreement between Nationalist and Sinn Fein candidates, to avoid splitting the anti-unionist vote. When agreement had not been reached on the eve of nomination, Cardinal Logue, the archbishop of Armagh, allocated the constituencies as between the two anti-unionist parties, provoking caustic comment from Carson on the subservience of his political opponents to bishops and priests. The Sinn Fein, or republican, element in the opposition to unionism has been a fluctuating one, because of the generally abstentionist attitude of the republicans, which has at times been extended not merely to parliament but to elections themselves. The Nationalists, on the other hand, have always collaborated to some extent in the northern parliamentary system, and have given it a semblance of reality thereby. Even at the height of the revolutionary struggle, Joe Devlin's little group elected in 1918 did not attend the first Dail in Dublin, but went, with the unionists, to Westminster. The combined votes of those who opposed partition and the constitution of Northern Ireland – representing about a third of the population of the area – have been sufficient usually to gain about eleven or twelve seats of the fifty-two in the Stormont house of commons. Most of these have been held as a rule by the Nationalists. The party has maintained such strength as it had largely through local Tammany-Hall-style organizations and local politics and through its association with opposition at local level to the Orange order, itself largely sectarian in character. In recent years, especially under the leadership of Mr Eddie McAteer, it has taken its policy line on broad issues from the Fianna Fail party of the Republic, and after the O'Neill–Lemass meetings, the National-ist party gave recognition to the Northern Ireland constitution by accepting the style of official opposition.

The rest of the opposition to unionism was fragmented and in recurring disarray. The 'step-by-step' policy was a Unionist one: it did not extend to the whole spectrum of politics in Northern Ireland. Liberalism never disappeared altogether, and from time to time it threw up sturdy champions like the Reverend James Armour of Ballymoney, a Presbyterian in the eighteenth-century tradition, who was a home-ruler at the beginning of the century; but it was not a political force. The labour movement was itself divided, indeed splintered, on the question of partition and the constitution, so that a political movement comparable to that which brought Labour governments to power in Westminster after the war never developed in Northern Ireland. A number of different traditions failed to come together in the movement: for example, that of trade unionism, which in theory should favour the solidarity of workers, irrespective of creed, but which has been divided on a number of issues – whether, for instance, unions in Northern Ireland should be branches of all-Ireland unions or branches of British unions. James Connolly, who had inspired the labour movement early in the century both in its industrial and in its political aspects, had been a separatist, strongly opposed to partition, and strongly opposed to any part of Ireland retaining a colonial status. His influence had waned, north and south; in the Republic in particular he had been turned into a nationalist plaster saint whose ideas were, as far as possible, suppressed. One of the paradoxical results of the 1966 formal celebrations of the 1916 rising was that they redirected attention to the 1916 ideas which had stood the test of time – those of Connolly – and aroused the

141

interest of young people, north as well as south of the border, in them. But this did not affect parliamentary politics. Another tradition in the labour movement in Northern Ireland was, of course, that of the British labour movement, and the Northern Ireland Labour party has been since 1949 a part of that movement. The Irish Labour party (of the Republic) also had some connections north of the border. Labour opposition tended to concentrate in Belfast where a variety of candidates labelled Republican Labour or Independent Labour or Northern Ireland Labour or otherwise have contested seats in most elections, and from time to time won them. But in so far as these drew unionist votes, they were liable to lose them back to the official Unionists whenever danger appeared to, or was made to seem to, threaten the Protestant cause. Thus, in 1949, after the great Mansion House Committee agitation about partition, the Unionists roundly defeated Labour candidates at the polls. Jobs, houses, and food were not in the end the issues on which the workers of Belfast voted, but the threat of Rome.

The religious professions of the population of Northern Ireland as recorded at the 1961 census are shown in Table 1. The religious practice of most of the people was not confined to entering a denomination on a census form: church attendance in Ireland remains extremely high by the standards of the post-Christian world of north-western Europe. The average attendance of Roman Catholics at church on Sundays in the 1960s was probably over 90 per cent in Northern Ireland, and of the various Protestant denominations probably over 50 per cent. That is on any one Sunday: the percentage of the whole population attending church, but not necessarily weekly, was probably over 80 per cent in the 1960s. In this respect, Northern Ireland is at once distinct from England and much closer in its patterns of behaviour to the Republic of Ireland, where, however, the proportions of the different denominations in the whole population are quite different, almost 95 per cent being Roman Catholic.

Church attendance and other religious practices reflected the strength of belief of the people in the various creeds they pro-

TABLE 1[61]

Roman Catholic	497,547	34.9 %
Presbyterian	413,113	29.0 %
Church of Ireland	344,800	24.2 %
Methodist	71,865	5.0 %
Brethren	16,847	1.2 %
Baptist	13,765	1.0 %
Congregational	9,838	0.7 %
Unitarian	5,613	0.4 %
Others	23,236	1.6 %
Not Stated	28,418	2.0 %
Total	1,425,042	100.0 %

fessed, but, while the Protestant group as a whole is divided up into a variety of confessions, Protestants have generally drawn together in opposition to the Catholics on many issues. In the eighteenth century there had been considerable opposition between Dissenters (but especially Presbyterians) and the established Church of Ireland. These differences had long been merged, so far as all major social and political questions were concerned, in the common front against Rome. What brought them together in this common front was fear: thus the General Assembly of the Presbyterian Church in 1950:

... One root of the Catholic–Protestant conflict, especially here where numbers are sometimes nearly equal, is the fact that the Roman Catholic Church is a world-wide religious organization that seeks to gain control of the institutions of mankind and of public life generally; it is not merely a Church, it is a political organization. ...

Thus the Protestant often fears the dangers of the violation of his freedom and/or ecclesiastical power in religious, political, and social affairs.[62]

It was, in other words, not so much that the majority quarrelled with the doctrines accepted by the Catholics (although they did) but that they feared that if ever the Catholics should come to power in Northern Ireland, a theocratic tyranny would be in-

143

stituted. The fact that no such tyranny had been instituted in the overwhelmingly Roman Catholic state on the other side of the border appears to have had little effect in dispelling this fear. But then among many of the Protestants of Northern Ireland, especially in the poorer part of the community which has had few opportunities for education, there prevailed an ignorance of what conditions were really like in the south which was enlivened by an imaginary demonology derived from the enthusiasms of various bethels and preaching-houses in the back streets of Belfast and elsewhere. Something like the Browne case, when it happened, was taken as proof positive of the reality of Rome rule in the Republic.

To Catholics in Northern Ireland, on the other hand, too many of their Protestant fellows appeared as canting bigots – hypocrites too, for the very liberties they feared to lose for themselves they deprived others of, and the very features of government they deprecated in a Catholic state they maintained in a Protestant one. Thus ministers of religion, sometimes more than one at a time, had held office in Northern Ireland cabinets; the government party was closely connected with the avowedly religious Orange order; the government had more than once altered its decisions because of pronouncements of the Presbyterian General Assembly or other religious bodies. In an atmosphere where there was no disposition on either side to make concessions, such recriminations were cumulative, and built up into a fabric of mutual distrust, fear and, at mildest, dislike.

This was helped by the segregation of the community. Catholic or Protestant: this was as fundamental a distinction, affecting as wide a range of activities and attitudes in Ulster as Black or White in the United States. Schools and social activities were segregated. In many, indeed most, towns residential areas were fully or partly segregated. Intermarriage between Catholics and Protestants was rare, and the application by the Irish bishops of the *Ne Temere* decree of the Council of Trent requiring the Catholic partner in a mixed marriage (which must take place in a Catholic church only) to obtain guarantees from the Protestant partner regarding, among other matters, the bringing up of the children as Catholics, was one of the sources of alarm to Protestants. The broad economic difference between the status of the two communities, which was and is marked, has reinforced segregation. And there are still cultural differences – apart from those involved in the very religious distinction itself. For example, Irish is often taught at Catholic schools, and Catholics tend to have a different view of their own and the country's history, and to be much more conscious of their Irishness.

Some tensions are inevitable in a society where two communities (in effect) live side by side with different outlooks and traditions, but in numbers which approach being equal. It has been pointed out that the minority in the Republic does not constitute a problem because of the great imbalance in size between it and the majority. However, special problems have arisen in the Republic from this very imbalance, problems revealed in the tendency of the already small Protestant population to decrease steadily. A very sharp decline of the number of Protestants living in the twenty-six-county area had taken place in the period in which the parliamentary union with England was broken, as revealed in the census figures:

1911 327,179
1926 220,723

This, however, is largely explicable by the great exodus of Protestants (who were mostly unionist in opinion in all parts of Ireland) which took place at the time of the setting up of the Free State. They left either because a sense of loyalty to England led them to refuse to serve under an Irish government or because an unwillingness to yield their ascendancy to Catholics brought them to the same decision. Those who stayed on continued to decline in numbers, and it seems likely that they were too small a proportion of the population (one too with a lower birth rate than the majority) to resist the steady if involuntary pressure exerted on them by the lack of intermarriage.

The refusal of the two communities to intermarry, leading as it inevitably must to segregation of the young at separate schools, and separate social occasions, has maintained in Northern Ireland the separation of cultural traditions. The genetic segregation has been so effective that, since it is also reinforced by minor distinctive cultural traits, it is common enough to hear in Ulster that someone 'looks like a Protestant'. Settlers and natives remained distinct, and it is the settlers, the Protestants, who continue to experience the feeling – and the fears – of being a minority, for they are very conscious of being a fifth of the population of the island, crowded into its north-east corner, and pressed upon by the faster-breeding Catholics.

The defence against the apprehended threat to Protestant liberties then, a threat which has always been kept before the minds of the Protestants at large by the rulers of the state, has been to operate an elaborate system of discrimination, along the line of religious cleavage. It has been operated throughout the area in employment in various ways. In some firms or offices, especially smaller, family businesses, no Catholics were employed. In larger establishments, no Catholics were employed except at the lower levels. This kind of discrimination at the level of the family business could be, and was, operated in reverse, by the Catholics, but when it came to larger-scale operations, especially in the public sector, they were in no position to resist the steady oppression exerted by the Protestant majority. Many tables of figures and facts have been made available in the past year or so, in connection with the civil rights agitation, which demonstrate in detail the kind of problem the civil rights workers were facing in public employment. A single example, which is representative, must suffice here. It is taken from Co. Fermanagh, where in 1948 Mr E. C. Ferguson, Unionist M.P. for Enniskillen (who became Crown Solicitor for Fermanagh in 1949), speaking at the annual Unionist convention, said:

The Nationalist majority in the county, notwithstanding a reduction of 336 in the year, stands at 3,684. We must ultimately reduce and liquidate that majority. This county, I think it can safely be said, is a Unionist county. The atmosphere is Unionist. The Boards and properties are nearly all controlled by Unionists. But there is still this millstone around our necks. . . . I would ask the meeting to take whatever steps, however drastic, to wipe out this Nationalist majority.[63]

The Catholic population of the county was 55.3 per cent of the whole in 1937, 55.6 per cent in 1951, and 53.2 per cent in 1961. The local government (County Council) employment pattern for Fermanagh in March 1969 (excluding people working in schools) is shown in Table 2.

TABLE 2[64]

	Catholics	Protestants
1. County Council Administrative & Financial:		
(a) Secretariat	0	10
(b) Finance	1	17
(c) Local Taxation	0	4
(d) Caretakers	0	2
2. Housing Department	0	10
3. County Library	1	14
4. Planning & Tourist Department	0	5
5. Architect's Office	1	8
6. Public Works Department	4	60
7. Education Office	4	120
8. Health & Welfare Department:		
(a) Health	17	63
(b) Welfare	4	25
Totals	32	338

A similar policy has been followed in the allocation of housing, with the added refinement that the boundaries of electoral wards are taken carefully into account here, housing being one of the chief devices by which the distribution of the population into segregated Catholic and Protestant districts is arranged for electoral purposes. Local and central government, employment, housing, electoral manipulation, the encouragement of divisive sectarianism especially in the trade union and labour movements: all of these have been operated over the years in a close-knit system to preserve, in every area and at every point and touching the lives of the people at every turn, the dominance both in numbers and in power of the Protestant ascendancy. The point of intersection and contact for all these activities was the Orange Lodge, reinforced by the Unionist party.

Since a great deal of this kind of control was exercised through local authorities and the manipulation of local government, the mode of election of these was of particular interest to the Catholics who were the victims of the control. The effects of Unionist control of local authorities may be judged from, to take the same example again, Co. Fermanagh, a county with a Catholic majority and one where discrimination in employment and other opportunities has caused a considerable economic differentiation between Protestants and Catholics in favour of Protestants. Of 1,589 county council houses built there from the war to 1969, 1,021 were occupied by Protestant tenants and 568 by Catholic tenants.[65]

The local government franchise included a property qualification and multiple votes for businessmen – limited companies being entitled to appoint one nominee for every £10 of the valuation of the premises, up to a maximum of six nominees. The effect of these provisions in the franchise may be judged by comparing the number of local government electors (including multiple-vote nominees) on the register with the numbers on the Westminster parliamentary register and on the Stormont register. The figures quoted are for the year 1967:[66]

Local government register	694,483
Stormont register	933,724
Westminster register	909,841

Apart from the device of multiple votes and the retention of property qualifications, the Unionists retained control in local and Stormont government in many areas where they were in minorities by the skilful use of the device of gerrymander. This is a device which can only be used effectively on the basis of a very accurate knowledge of how particular groups of people will vote. It is relatively ineffective in a political situation where voters are liable to change their minds, but in Northern Ireland the line of political division approximated so closely to the line of religious division that for a party in full control of the electoral machinery gerrymandering was relatively easy.

The arrangement of three constituencies which returned members to Stormont from Co. Fermanagh in 1949 (see Table 3) will illustrate the method. Here, what has been done is to

TABLE 3[67]

Constituency	Unionist vote	Nationalist vote	Unionist majority	Nationalist majority
Enniskillen	5,706	4,729	977	
Lisnaskea	5,593	4,173	1,420	
S. Fermanagh	2,596	6,680		4,084
Totals	13,895	15,582		1,687

draw an electoral boundary, giving an unlikely-looking shape on the map, to include as many Nationalist and as few Unionist votes as possible and to create the constituency of South Fermanagh. The remainder of the county, where there is now a slight Unionist majority, is then divided in two. Thus a county with a Nationalist majority of voters returns two Unionist and one Nationalist M.P. to Stormont.

The classic instance of gerrymander, before 1969, was the city of Londonderry, symbol to Protestant Ulster of their whole beleaguered defiant situation ever since it withstood siege by James II. Unfortunately for the symbol, the city in the twentieth century had a large majority of anti-Unionist Catholics. At the beginning of the Northern Ireland state the city therefore returned a Catholic nationalist to the Northern Ireland parliament. In order to change this, in a rearrangement of boundaries the city was divided in two, the bulk of the urban population, crowded into the Catholic ghetto on the west side of Derry, being taken into the 'Foyle' constituency, and the 'City' constituency having its boundaries extended eight miles to the east into the countryside of Co. Derry to create a Protestant majority, so that the city whose 'prentice-boys had

149

closed the gates in James's face would be represented at Stormont by a Protestant Unionist.

The most skilful manoeuvre was carried out, however, in arranging the electoral wards of Derry for local government purposes. The 1966 revision gave eight local government representatives to each of three wards, a total of twenty-four. These were arranged as follows:

South Ward (the area which includes the Bogside)	14,125 anti-Unionist voters
	1,474 Unionist voters
North Ward	3,173 anti-Unionist voters
	4,380 Unionist voters
Waterside Ward	2,804 anti-Unionist voters
	4,420 Unionist voters [68]

By this division, the 20,102 anti-Unionist voters of Derry returned eight representatives to the city council, and the 10,274 Unionist voters returned sixteen representatives – who maintained the South Ward ghetto by every device at their disposal. A Catholic, even with money in his pocket, could only with the greatest difficulty, and only by subterfuge, buy a house in a Unionist ward.

By the late 1960s Northern Ireland was virtually a one-party state, where the Unionist manipulators of prejudice, of genuine fears and traditions, and of the forms of parliamentary democracy had produced a system of tyranny that operated on more than a third of the population like the body's rejection mechanism on a transplanted organ. The system had two areas of weakness where it was exposed to new forces. One was the tendency of the labour movement to redefine the social categories in terms of class, which would produce an analysis of the Northern Ireland situation that would ultimately be detrimental to the Tories who exploited the sectarian division of the workers. The other was the penetration of parts of the system by English social democracy as the result of Labour policies in England, the maintenance of the Union, and the consequent 'step-by-step' policy of the Unionists.

These two forces converged in the 1960s in the civil rights movement. The trade union movement in Ireland had been organized originally on an all-Ireland basis, and although the creation of the Irish Free State and of Northern Ireland subjected trade unionism to many strains, this concept remained. In the war years, when the Irish Trade Union Congress split, the main unions in the south breaking away from it, there were demands in Northern Ireland for a separate T.U.C. for that area. Since any such move would introduce sectarianism – which had manifested itself so violently among the Belfast workers in the middle 1930s – not only among the workers, but into the structure of trade unions themselves, these demands were opposed. A split into Catholic and Protestant unions and congresses, even in Northern Ireland, was too obviously contrary to the spirit and meaning of the movement. Northern Ireland retained, in this field, its connections with the south. After 1959 there was a single Irish congress again, the I.C.T.U., which was organized on an all-Ireland basis. Labour in the north was cautious on the whole question of partition. The Northern Ireland Labour party, associated with the Labour party in England, was officially committed to the constitution of Northern Ireland, and drew its support from Protestant as well as Catholic voters, mainly in Belfast. Labour politicians who were opposed to the union belonged to separate or independent labour parties, like the Republican Labour party. All of these, however, as well as most trade union organizations, were opposed to the toryism of the Unionist party, and were seeking a way, in the changing post-war world, out of the dilemmas and rigid postures of Northern Ireland politics. The way was found in developing pressures on the government in the matters of jobs, discrimination, houses, and civil rights. Proposals for a civil rights programme were worked out in Belfast in the early 1960s by trade union leaders cautiously feeling their way: it was laid down from the start that no question was involved of changing the Northern Ireland constitution unless the majority of the people in the area should wish to change. The Belfast Trades Council, representing most of the northern unions, took up the programme, and the (English) National Council of Civil Liberties established a link with the Northern Ireland trade union movement. This beginning was an effort to cross the sectarian lines and work in one area of politics which might (in terms of the national-sectarian politics of the previous fifty years) be 'non-controversial' among the working people of Northern Ireland. Captain O'Neill, installed as prime minister since 1963, was beginning his career as a political conjuror, producing liberal promises out of a Unionist hat, and making them disappear before the very eyes of his mesmerized audience. He declined to accept the principle put to him by the Trades Council early in 1966 that equal citizenship should confer equal rights, but he produced one of his promises later in the year – to abolish the business vote in local elections – and rejected the rest of the civil rights programme.

In the meantime ancestral voices had begun prophesying war. One of the main world events of the beginning of the decade of the 1960s was the council called in Rome by Pope John XXIII, who in his brief pontificate (he became pope in 1958 and died in 1963) brought about the beginning of major changes in the institutional fabric of the Roman Catholic church, and administered a shock of explosive effect to that fabric so that some of the calcified accretions of centuries fell away, and something different was revealed beneath. He urged and encouraged in many ways the ecumenical spirit – the reaching out to 'separated brethren' – and met with response from leaders of other churches, in kind. But the new ecumenism met with a different response from the Ulster Hall and the streets of Belfast. 'I have hated God's enemies with a perfect hate', said the Reverend Ian Paisley, the leader in the late 1950s of a group known as Ulster Protestant Action and a minister of the Free Presbyterian church. Dr Paisley had been preaching and agitating for a number of years, his main theme being the need to defend Protestantism and the Reformation against liberal unionists or liberal churchmen, who would betray them to 'the forces of popery and the scarlet whore drunk on the blood of the churches'. He was and is a sane intelligent but fanatical man, good at thinking on his feet and handling a crowd, a heckler, or a television interviewer, superb at following the dire logic of his argument almost but not quite to the point of violence. He made himself the spokesman for the poor sectaries of Belfast, whose bitter prejudices had for years been exploited by the inflammatory speeches of Unionist leaders, but who now found themselves abandoned in a topsy-turvy world where the Belfast City Hall lowered the Union Jack in mourning for Pope John, and where bishops and ministers of reformed religion went to Rome to exchange the kiss of peace with the Whore of Babylon. Them Ian Paisley led; to them he preached.

In 1964 Dr Paisley was involved in what became known as the 'tricolour riots' in Belfast, when, during the Westminster general election campaign of that year, the tricolour flag of the Republic was being flown from the headquarters of the Republican party (which had a candidate in the election) in Divis Street in a Catholic area of Belfast. The Unionist candidate in the constituency, James Kilfedder, sent a telegram to the Stormont Minister of Home Affairs, Brian McConnell: 'Remove tricolour in Divis Street which is aimed to provoke and insult loyalists of Belfast.' Paisley threatened that if the police did not remove the tricolour (prohibited from display in Northern Ireland under the Flags and Emblems Act, 1954), he would lead his followers in to do so. McConnell ordered the R.U.C. in to seize the flag and at the same time issued an order restricting Dr Paisley's protest parade to an area near the City Hall, away from Divis Street. A force of R.U.C. with sten-guns, revolvers, and riot equipment, backed by armoured cars, forced their way through a large crowd which blocked Divis Street and seized the flag, while the Paisleyite gathering held a prayer-meeting (with speeches) at the City Hall. Two days later another tricolour was hoisted on the Divis Street building, as a crowd sang the national anthem of the Republic, and again an armoured car came, and police with guns and crowbars broke down the door to seize the flag. A crowd of republicans gathered in the evening, armed with sticks, stones, and petrol bombs, and a fight developed with the R.U.C., as a result of which thirty

153

people, including eighteen R.U.C. men, received hospital treatment. Five days later, on Sunday, 5 October 1964, the republicans carried the tricolour at the head of a march through west Belfast to an election rally, but this time the police did not intervene. Mr Kilfedder, who won the seat, thanked Dr Paisley, without whose help 'it could not have been done'.

This episode, occurring in the middle of a British general election campaign, was in part covered by television. It was the first time that Dr Paisley had moved on to the centre of the stage in Northern Ireland politics, but he now occupied that position more and more frequently. He and his followers called on the government to ban all commemorations of the Easter rising; he vigorously attacked the O'Neill–Lemass meetings; he went to Rome to protest vociferously against the Archbishop of Canterbury's visit to Pope Paul ('Dr Ramsay is a Romanizer, an idolater and a blasphemer'); he organized a march, through a Catholic area (Cromac Square), where a brief but violent riot occurred on the way, to the General Assembly of the Presbyterian church – which, apparently, was on the way to Rome too – and he and his followers took the occasion of their arrival at the Assembly meeting to attack and insult Lord Erskine (Governor of Northern Ireland) and Lady Erskine, who were attending the opening. The Minister of Home Affairs, who had permitted the Paisleyite march through the Catholic area of Cromac Square and to the Assembly building, appeared at the Assembly and spoke to a silent gathering, expressing regret. The Moderator, Right Rev. Dr Martin, received him coldly, as did the Assembly:

> We accept the expression of regret which you have brought. We have asked for a written assurance that such happenings will not occur again. When we receive this it will be recorded in our minutes.

In this same summer of 1966 a programme of violent action was announced to the newspapers by the 'Adjutant of the 1st Belfast Battalion of the Ulster Volunteer Force', who said that war was being declared on the I.R.A. and its splinter groups, and that known I.R.A. men would be 'executed mercilessly and without hesitation'. Shortly afterwards a young engineering worker, John Patrick Scullion, was murdered at night, and a few weeks later four Catholics (three of them hotel workers) were shot as they left a public house called the Malvern Arms at two o'clock in the morning of 27 June, one of whom, Peter Ward, died almost immediately. Three men, Augustus Andrew Spence, Hugh Arnold McClean, and John Williamson, were arrested within a matter of hours and charged with murder. McLean, on being charged, said: 'I am sorry I ever heard of that man Paisley or decided to follow him.' But Dr Paisley's newspaper, the *Protestant Telegraph*, in reply to the publication of this, spared a few lines from its customary incitements against liberals, Catholics, and 'Romanizers' to say:

Mr Paisley has never advocated violence, has never been associated with the U.V.F., and has always opposed the hell-soaked liquor traffic which constituted the background to this murder.

Mrs Matilda Gould, a seventy-year-old Protestant widow, died on 28 June of burns received when a petrol bomb, intended for a Catholic-owned public house next door, was thrown into her home in one of the little narrow streets that link the Shankill Road with the Crumlin Road in west Belfast.

Spence, McClean, and Williamson, two of them members of the Prince Albert Temperance Loyal Orange Lodge No. 1892, and all three members of the U.V.F., were accused of murder, and of murder in furtherance of seditious conspiracy (a capital crime): that they

on divers dates between 1 March and 27 June 1966 conspired together, and with other persons unknown, to incite illwill among the different classes and creeds of the Queen's subjects, to create a public disturbance and disorder and to injure and murder persons who might be opposed to their opinions.

They were found guilty and sentenced to life imprisonment.

Dr Paisley meantime had been charged with unlawful assembly after the demonstration against the Presbyterian Assembly and Lord Erskine. He refused to be bound over to keep the peace for two years – telling his supporters that he was prepared to go to jail to preserve the right to protest – and he was sentenced to three months' imprisonment. At the beginning of 1967 he was active again in another noisy protest. The Irish Church Association, a body of the Church of Ireland of ecumenical disposition, decided to invite Dr John Moorman, the Anglican bishop of Ripon, to preach in St Anne's Cathedral in Belfast, and to give an account of the Gazzada conference, where he had led a delegation from the Church of England to have discussions with Roman Catholic theologians. A special conference of Orange leaders met in Belfast at the end of January to protest; the lead given by the Belfast County Grand Lodge was followed by various Protestant groups, and Dr Paisley rallied his supporters with fiery sermons and speeches. A march of '100,000 Orangemen' was threatened. The Dean of St Anne's, having consulted the Prime Minister, Captain O'Neill, withdrew permission for the use of the Cathedral, and Dr Moorman's visit was cancelled.

The kind of sectarianism which passed in the hungry 1930s, when enunciated from unionist and government platforms, looked antiquated and archaic in the 1960s. Captain O'Neill's chief function and purpose was to save what he called, in relation to the Moorman episode, 'the image of Ulster', but from the outset he ran into serious difficulties because 'extremists' like Dr Paisley insisted on revealing the realities of the situation that Unionism had created over a period of more than forty years of uninterrupted rule and uninterrupted fostering of sectarianism. Captain O'Neill himself was addressing his words chiefly to the outside world – and especially to that part of the outside world which had money to invest in industry in Northern Ireland. His words were not matched by deeds within Northern Ireland, except when these were forced on him. He belonged to that faction within the Unionist party which realized that the old mechanisms by which Tory power and wealth had been maintained would no longer serve the purpose in the new 'affluent society' with its instant communications, in which the values, such as they were, of the old colonial settlers would be eroded by the new materialist values of advanced capitalism. He belonged to the group which had some apprehension of the differences between colonialism and 'neo-colonialism'. His difficulties stemmed from the fact that a difficult transition was necessary from old unionism to new unionism, and that old unionism had called up forces which had never been easy to control. He succeeded for a while, largely because he had personal qualities which fitted him for the task. He allowed himself to show the distaste which the landlords, of essentially English background (Eton and the Brigade of Guards in Captain O'Neill's case), had always felt for the squalid bigotry of the basically proletarian Orange movement, and by seeming aristocratically aloof from it, from sectarianism, from the mere middle-class politics of people like his Minister of Home Affairs, Mr William Craig. But power is power, and, however much his nose might twitch, Captain O'Neill, like his cousins and kindred of the settler squirearchy who occupied commanding positions within the Unionist party, was an Orangeman, a member of the Order, and so was involved in the whole paraphernalia of drums, sashes, bowler hats, crudely-lettered temperance banners, and the vulgar enthusiasms of industrial-revolution religion.

The civil rights programme was rejected by Captain O'Neill in 1966 when the Northern Ireland Labour party and the Irish Congress of Trade Unions put forward their demand for democratic rights. In the same year meetings were held by other groups interested in civil rights, groups which included liberals, republicans, members of various parts of the labour movement and of the Northern Ireland Communist party, and which included both Catholics and Protestants. Attempts were being made to draw together all who were opposed to Unionist totalitarianism – not, this time, on the basis of demands for the reunification of Ireland, but on the basis of demands for the extension to Northern Ireland of the civil rights enjoyed by citizens in the rest of the United Kingdom. An *ad hoc* committee was formed, which called a meeting at which, on 6 February 1967, the Northern Ireland Civil Rights Association was founded. It issued a statement of its objectives, summarized in five points:

To define the basic rights of all citizens;
To protect the rights of the individual;
To highlight all possible abuses of power;
To demand guarantees for freedom of speech, assembly, and associations;
To inform the public of their lawful rights.

Other organizations joined in the movement of agitation for civil rights, including the Campaign for Social Justice, and a group within the British Parliamentary Labour party at Westminster known as the Campaign for Democracy in Ulster, who based their interest in the matter on the section of the Government of Ireland Act, 1920, which affirmed the ultimate authority of the Westminster parliament in Northern Ireland affairs.

Although the C.R.A. proceeded very circumspectly at first, the civil rights campaign alarmed and disquieted the Unionist government, chiefly because it was non-sectarian, and so attempted to cut across the lines of division in the community which Unionist rule had been so careful to emphasize. Since, however, the denial of civil rights in Northern Ireland was largely organized on a sectarian basis (although it must be remembered that Protestants who rejected Orangeism and the Unionist party also suffered), the obvious strategy by which the government attempted to counter the movement was to reintroduce sectarianism and to treat the movement as if it were simply a Catholic or anti-partitionist agitation.

The civil rights movement, at a conference in London in February 1968, at which Westminster Labour M.P.s and members of the opposition at Stormont were present, decided to proceed beyond the cautious protests and complaints of its beginnings to a more open challenge of the Stormont government, taking as their point of attack the discriminatory allocation of housing by Unionist-controlled local authorities.

In east Co. Tyrone, where many Catholic families had been for years waiting for council houses, and were meantime living in inadequate and often squalid accommodation, the Unionist councillor, who had the effective responsibility for allocating council houses in the village of Caledon, gave a council house to an unmarried Protestant, Miss Emily Beattie. Two Catholic families from a neighbouring district, where the building of houses for Catholic tenants had been prevented by Unionist opposition, had moved into Nos. 9 and 11 Kinnard Park, Caledon, as squatters. The family in No. 9 left, and Miss Beattie moved in. In the words of the Cameron Report:

> There had been squatting in two new houses at Kinnard Park, Caledon, during the previous months encouraged by Mr Austin Currie, M.P. (N.I.) and others. No 11 was occupied by the Goodfellow family and No. 9 by the McKenna family. These families came from another district in the area of the Rural District Council, where the Unionist Councillor had, in effect, opposed the building of houses for Catholic tenants. . . .
>
> Miss Beattie took possession of her house on the 13th June. She was 19 years old, a Protestant, and secretary to the local Councillor's Solicitor, who was also a Unionist Parliamentary candidate living in Armagh. . . .
>
> In concentrated form the situation expressed the objections felt by many non-Unionists to the prevailing system of housing allocations in Dungannon Rural District Council. By no stretch of the imagination could Miss Beattie be regarded as a priority tenant. On 18th June, within a few days of Miss Beattie taking possession, the Goodfellow family, squatting next door, were evicted with full television coverage. . . .[69]

On 20 June, Mr Austin Currie, of the Nationalist party, occupied Miss Beattie's house, with two others, for a few hours until Miss Beattie's brother, a policeman, evicted them in the presence of some of his police colleagues. Mr Currie, before resorting to this action, had raised the matter at every level, including the Northern Ireland House of Commons, without receiving any satisfaction. Television news cameras (soon to become almost as detested by Paisleyites, Orangemen, and the R.U.C. as the Pope) covered the evictions.

Mr Currie now pressed on to a more general agitation about housing policy in the area, where studies by the Campaign for Social Justice had demonstrated a clear pattern of discrimi-

159

nation. The C.S.J. agreed to organize a protest march from
Coalisland to Dungannon. A meeting with the C.R.A. was held
on 27 July at Maghera, and a march was announced for 24
August, from Coalisland to Market Square, Dungannon. There
was no objection from the police until the Unionist politicians
of the area raised the threat of a counter-demonstration. In the
cautious words of the Cameron Commission's report:

> Senator Stewart (Chairman of the Urban District Council and
> a prominent resident) told the police that there would be trouble if
> the march entered the Square and proposed a re-route to Quarry
> Lane to Anne Street. Mr John Taylor M.P. also told the police that
> there would be trouble if the march entered the Square. We think it
> is to be inferred from their own evidence that whether these local
> Unionist leaders would have organized, they at least would not have
> discouraged, the organization of a counter demonstration if the
> march had been allowed to enter Market Square. Such a counter
> demonstration, if organized, would almost certainly have led to an
> outbreak of violence – as persons occupying positions of such public
> responsibility cannot have failed to appreciate.[70]

The policy underlying the Unionist demand for a rerouting of
the procession was to apply the principle, accepted fairly generally in normal times (if such a term is appropriate of any
times in Northern Ireland), that Protestant marches should be
conducted in Protestant areas and Catholic marches in Catholic
areas, to avoid provocation. It was to categorize the demand for
civil rights as a Catholic agitation, and to attempt to force the
campaign for democracy back into the sectarian mould. To
reinforce the threat to the civil rights march, the Ulster Protestant Volunteers announced a meeting for the Market Square
for the same day as the march. The police issued a direction late
on the eve of the march rerouting it as directed by the local
Unionists.

The march took place, but was prevented by a police barrier from entering the Market Square. The demonstrators
halted at the barrier and a meeting was held, at which Miss
Betty Sinclair of the C.R.A. presided. One of the speakers was
Mr Currie. Another was Mr Gerry Fitt, who in the general

election in March 1966 defeated Mr Kilfedder for the West Belfast seat (which Mr Kilfedder, according to his own account, had owed in 1964 largely to the help of Dr Paisley) at Westminster, and was the only non-Unionist among the twelve members representing Northern Ireland constituencies there. He was also M.P. at Stormont for the Dock division of Belfast, and a member of Belfast Corporation. His speech roused the crowd on general civil rights and anti-Unionist issues (his own party was Republican Labour), while the other speakers dealt mostly with local social issues.

The Dungannon march had been peaceful, but the demonstrators had accepted the restriction which gave them the appearance of engaging in a sectarian agitation. Now the civil rights movement turned its attention to the place where the evils of Unionist rule – discrimination, gerrymandering, unemployment, demoralization, sectarianism, partisanship in the operation of public services, police oppression – could notoriously be seen at their worst, to the Catholic city which was the sacred symbol of Protestant intransigence, to Derry.

6   The Fifth of October

It is also certain that they are much mistaken that think the poverty of a
nation is a means of the public safety. Who quarrel more than beggars?
Who does more earnestly long for a change than he that is uneasy in
his present circumstances? And who run to create confusions with so
desperate a boldness as those who have nothing to lose, hope to gain by
them? If a king should fall under such contempt or envy that he could
not keep his subjects in their duty but by oppression and ill usage, and
by rendering them poor and miserable, it were certainly better for him
to quit his kingdom than to retain it by such methods as makes him,
while he keeps the name of authority, lose the majesty due to it. Nor is
it so becoming the dignity of a king to reign over beggars as over rich
and happy subjects. *Sir Thomas More* [71]

The division of Ireland, and of Ulster, runs through the heart of
Derry. To its Catholic population (and they are a majority of
two to one) it is, as it was known for centuries to the Irish,
Doire Cholmcille, Columba's Derry, where St Columba had
founded a monastery in the sixth century. The place-names of
the area below the walls to the west, the area farthest from the
river – the Bogside as distinct from the Waterside – preserve
these memories: Long Tower Street and Long Tower church
(where the belfry tower of the early Irish monastery had been),
Columb's Well, and so on. In the sixteenth century, not long
before the conquest of Gaelic Ulster by the English, Manus
O'Donnell of Tyrconnell wrote (in Irish) a life of St Columba
which included verses attributed to the saint – although their
composition was of much later medieval date:

> ... Nochan fhuil duilleóg ar lár
> i nDoire chuanna chomhlán

gan dá aingeal go n-óige
i n-aghaidh gach duilleóige.

Ní fhaghaid ionadh are tír
d'iomad na n-aingeal maith min;
ar naoí dtonnaibh amach dhe
is eadh ghabhaid ó Dhoire . . .

Ó na gáirthibh-se ad-chluinim
créad fá bhfuilim im beathaidh?
gáir mhór muintire Doire
do bhris mo chroidhe i gceanthair.[72]

(There is not a leaf throughout
all of lovely Derry
but there are two angels
for every leaf.

There is not space on land
for all of the good angels:
for a full nine waves out
they extend from Derry . . .

Why do I still live and hear
these lamentations?
the lament of Derry's people
has broken my heart in four.)

To its Protestant minority, Derry was the city founded at the beginning of the seventeenth century, at the end of O'Neill's and O'Donnell's war against the Queen, garrisoned by Dowcra, and then taken over by the City of London: it was Londonderry, which closed its gates against King James in favour of William, and withstood successfully the long siege. Its heroes were the apprentice boys, and the rector of Donaghmore, George Walker, who was chosen to govern the city in the siege, and whose cry of 'No surrender!' has ever since been a slogan of Protestant Ulster. The Walker monument, commemorating the siege of 1689, is a tall column surmounted by a statue, which stands on the eminence of Derry's walls on the west, at a point where their height is augmented by a sharp fall of ground, and where they look down on the crowded poor dwellings of the Catholic Bogside below. Here, at this monument, the anniversary of the relief of Derry was celebrated each year on 12 August (it was on the 30 July, old calendar, that the original relief occurred), and nowhere in Ireland was the Protestant ascendancy more arrogantly symbolized than by the firing of cannon, the beating of drums, and the chanting of Orange songs of triumph on this high spot overlooking the narrow streets and crowded dwellings where more than twenty thousand Catholics lived in subjection in their ghetto.

Derry in 1968 had very high unemployment, notorious gerrymandering, inadequate housing; by this time all sections of its community had a sense of grievance due to what appeared to them to be a policy of discrimination by the government against, not only Catholics, but in general those parts of Northern Ireland which lay west of the Bann (although if they had looked south to the Republic the people of Derry might have realized that this was a problem which transcended the borders of Northern Ireland). The Great Northern railway line to Derry had been closed, the docks had gone into decline, shipping lines which once served Derry had ceased to do so, industries, including especially the factory of British Sound Reproducers Ltd, had closed, the new town planned for Northern Ireland had been located in the east (and given the provocative name of Craigavon). Above all, the new university of Ulster, in spite of the fact that there was the nucleus of a university in Derry already in the form of Magee University College, had been located in Coleraine, a town which, to the outsider at least, would seem to have little to recommend it as a university centre, apart from a supply of Protestant landladies. The university question in particular had brought all sections of the community in Derry together, for the first time, Catholic and Protestant together, in opposition to a Stormont policy – which had nevertheless been forced through.

The Derry Housing Action Committee, after the Dungannon march, asked for a civil rights demonstration in the city. The committee had been active for some time in trying to organize protest against the discriminatory policies of the corporation, and there had been some sit-downs and demonstrations. Two members, Mr Éamonn McCann and Mr Éamonn Melaugh, who were especially active, invited the officers of the C.R.A. to a meeting held in Derry on 31 August to discuss the holding of a protest demonstration in the city, and invitations were then sent out to other groups to participate. The Northern Ireland Labour party (in Derry, the local organization of the party had departed somewhat from official policy), the Young Socialists, the Derry Housing Action Committee, the Derry City Republican Club, and the James Connolly Society became involved in organizing the protest. Mr Gerry Fitt, M.P., of Belfast, was associated with the arrangements, but the local organization was mainly carried through by Mr McCann.

Derry was chosen for a direct challenge to the Unionist strategy of making the civil rights agitation appear to be a sectarian one by restricting civil rights demonstrations to Catholic areas. In Derry the Civil Rights Association gave notice of a march which was to follow a traditional *Protestant* route: to start at the Waterside Station on the east side of the Foyle, cross Craigavon Bridge (the only bridge over the river at Derry) and proceed into the area within the walls (sacred to the Protestant myth), ending in the Diamond, where the memorial for the 1914 and 1939 wars stood. This provoked a reaction similar to that brought by the notice of the Dungannon march in August. The local Unionists objected to the route proposed, and the Middle Liberties Young Unionist Association threatened a counter-demonstration. However, there was not much force in the protests of the Derry Unionists, who had a feeling of having been abandoned or of being about to be abandoned by Stormont (just as their fellows in Donegal, Cavan, and Monaghan had been in 1920) as a result of the university dispute. A protest was also submitted on 30 September (the march was scheduled for 5 October) by the General Committee of the Apprentice Boys of Derry, a local Orange organization, and on the following day the same organization served notice of an 'Annual Initiation

Ceremony', involving a march of Apprentice Boys from the Waterside Station to the Diamond, and then to the Apprentice Boys Memorial Hall, on 5 October. Of this, the Cameron Commission says:

It may be true that private initiation of members could have been planned for that date, but we are quite satisfied in the light of the facts that this proposed procession was not a genuine 'annual' event, and we regard the proposal to hold it at the precise time indicated as merely a threat to counter demonstrate by political opponents of the Civil Rights march. To put forward proposals for a march or demonstration which, if pursued, would clash in time or place with another already proposed on behalf of an organization of an opposite political colour has been for long a recognized tactic of obstruction in Northern Ireland. In such an event the purpose of the proposed counter demonstration or march is to secure the prohibition or re-routing of the original march or demonstration. Once this is achieved the proposed counter demonstration is allowed to lapse. In the event no march by Apprentice Boys took place. Those to be initiated travelled by car to the place of initiation in the forenoon of 5th October.[73]

It was Mr Craig, the Minister of Home Affairs, who drew public attention first to this 'annual initiation' and gave it as grounds for issuing a restriction on the march, in which he prohibited all processions in the Waterside Ward (east of the river Foyle) or within the city walls. The prohibition came on 3 October, two days before the march was due, and caused much discussion among those involved. Mr Eddie McAteer, the Nationalist M.P. at Stormont, who was not in fact involved, since the Nationalist party as such had not taken up the civil rights cause, called for observance of the Minister's ban. The civil rights movement itself was divided on how to react. A long meeting of the organizations involved in the demonstration, held in the City Hotel in Derry on the evening of 4 October, ended in a unanimous vote to go ahead with the march as originally planned. This unanimity, however, was achieved only after long argument, and only after it had been made clear that some of the organizations involved would go ahead even if the

C.R.A. itself decided to accept the restrictions imposed by the Minister. The view which prevailed was that of Mr McCann.

The issue was now clear. The immediate point was that of right of assembly, but the real question was whether the Unionist government could treat every protest against its own policies as a sectarian one. If the civil rights movement at this point had accepted the restrictions imposed by the Minister they would have accepted his imputation that they were a sectarian organization, since he was restricting them to demonstrate only in 'their own' Catholic areas of Derry. His restriction itself, even under the draconian legislation of Unionist Stormont, was of dubious legality.

On the morning of 5 October, a Saturday, loudspeaker vans went through the streets urging people to join in the march. Mr McCann, while engaged in this activity, was arrested, but he was released later. At half past two in the afternoon a final meeting of organizers was held in the City Hotel, and meantime a crowd began gathering on the other side of the river at the Waterside Station, where the march was to begin. Mr Gerry Fitt arrived at the City Hotel meeting accompanied by Mr Russell Kerr, M.P., Mrs Anne Kerr, M.P., and Mr John Ryan, M.P., all of whom represented English constituencies in the Labour interest in Westminster, and who had come to observe the events of the day at the invitation of Mr Fitt (an invitation which the Cameron Commission appeared to find reprehensible). The meeting made the final decision to go ahead, as far as possible, with the march as originally planned – the police activity during the day in Derry suggested that the possibility might not be very large.

At the Waterside Station, surrounded by police, there was much confusion before the march began. There was a moderately large milling crowd in the station yard, composed of members of the organizations involved in the march as well as Derry people who had come along to join the demonstration. There were many roughly lettered placards; there was much pushing and pulling. The police came and informed such organizers as were present of the restrictions imposed by the ministerial order. The M.P.s and a few others were interviewed for television in the middle of the crowd; then the arm-banded marshals did their not very successful best to form the crowd into a column of march. The start, however, which had to press out of the station yard through a thin screen of police, was held up for a number of minutes by a sudden press of oncoming motor traffic along the route, due to a traffic diversion. Then, finally and unexpectedly, the column set off, Mr Fitt and Mr Austin Currie, who had by this stage been joined by Mr Eddie McAteer, in the front rank with the Westminster M.P.s. The pace was fast – almost a trot – as if the procession were trying to cover as much ground as possible before the police moved in, and the column was swelled as it moved by numbers of people, mostly very young, who converged on the route to join it.

Even with these additions, the crowd taking part in the demonstration was not remarkably large, and was numbered in hundreds rather than thousands. It included members of the Nationalist party, who had taken no part in the organization of the protest but could not ignore such a demonstration in the city of Derry, members of the Northern Ireland Labour party, members of the Liberal party, members of the Republican Labour party, members of the Young Socialists. There were some members of the I.R.A. present, some of them acting as stewards, although the I.R.A. had not been involved in the organization of the march. There were a few people from the Republic present, among them Professor David Greene of the Dublin Institute of Advanced Studies, who was engaged at the time in advocating the retention in the Republic (where Fianna Fail wished to abolish it) of the system of proportional representation, whose abolition in Northern Ireland had helped to make such abuses as the gerrymandering of Derry possible. Most of the crowd, however, was made up of ordinary young working people of Derry, many of whom came along in response to the loudspeaker appeal.

The route (not the one originally scheduled) which was taken to Craigavon Bridge led uphill along Duke Street – narrow and with few side-streets – through a Protestant quarter of the city.

As the procession moved up the hill, its leaders could see ahead, at the crest, a cordon of uniformed police drawn across the narrow street, and behind them a barricade of police tenders. The march, loose and disorganized as it was, none the less pressed on without slackening pace, and as its head came up to the cordon the front line of police drew their batons, stepped forward a couple of paces, and struck down the leaders. Gerry Fitt was felled, and the police ranks moved forward with batons swinging to drive the crowd back down the hill, but there was not much vehemence in their drive, and it was unsuccessful. After a few minutes of confused struggle the police re-formed their ranks across the street and the crowd remained halted, pressed up against them. For a short while the crowd chanted, shouted, or sang. At one point many people sat down in the street, and an effort was made to start singing the American civil rights song 'We shall overcome', but the crowd was unfamiliar both with the song (Ulster was to learn it in the coming months) and with the tactic of sitting down. At about this point, while, unknown to those behind the first two or three ranks of the march, Mr Fitt was being taken away by ambulance, Miss Betty Sinclair arrived and obtained a chair, and an impromptu meeting was held at the head of the march, up against the police barricade.

The meeting lasted for about half an hour. In the meantime a further body of police moved in at the rear of the column, and created another barricade of tenders, boxing in the crowd. An Ulster Transport bus, caught in the crowd, had begun to cause anger because the driver kept his engine running and in the narrow confined and crowded street the exhaust fumes were causing distress. When there were signs that violence might be used on the bus, it moved down the hill and away, just before the second barrier closed the line of retreat for the demonstration. Miss Sinclair acted as chairman of the meeting, and she, like Mr McAteer (who had received a glancing blow from a police baton) and some other speakers, urged the parade to disperse quietly now, having made their point by technically infringing the Minister's restriction. Such moderate counsels were not well received by most of the crowd, and advice to disperse was shouted down by people who loudly insisted on their right to march in their own city. It was in any case difficult to see how people who were tightly hemmed in by buildings on either side and by police cordons before and behind could disperse. In the event the moderate counsels did not prevail. One or two speakers – notably Mr McCann and Mr Currie – did not give this advice. Miss Sinclair wound up the meeting with a repetition of it and as she finished a police loud-hailer broke in on the proceedings, but its first few words produced a surge of people against the police barricade, and this was followed immediately by a series of baton charges. Banners, placards, Miss Sinclair's chair, all became weapons. The police charged in among the penned-in crowd, slashing at skulls and genitals with their batons. The crowd was driven, running, falling, and stumbling, back down the hill, against the lower cordon, through which ultimately all of them passed, running a gauntlet there too of swinging clubs. Below this the crowd was driven to a section of the street where there was a large vacant lot, littered with bricks and stones. Here part of the crowd, notably the Young Socialists, rallied, finding ammunition ready to hand, and the bricks and stones were used against the police, until a water-cannon arrived and succeeded in scattering the crowd. The police now followed through, pursuing the dispersed crowd, and coming ultimately on to Craigavon Bridge, where they attacked the populace at large, mostly Saturday afternoon shoppers.

At Altnagelvin Hospital, on the eastern outskirts of Derry, ambulance after ambulance brought in the injured to the casualty station. Most suffered from head wounds, and numbers of the injured were young girls.

Derry, as dusk gathered, was electric with tension, and with a feeling that something had been done that could not be undone. It was in some ways a new feeling. Protestants had taken part in the march, and among them Mr Ivan Cooper, of the city itself, had been one of the speakers at the barricade meeting. People who were not opposed to the union with England had taken part in it. The brunt of the street fighting with the police had been borne, not by any traditional Nationalist element, but by the Young Socialists, who had shown great courage. No sectarian feeling had been displayed – not even in Duke Street, where the marchers had been trapped by the police cordons in a Protestant area. There had been a straight confrontation between the people of Derry and the Stormont government. The government, in purely physical terms, had won this first round, by methods which had been recorded all afternoon by television news cameras. Within a few days, the films of the brutality in Duke Street were being seen around the world. It became plain that it was not the civil rights movement that had walked into Mr Craig's trap. Mr Craig had walked the Unionist government into Mr McCann's trap.

7 Guns and Drums and Wounds

We had fed the heart on fantasies,
The heart's grown brutal from the fare;
More substance in our enmities
Than in our love; O honey-bees,
Come build in the empty house of the stare.
William Butler Yeats[74]

The Derry confrontation of 5 October 1968 began a period of
agitation and sporadic violence in which it seemed to some of
those involved, on more than one side, that revolutionary
changes were taking place, or about to take place. Stormont was
faced suddenly, not by the traditional anti-partitionist physi-
cal-force movements, but by people who demanded the rights
of British subjects. The violence came from those who opposed
drastic change – first from Stormont itself, then from its supporters on the right, then from old-fashioned republicanism.
The British Government intervened with force, a process easier
to begin than to end. From many months of confused struggle
there emerged, however, initially not revolutionary change but
some limited and grudging reforms and, in effect, a reiteration
of the Lemass–O'Neill policies, with the addition of the intervention of Britain as guarantor and enforcing agent. Ireland,
north and south, was to conform to the ideology of Common-
Market Western Europe. But this attempt, backed though it was
by massive British force, to return in general effect to the situation of the early and middle sixties, in turn set off another
phase of confused struggle. The fifty-year experiment of
'Northern Ireland' was ending in failure.

The conduct of the R.U.C. in Derry on that day was no worse than that of any other police force in similar circumstances acting on similar instructions. Once violent force is used against a crowd it tends to be indiscriminate or to discriminate against those least capable of resisting it, and it tends also not to be over-scrupulous in manner. The official casualties for that weekend in Derry were seventy-seven (mostly treated for bruises and lacerations of the head) but, including those who did not report to hospital, the true figure is almost certainly a good deal higher. There were no very serious injuries and no deaths. The main fault to be found with the action was that it was unjustified and unnecessary and was carried out in an un-disciplined manner.

A baton charge, however, is extremely unpleasant to observe, especially in close detail, and the police behaviour of 5 October was closely watched by television cameras. It certainly had a bad effect on the 'image of Northern Ireland' which had con-cerned Captain O'Neill, but it also had considerable impact on opinion within Ireland, north and south. In Derry itself its effects were immediate: late on the evening of 5 October fighting broke out in the Diamond, when the police, feeling perhaps that the afternoon's assertion of Protestant supremacy was not enough, attacked a small group of demonstrators to remove a banner from them. The fight spread, until the police drove the crowd down into the Catholic Bogside area – outside the sacred Protestant walls – where attempts were made un-successfully to erect barricades. Fighting continued on the fol-lowing day, Sunday, and then died down.

In Belfast, the university term was just beginning when these events took place, and they had their impact too on student opinion. A small protest march was organized on Sunday, 6 October, to the home of the Minister of Home Affairs, Mr William Craig, who expressed the opinion that students in gen-eral were 'silly bloody fools'. On Monday, 7 October, a meeting of somewhat less than a thousand students was held in the Queen's University. These decided to hold a protest march to the City Hall on Wednesday, 9 October, and they notified the police accordingly, declaring a route which would bring them through Shaftesbury Square. The march was to start at 2 p.m. Dr Ian Paisley immediately announced that he would hold a meeting at 2 p.m. in Shaftesbury Square.

The students rerouted their march to avoid Shaftesbury Square, where Dr Paisley had duly presented himself at two o'clock on Wednesday with about a thousand followers, but as they were approaching the City Hall by another route they found that there too a number of Paisleyites had assembled ahead of them. The police halted the march. The students, continuing to show restraint, obeyed, and sat down in the street at Linenhall Street, blocking traffic for three hours. Those who took part in this first protest march of students were of very varied political opinions, and included unionists. The rebuffs they had received, and the acquiescence of the authorities in Dr Paisley's obstructionist tactics, produced a mood of militancy, and a meeting was held at the university to establish some formal organization for the movement. The group formed was designed to be open to membership to those who were not students – former students like Mr Michael Farrell and Mr McCann, or even people who had no connection with the university. The new group, which was shortly to be known as 'People's Democracy', agreed to Mr McCann's proposal that a further protest march should be held to the City Hall on Saturday, 12 October, but this was then postponed to 16 October. Since the law required that full details of such a march must be given in advance to the police, someone had to be delegated to hand in this notice. Miss Bernadette Devlin, a student in her fourth year at the university, was chosen to do so.

People's Democracy from its formation had a strongly 'left-wing' character, which it received from its leadership, some of whom were Marxists (at least by inclination: it is doubtful if many had read Marx). It resembled student radical movements elsewhere in Ireland and outside in the late 1960s in that it had no fixed membership and no established constitution or rules. It played a part of some importance in the period immediately following the beginning of violence in Derry. When the civil rights movement otherwise showed a tendency to accept assurances and promises from the Unionist government, and to ease up on its pressure accordingly, the radical leadership of People's Democracy forced the pace by keeping up a pressure of demonstrations and demands. The march of 16 October to the Belfast City Hall was again rerouted from Shaftesbury Square. It was without incident, and the centre of interest moved away from Belfast again to the struggle to establish right of assembly and of protest elsewhere.

In Derry a committee of sixteen was chosen on 9 October after a meeting, with Mr McCann in the chair, of persons representing various groups and elements in the city – especially the organizations which had planned the 5 October march. The committee called itself the Derry Citizens Action Committee. Mr McCann refused to take part further, and described the group as 'middle-aged, middle-class, and middle-of-the-road'. One of the sixteen at the beginning was a Unionist, but he resigned at the first decision made, which was to hold a sit-down in the Diamond on 19 October – a form of protest which went off peacefully, as did a march by the fifteen remaining members of the committee from the Waterside Station to the Diamond on 2 November. A week later Dr Paisley held a march, with his associate of the time, Major Ronald Bunting, and a group known as the Ulster Protestant Volunteers, again to the Diamond, and this passed off peacefully. Finally, in this stage of the campaign, the Derry Citizens Action Committee announced a major march from the Waterside Station to the Diamond – the march-route of the 5 October procession. Mr Craig issued another ban, this time prohibiting for a month all processions within the walls of Derry. Now, however, the R.U.C. were not confronted with a few hundred people whom they could baton to the ground, but with well over 15,000, a great human tide flowing irresistibly over Craigavon Bridge towards the walls. The civil rights stewards halted the march at the police barriers erected in Carlisle Square, where the police would have been powerless to stop the march. A small number of representatives of the marchers made a token breach of the police line and of

the Minister's restriction by vaulting over the barricades – the
police not interfering – and then the crowd broke up, made
their way individually in through the city gates, and reassembled in the Diamond. Just under 280 years after the Apprentice Boys had closed the gates in 1688, the walls of Derry
had been breached. Such symbolism is important in Northern
Ireland, but more important in this episode perhaps was the fact
that, virtually for the first time since the setting up of the northern state, the police were faced with a situation where they were
not in the dominant position. From this point on, the morale of
the R.U.C. began to deteriorate.

Among the leaders who had emerged in Derry at this period,
with the formation of the Citizens Action Committee, were
John Hume and Ivan Cooper, moderates who differed from
Eamonn McCann, People's Democracy, the Young Socialists,
and some other groups involved in the early stages, in that their
aim was to apply steady pressure on the government towards
the yielding of reforms in the political and social system. The
left-activists wished to replace the system.

In the meantime, Unionism, already suffering from severe
internal stress from its efforts to adapt to new conditions over
the previous ten years or so, now began to suffer this to an even
greater extent. The assertion by Mr Craig of Protestant and
Unionist supremacy in the old style, by force, on 5 October, had
triggered off the release of forces which were becoming increasingly difficult to control. Civil rights organizations sprang up
everywhere in Northern Ireland. The efforts of Captain
O'Neill's government to retain the substance of power while
achieving a new manner which would be acceptable in the new
period of mass communications were vitiated by the rebellion
of the sectarian right, and by the emergence of fascist-type organizations such as the Ulster Constitution Defence Committee,
the Ulster Protestant Volunteers, and the Ulster Volunteer
Force (the extent to which these were separate organizations is
uncertain).

The system of accommodation to change which had been
worked out in the middle 1960s began to break up almost im-

mediately. On 15 October the Nationalist Party, finding that its co-operation (under Fianna Fail stimulus) with Unionism was rendering it even more irrelevant than it had been for many years, withdrew as the official opposition in Stormont. Little notice, however, was taken of this, since the political struggle was taking place, not in parliament, where it was ineffective and stultified, but on the streets. On 4 November, Captain O'Neill, Mr Craig, and Mr Brian Faulkner, Stormont Minister of Commerce at this date, went to London and were seen by the English Labour Prime Minister, Mr Wilson, at Downing Street. The following day Mr Wilson told the Commons that he wanted a full impartial inquiry into the events of 5 October. He stressed his support for Captain O'Neill, but said he would like to see an early change in the franchise for local government in Northern Ireland. It was now plain that the 'devolution', which some Unionists had seen taking place in the Northern Ireland constitution, could be reversed: the threat of the exercise by Westminster of its supremacy over the Stormont parliament and government was added to the pressures on Captain O'Neill.

Spontaneous marches and demonstrations were occurring with increasing frequency, including a march by dockers and factory workers within the walls of Derry on 18 November, which was followed by a call from Mr Cooper (chairman of the Derry Citizens Action Committee) for a halt to such marches. On 22 November the Stormont government announced a programme of reforms, which included abolition of the company vote in by-elections (this had been promised some years before) and the appointment of an 'ombudsman'. One actual change (as distinct from a promised 'programme') was made immediately, in the replacement of Londonderry Corporation by a government-appointed development commission. Universal adult suffrage in local elections was not yielded, and the civil rights movement retained its simple and effective slogan: 'One man one vote'.

The confrontation between the civil rights movement on a broad front on the one hand and the government on the other did not for long remain a simple one. The irregular forces on the Unionist right now began to take more direct action against the civil rights agitation, and no longer confined themselves to the old tactics of trying to have demonstrations prohibited by announcing rival demonstrations for the same place and time – since it was now plain that such prohibitions would no longer be effective. Clashes occurred twice in Dungannon towards the close of the year, first at a People's Democracy demonstration and then at the formation of a local civil rights committee – in this incident a member of the unionist crowd fired a shot at a press cameraman, narrowly missing him.

In Armagh, the ecclesiastical capital of Ireland, a local civil rights committee was formed at a public meeting on 8 November and decided to hold a march through the town. Mr Denis Cassin of Armagh and Mr Frank Gogarty (later chairman of the Northern Ireland Civil Rights Association) were the organizers of the march, and a route was agreed on with the local police. The local Unionist and Orange organizations, however, demanded that the Minister ban the parade. Dr Paisley now came to Armagh and went with a local Protestant extremist to interview the police, demanding that the march be prohibited, and threatening that if the police did not prevent it, the Ulster Constitution Defence Committee would take 'appropriate action'. Warning leaflets printed in red were distributed through the town, ending a threatening text with the slogan 'O'Neill must go', and posters were pasted up. Dr Paisley's strange comrade-in-arms, Major Bunting (a believer in Love), announced that a 'trooping of the colour and cavalcade' would be held on Saturday afternoon in the Catholic area of Armagh by 'Apprentices and Fellowcraft, Tubal Cain Group (Masters and Purplemen) and Knights of Freedom' (organizations whose titles, according to the Cameron Commission's report, 'appear to represent Major Bunting's fantasies, and Major Bunting's supporters were Dr Paisley's'). The police ordered a rerouting of the 'trooping of the colour' into a different part of the town, and its deferment until a late hour on Saturday, 30 November.

Soon after midnight the Major and Dr Paisley arrived in

Armagh with about thirty cars, to spend the night 'holding a religious meeting' at points along the routes of the proposed civil rights march, armed with heavy sticks. Their supporters were relieved of two revolvers and 220 other weapons at police road-blocks as they arrived in the town during the morning. The police tried, by argument, to dislodge the large Paisleyite crowd from the position they occupied athwart the route, but failed. They finally blocked the march-route with two barricades, creating a no-man's-land seventy-five yards wide between about five thousand civil rights marchers who were halted at one barrier, and the armed Paisleyites who awaited them at the other. The marchers were not carrying weapons of any kind. They dispersed peacefully, but later in the day the police baton-charged a Catholic crowd in another quarter of the city.

The Paisleyites were triumphant in their victory, which they had scored not only over the civil rights march but also over the television cameras which watched and recorded. A B.B.C. camera was smashed (by the police: damages were successfully claimed from the local authority later) and an Independent Television cameraman was badly injured by Paisleyites. In spite of the satisfaction gained from smashing cameras and cameramen, however, the Paisleyites nonetheless had to suffer seeing their own activities on the television news broadcasts, and Captain O'Neill, who denounced them as thugs and bully-boys in a broadcast of 9 December, had to endure a further deterioration in 'the image of Ulster'. In this same broadcast of 9 December, Captain O'Neill appealed for support for his policies and for the limited reforms he had announced. The Derry Citizens Action Committee called off marches until 11 January, but People's Democracy declared its dissatisfaction with the proposals and demanded full adult suffrage in local government elections and action on the unemployment and shortage of housing west of the Bann. A march on Belfast was called off, but after several meetings in the Queen's University it was decided to organize a march from Belfast to Derry, beginning on 1 January.

Not only the Unionists objected to this march. Mr McAteer and the Nationalists also called on People's Democracy to call it off. The Northern Ireland Civil Rights Association made a grant of £25 to defray the expenses of the march, and Derry Citizens Action Committee agreed, somewhat reluctantly, to meet the marchers when they arrived in Derry. Captain O'Neill had dismissed Mr Craig from the Ministry of Home Affairs on 11 December. The new Minister, Captain Long, did not impose a ban on the Belfast–Derry march, although he tried to dissuade the organizers from going ahead with it.

The march, which began from the City Hall in Belfast, was impeded from the start. Major Bunting had assembled, at the starting point, a group calling itself the 'Loyal Citizens of Ulster', with the proclaimed intention of harassing the march, and scuffles broke out before the students had left the City Hall. There was sporadic trouble all along the way from there – a gauntlet of abuse to the outskirts of Belfast, then relative peace until mid-afternoon when the seventy-odd marchers were met by a hostile group, including Major Bunting again, and were held up for several hours. Although the marchers were within their legal rights, the police too were hostile to them. Occasional outbreaks of violence were interspersed with sermons and recitations on the religion of love and the evils of Rome delivered through the loudhailer by Major Bunting from under the Union Jack. Eventually a Unionist M.P. intervened, and the marchers were taken on by police tender to a community hall beyond Antrim, where they spent the night. After this they were again required to make a detour in the morning, their route being blocked by a combination of police and counter-demonstrators. The detour took them through Toome, where the population was friendly. Beyond Toome they were stopped by police, who had been in consultation with Major James Chichester-Clark, then Minister of Agriculture (later in the year to become Prime Minister) and his brother, who was a Unionist M.P. in Westminster. The march was ordered, after these consultations, to take another detour, along a by-road through a bog where they came to a stop after two miles, faced with yet another police

cordon, behind which were ranged Major Bunting and a large
force of his 'Loyal Citizens'. At this point Michael Farrell conferred with the marchers and it was agreed that this time they
would insist on their right to pass. The police, after making an
attempt to disperse them, were deterred by the arrival of re-
inforcements for the marchers from Toome, and, for the first
time, cleared a way through the 'Loyal Citizens' – but in a
fashion which gave the 'Loyal Citizens' ample opportunity to
shower missiles of various kinds on the marchers as they proceeded. The march moved on towards Maghera, and when they
reached the village of Gulladuff, on the way, where they were
welcomed by the local people, they learned that large numbers
of men armed with cudgels were gathering ahead of them. It
was now dark, and it was agreed that they would accept the use
of cars supplied by local people and make a further detour,
passing beyond Maghera to Brackareilly Hall, where accommodation would be supplied. In Maghera itself there was some
rioting that night.

The following day the marchers had a peaceful progress to
Dungiven. In Belfast the Minister of Home Affairs, Captain
Long, conferred with Dr Paisley and Major Bunting. Later he
appeared on television and said that the two gentlemen had
been very courteous, that their followers had been wholly non-
violent during the march, and that there was no threat or hint of
violence from them for the march as it arrived in Derry. Dr
Paisley and Major Bunting gave a press conference after their
meeting with the Minister, in which Major Bunting said:

I have given a request to the Loyal Citizens of Ulster and thank
God that they have responded – I thank you very much indeed, God
– to hinder and harry it. And I think they have hindered it, and I
think to a certain extent they have harried it.[75]

By night the marchers reached Claudy, where they were generally welcomed. In Derry, Dr Paisley and Major Bunting were
now addressing a 'prayer meeting' in the Guildhall, calling on
their audience not to tolerate the entry into the city of the
Apprentice Boys of a march of people who were no better than

republicans. Outside the Guildhall, in the largely Catholic city, a large hostile crowd was gathering, and the civil rights leaders addressed it appealing to the people not to attack the meeting in the Guildhall. Mr Ivan Cooper asked the crowd to spare all their efforts for welcoming the courageous students on the following day. Mr McCann made a similar appeal:

You know I am not a moderate. I want to see a lot of radical changes in our society, and I want to see them as soon as possible. Tonight I would achieve this if it could be done. But nothing, nothing whatsoever, can be gained by attacking or abusing the people in the Hall. Don't you see that this kind of action is precisely what the clever and unscrupulous organizers expect and hope will happen? Paisley and Bunting will be delighted if there is uproar and disturbance here tonight. It will give strong support to the idea that the Civil Rights movement is anti-Protestant, set on destroying one section of the population on sectarian grounds. . . .

No, you must not attack these people. They are your proper and natural allies.[76]

In spite of this, while most of the crowd dispersed after a while, an intransigent element remained. Major Bunting's car, parked behind the Guildhall, was burned. Then some of the people within the Guildhall broke up furniture to make clubs, and charged out, with the police, to disperse what remained of the crowd outside.

While the marchers were at Claudy, where they were subjected to threats during the night, an ambush was being carefully prepared. Several lorry-loads of freshly quarried stones in eight-stone sacks were distributed, clubs and cudgels with nails driven through them were prepared, large numbers of Special Constabulary – the 'B Specials' – out of uniform prepared to move into position. In Claudy, in the morning, Eamonn McCann and Michael Farrell addressed the marchers: they were warned that all the signs were that this day, the last of their journey, they might face provocation beyond anything they had yet seen, but they were urged to remain non-violent. McCann put this strongly:

I am afraid this is the policy we must support to a lunatic extreme. We must agree that not one single person will retaliate even
to save himself from injury. . . .

. . . Remember the nature of those who have hindered us during
the last few days. They are not our enemies in any sense. They are
not exploiters dressed in thirty-guinea suits. They are the dupes of
the system, the victims of landed and industrial Unionists. . . .

The Protestant poor have been bullied and bribed to the stupid
belief that they are in some way privileged beyond other people,
beyond Catholic people. . . .[77]

Some distance beyond Claudy, where the route debouched on
to the Dungiven–Derry road, the marchers were halted by the
police and warned that a hostile group was assembled on high
ground to the right-hand side of the road about thirty yard
ahead. The police this time did not suggest rerouting the march,
but merely advised that the marchers keep close to the right-
hand bank, which would give protection against any chance of
flying stones.

The march moved on to the main road, about seven miles
from Derry, towards the bridge of Burntollet. Some police vehicles preceded the marchers, followed by a small group with a
Union Jack who had smashed the windscreen of a car carrying
newsmen from Derry a short while previously. After them
came a district inspector leading steel-helmeted police equipped
with riot shields, then about five hundred marchers, and finally
more police tenders. A screening force of police, without riot
equipment, moved into the fields on the right. The marchers
were battered with large stones of several pounds' weight, with
bottles (delivered by lorry in crateloads during the night to
the ambush site) and by nail-studded cudgels. On the left of the
road the ground sloped down a short distance to a stream, th
Faughan, and many of the marchers were driven down here.
Numbers of girls were thrown into the stream by the attackers,
into water which was about three feet deep. Stones were thrown
at them in the water, and when they attempted to come out they
were beaten back again by home-made cudgels. Other girls

were thrown off a bridge into the stream; some were beaten while in the water with clubs from which large nails protruded; others were threatened with rape.

A further ambush, conducted largely by the same people who had taken part at Burntollet, met the bloody and battered marchers who finally made their way into the outskirts of Derry. In Irish Street, large numbers of heavy stones, bottles and petrol bombs were thrown by the attackers from high ground on to the procession. Before the marchers reached Craigavon Bridge and could cross the River Foyle into Derry, they were held up for some time in Spencer Street by a police cordon, while missiles rained down on them. At last they crossed the bridge, and, having been kept out of the walled area by a last rerouting by the police, they came into the Guildhall Square, where the people of Derry waited to welcome them. In the late afternoon of that Saturday, 4 January 1969, the Burntollet attackers gathered again in the high central part of the city and on the walls, shouting, drinking, singing, dancing in triumph. They now began to shower bottles and stones down into the Guildhall Square on the dispersing crowd which had greeted the marchers, most of whom now were having their wounds dressed. The police formed a human barrier across the gates, keeping apart the Protestants armed with sticks, stones, and bottles up on the walls, and the crowd in the Guildhall Square below. By the end of the afternoon the police had begun to drink and to abandon pretence of impartiality, joining openly with the Protestant mob, and becoming themselves a mob. This culminated, in the small hours of the morning, in an invasion of the Catholic Bogside area of the city by unruly police, many of them drunk, banging on their riot shields and shouting obscenities, to smash in the windows of the working-class houses and hammer on the doorways with their batons. Many of the residents later testified in such depositions as:

At a quarter to three in the morning, a crowd of police in our street were shouting, 'Hey, hey, we're the Monkees. We'll Monkee you around 'til your blood is flowing on the ground . . .' I looked out the window and one shouted, 'Come on out you Fenian, 'til we rape you.'[78]

Following this episode, the police for some days were excluded wholly from the Bogside area, which was patrolled by vigilantes appointed by the local people.

The Burntollet ambush and its Derry sequel were of great importance for subsequent developments in Northern Ireland in 1969. In Derry especially, the police from this point on were regarded as totally partial, sectarian, and criminal. The B Specials had fully justified the reputation they had enjoyed since their establishment. But, perhaps most significant, Captain O'Neill, whose bland manner and promises of reforms – even if the promises had not been followed so far by any substantial actions – had convinced some people at least that Unionism might be changing, now issued a statement, on 5 January, which alienated the great majority of Northern Ireland Catholics:

I want the people of Ulster to understand in plain terms the events which have taken place since January 1. The march to Londonderry planned by the so-called People's Democracy was, from the outset, a foolhardy and irresponsible undertaking. At best, those who planned it were careless of the effects it would have; at worst, they embraced with enthusiasm the prospect of adverse publicity causing further damage to the interests of Northern Ireland as a whole. . . .

But in the event, two things have happened. Some of the marchers and those who supported them in Londonderry itself have shown themselves to be mere hooligans, ready to attack the police and others. And at various times people have attempted to take the law into their own hands in efforts to impede the march. These efforts included disgraceful violence, offered indiscriminately both to the marchers and to the police, who were attempting to protect them. . . .

The maintenance of law and order in a democracy depends quite as much upon support for the law and respect for the law by the population at large as it does upon the actions of the police.

They have handled this most difficult situation as fairly and as firmly as they could. Their advice throughout has been that the imposition of a ban in the particular circumstances of this march would be likely to hinder rather than help them in their task. They are the professionals in this matter and it would be a grave step to set their advice lightly aside.

But clearly Ulster has now had enough. We are all sick of marchers and counter-marchers. Unless these warring minorities rapidly return to their senses we will have to consider a further reinforcement of the regular police by greater use of the Special Constabulary for normal police duties. . . .

I think we must also have an urgent look at the Public Order Act itself to see whether we ought to ask Parliament for further powers to control those elements which are seeking to hold the entire community to ransom.

Enough is enough. We have heard sufficient for now about civil rights; let us hear a little about civic responsibility. For it is a short step from the throwing of paving stones to the laying of tombstones and I for one can think of no cause in Ulster today which will be advanced by the death of a single Ulsterman.[79]

This statement, with its praise for the police and its threat of further use of 'B Specials', did not have the effect which appeared to be intended but infuriated in particular the Catholic population of Derry. To understand why, it is sufficient to quote from the report of the Cameron Commission of Inquiry into the disturbances, set up a few days later by Captain O'Neill's government, at the behest of the British government:

We have to record with regret that our investigations have led us to the unhesitating conclusion that on the night of 4th/5th January a number of policemen were guilty of misconduct which involved assault and battery, malicious damage to property in streets in the predominantly Catholic Bogside area giving reasonable cause for apprehension of personal injury among other innocent inhabitants, and the use of provocative sectarian and political slogans. While we fully realize that the police had been working without adequate relief or rest for long hours, and were under great stress, we are afraid that not only do we find these allegations of misconduct are substantiated, but that for such conduct among members of a disciplined and well-led force there can be no acceptable justification or excuse.[80]

These events marked the end of the first phase of the political process set in train by the civil rights movement. The situation had been pushed beyond the possibility of moderation: the strategy of People's Democracy had succeeded – for the moment – in breaking away from the 'middle-aged, middle-class, and middle-of-the-road' line of the Derry Citizens Action Committee and of most of the civil rights groups. John Hume, Ivan Cooper, and other 'moderate' leaders nonetheless remained very effective. They undoubtedly represented a large and very important body of opinion, which the activists were still trying to commit to a fully anti-establishment position. The defiance shown to them had demoralized the police, whose violent reaction appeared to have confirmed the P.D. marchers in their provocative tactics. The Unionist government had lost control of a difficult situation and the British government was beginning to involve itself in the internal affairs of Northern Ireland. One effect of the violent confrontations forced by People's Democracy was to bring about a reinforcement of the sectarian character which the conflict inevitably had – this in spite of the insistence of P.D. spokesmen on the non-sectarian character of their cause. By provoking violence they re-emphasized sectarianism: after almost two hundred years of precedence this was the character that violence assumed in Ulster.

There were further marches after Burntollet, but civil rights marches as such now ceased to be the main theme of further developments. A P.D. march announced for Newry for 11 January 1969 was met by the standard announcement of a counter-demonstration – again, as at Armagh, a 'trooping of colours and cavalcade' by Major Bunting's 'Loyal Citizens of Ulster'. This, however, was abandoned at the last moment, and the march, badly organized and inadequately stewarded, was something of a fiasco, which ended in the burning of some abandoned police tenders by a mob of Catholic adolescents.

As divisions were accentuated among leaders of the various groups and factions of the civil rights movement, divisions developed also within the Unionist party, under pressure from the right demanding that 'O'Neill must go'. On 3 February Captain

O'Neill announced that a general election for Stormont would take place on the 24th of the month. He was already losing support at this time, and he had lost by now the confidence of most of those Catholics (a minority to begin with) who had been prepared a few months earlier to believe that he might carry through effective reforms. By calling an early enough election he hoped to win moderate Protestant and Unionist support and also to appeal to Catholic voters as a man more likely to grant concessions to the minority than a more right-wing Unionist prime minister. It was too late: he failed. There was an unusually high number of candidates. It had long been customary in Northern Ireland not to contest many of the seats, where these were obviously 'safe', but now a divided Unionist party appeared. Official Unionist candidates, chosen by the local constituency organizations, were divided into pro- and anti-O'Neill Unionists, and in a number of constituencies were opposed by unofficial anti- or pro-O'Neill candidates. On the anti-Unionist side, too, there was division. In spite of the opinion of some civil rights leaders that the movement should stay out of party politics, John Hume and Ivan Cooper offered themselves as candidates, both challenging Nationalist leaders. People's Democracy put up its own leaders, mainly in east Ulster.

The election result left Captain O'Neill in a weakened position. He failed to attract any substantial Catholic vote, and he found himself with a small and very precarious majority within his own party. In parliament he now faced a new-style opposition, for three civil rights leaders had been elected – John Hume, Ivan Cooper, and Patrick O'Hanlon. Eddie McAteer, the leader of the Nationalist party, and Patrick Gormley, one of his colleagues, lost their seats. In a three-cornered contest in his own constituency of Bannside, Captain O'Neill secured only 47 per cent of the vote, 7,745, as against the very imposing total of 6,331 for Dr Paisley. The prime minister had gone into the election largely because his government had begun to break up as he gradually lost the confidence of business and professional interests – who had no great regard for the landlord tradition

Guns and Drums and Wounds

which he himself and his brand of toryism represented – and his announcement of the dissolution had followed shortly after the significant resignation of Mr Brian Faulkner from the government. His position now was that he could draw on only a limited section of the party to form his government: he clearly could no longer command the party; he must go. A bitter struggle for power went on, semi-publicly, within the Unionist party.

A struggle went on within the civil rights movement too. The young radicals, who had played a major part in bringing about the confrontation with Unionism but had yet to show themselves capable of a sustained follow-through, now found their influence increasingly resisted by some of those in the Northern Ireland Civil Rights Association (such as Miss Betty Sinclair of the Communist party) who had aimed at a broader-based, clearly non-sectarian, movement, which would follow a more cautious strategy. The republican element in the civil rights movement tended on the whole, at this stage, to throw its weight behind the radical approach, although within the republican movement itself there were two wings, the influence of the movement in the Republic being directed towards radical and socialist policies. A series of resignations tended to shift the civil rights movement to the left, but important bases of power and influence were held west of the Bann for the relatively conservative policies and approaches of Mr Hume and Mr Cooper.

The death of one of the Unionist Westminster M.P.s, Mr Forrest, left a vacancy in the constituency of mid-Ulster, where there was traditionally a large republican vote. In the by-election, on 18 April, the dead M.P.'s widow was entered as the Unionist candidate. On the anti-Unionist side, after discussions among various groups, the republican, Mr Kevin Agnew, withdrew in favour of Miss Bernadette Devlin to present a united opposition. Miss Devlin won the seat with 33,600 votes to Mrs Forrest's 29,337. People's Democracy, and the radical wing of the civil rights movement, now had a voice, and a very distinctive one. It was soon heard at Westminster, in a maiden speech to a packed house, where Northern Ireland was now represented by ten Unionists and two anti-Unionists (the other being Mr Fitt).

The campaign against Captain O'Neill was now renewed, and there was more violence. The C.R.A. in north Derry had proposed a march on 19 April from Burntollet bridge to the outskirts of Derry. The Minister of Home Affairs (Mr Porter at this stage) banned the march, and after some discussion the organizers withdrew. A sit-down was organized instead in Derry itself, as a protest, and while it was in progress Protestant militants, who had come together at Burntollet to oppose the march, entered the city. Fighting between the two groups developed. Again, by night, the R.U.C., accompanied by B Specials, invaded the Bogside, smashing windows and breaking into houses. In one, that of the Devenny family, they beat Mr Devenny: he died three months later as a result. The following morning, when riot police with full equipment had assembled for action in the Bogside, Mr Hume succeeded in persuading the inhabitants to withdraw temporarily from the area. He later negotiated successfully with Mr Porter to have the R.U.C. withdrawn from the Bogside.

In east Ulster sabotage began on a large scale, with explosions in public utilities, the simultaneous burning of a number of post offices through the city of Belfast, and then further explosions cutting off a large part of the city's water supplies from Templepatrick and the Silent Valley. The government ordered the call-up of a thousand B Specials, there were more violent confrontations between civil rights demonstrators and extreme Protestants, and the tensions in the state began to tighten again. Government announcements and actions implied that the sabotage was the work of the I.R.A. or an associated splinter group. But it later emerged (and must have been known to many in authority at the time) that the violence again came from the Unionist right. It was the work of the Ulster Volunteer Force and was designed chiefly to create a state of emergency, involving the call-up of the Specials, and to force Captain O'Neill out of office. It succeeded. The prime minister, misinformed, had played into their hands. Late in April he returned from London, after another meeting with Mr Wilson, to demand from his cabinet acquiescence in a proposal for 'one man one vote' in local government elections. This passed only by the narrowest margin, and it was plain that he was at the point of failing to command a majority in his cabinet. Then one of his chief supporters, the Minister of Agriculture, Major Chichester-Clark, resigned. The move may have been designed to forestall a take-over by Mr Faulkner or another of the more powerful dissident members of the parliamentary party. At any rate, Captain O'Neill now finally resigned, and Major Chichester-Clark defeated Mr Faulkner by a margin of one vote (17–16) for the leadership of the party. Both wings of the party were represented in the new government. Mr Faulkner received the Ministry of Development, in a cabinet which was reshuffled but not essentially changed. Major Chichester-Clark declared an amnesty – which may have been intended as a gesture of goodwill to the civil rights movement or the Catholic minority, or may have been a gesture to the Unionist extremists and the police, who probably derived more benefit from it. Dr Paisley and Major Bunting, both of whom had been in jail since March, were released under the amnesty. For a number of weeks, Northern Ireland, for the first time since October, was relatively quiet.

While the lull persisted in the north, a general election was held in the Republic early in June. It had been expected that the main interest in this would be provided by the vigorous and reorganized Labour party, which had adopted a fully socialist programme and which, although it was a small minority party, had made gains in the previous two elections. Most observers expected Fianna Fail, now led by Mr Jack Lynch, which had badly misjudged the feeling of the electors in a referendum on the electoral system in October, to lose power, probably to a minority government of the conservative Fine Gael party, the second largest in the Dail. The government party launched a vigorous and successful attack on the Labour party's socialist policies and deprived them of seats in the south and in rural areas; it held Fine Gael in check, and increased its majority.

Discussion of affairs in Northern Ireland, in spite of the events of the previous nine months, played little part in the election campaigns.

In the summer, the slow fuse which had been burning in Northern Ireland since Burntollet and the attack on the Bogside in January reached explosion point. None of the government's promised reform programme had come into being, and at the end of June protest was resumed, with a demonstration in Strabane. The widening rift within the civil rights movement now showed itself in the form of an attack made by Mr Eamon McCann on the timidity and weakness, as he saw it, of the C.R.A. He was supported by Miss Devlin but rebutted by Mr Currie. His argument was that by suspending demonstrations the movement was allowing the conflict to become one between Catholics and extremist Protestants instead of an organized challenge of inter-denominational character to Unionism.

Violence came at the traditional date for it, in July. After Orange demonstrations on the 12th, disorganized fighting and vandalism broke out in Derry, with mobs of Catholic youths rampaging through the city centre, wrecking shops and installations. There was some gunfire, and the Derry Citizens Action Committee, condemning the 'hooliganism', moved to help check the violence, which, however, lasted for several days. Elsewhere there was also violence in the aftermath of the Orange celebrations, and in Dungiven an elderly man died after a police baton charge. There were flickerings of violence at various centres through July, and then, at the beginning of August, a serious outbreak in Belfast. B Specials were now on standby duty, and in Belfast sectarian tensions had been building up since 12 July. C.R.A. groups were organized to try to prevent violence as some Catholic families in the Ardoyne area left their homes. On 2 August a crowd retaliated after an attack on an Orange procession, broke into Catholic flats at the foot of the Shankill Road, and then turned on the (largely Protestant) Shankill Road itself, looting and smashing shops in a serious and destructive outburst of rioting. Rioting spread to the Crumlin Road, and barricades began to be erected.

The situation had barely eased in Belfast when the main explosion came, where most people watching developments in Northern Ireland predicted it would – in Derry, on 12 August. This, rather than 12 July, is the chief Orange day in Derry, when the raising of the siege in 1689 is celebrated by parades of the 'Apprentice Boys' and other Orange-type organizations, and by provocative displays on the walls overlooking the Bogside. In general, Derry had nothing like as bad a record of sectarian bitterness and rioting as Belfast, but it had now become for Orangemen the symbol of impertinent defiance of the Protestant supremacy. The sacred walls had been breached by civil rights marchers, and Orangeism now planned to have the biggest parade for many years, and contingents from all over Northern Ireland and farther afield were to bring thousands of Orangemen with their drums and banners to assert again Protestant supremacy in Derry. Appeals to the government to ban *this* parade at this time were ignored, and the celebrations took place, peacefully enough for some hours.

If on the one side there was a determination, by reassertion, to restore the situation in Derry to the old position, on the other side there was by now an equal determination. For decades, since the bloody days of 1922 and 1935, the minority in Northern Ireland had been largely passive. Many felt abandoned by the people and governments of the Republic. The civil rights movement had given a lead to what became a mass movement which the people of Derry especially, with its large Catholic majority, associated with a feeling that, as many of them put it, they had 'got up off their knees' and would not be beaten down again. And the precedent, established by Mr Hume and others in January and April, of forcing a withdrawal of the hostile police force from the Bogside, was remembered.

Trouble began when some stones were thrown at the marchers in the city centre, and fighting at once broke out. The government had taken the precaution of drafting into Derry large numbers of riot police with full equipment, including armoured cars and water-cannon. These went into action, not only to clear the city centre, but to press on to invade the Bogside yet again, this time with the help of large contingents of the Orange marchers. Barricades were thrown up, and a battle of stones and petrol bombs began, after an initial period of confusion and uncertainty. The fighting became heavy. The police and their Orange allies forced their way in towards the heart of the Bogside on the first day, clearing barricades, until a petrol-bomb attack drove them back, and the Bogsiders regained much of the lost ground. A tower-block of flats just beyond the highest part of the walls of Derry became the centre of the fight. The tricolour of the Republic was flown from its top, where, on the flat roof, a group of young men and women were stationed. These commanded a view of the narrow streets below, which they bombarded with flaming petrol bombs. Box-loads of fresh supplies were brought up in relays by children, while elsewhere other defences were prepared and more solid and permanent barricades were built. The organization of the battle was taken over within the Bogside by a group formed some weeks earlier, the Derry Citizens' Defence Association, headed by Mr Sean Keenan and Mr Paddy Doherty. Radio communications were established, first-aid posts set up, centres for the manufacture of petrol bombs were organized and arrangements were made for policing the besieged area. Fighting went on into the night as the battle settled down into a siege, carried on by increasingly weary and demoralized police, who began a systematic bombardment of the crowded houses and flats of the Bogside with C.S. gas. As hundred after hundred of the canisters and grenades of gas were launched over the blazing barricades and burning buildings of the Bogside, it seemed that civil war must spread across the north. The C.R.A. issued an urgent appeal to the government of the Republic to act immediately to have a United Nations peace-keeping force sent into Northern Ireland. Miss Devlin, who was active on the barricades, called for suspension of the constitution of Northern Ireland.

The Bogside's previous experiences of the police gave to its thousands of people unity as a community in face of police attack, so that they had almost spontaneously established a commune and were now, under siege, running their own affairs.

They withstood two days of siege, but felt desperately in need of help, and sent appeals out to different quarters. One response came from the C.R.A. which attempted to organize demonstrations elsewhere in the north, mainly to draw off some of the R.U.C. from concentration on the Bogside. This led to outbreaks of violence elsewhere.

Another response came from the Dublin government. This had been meeting in special session and was divided almost evenly on what should be done. A group of ministers urged intervention in support of the Bogsiders. A military appreciation of the situation was received, but was not encouraging. Even those who wished to send immediate help to Derry were aware of the dangers of the situation – that, in the words of the C.R.A. declaration, 'a war of genocide is about to flare across the North'. The danger of any intervention from Dublin was that this might be precipitated. On the evening of Wednesday 13 August, on the basis of these discussions and of a narrow majority in favour of a more restrained course of action, Mr Lynch spoke on radio and television to say that the Irish government could not stand by while the situation deteriorated still further in the north. He announced that Irish army units were moving to the border and that they would there set up army field hospitals and would look after refugees or any patients who might not wish to enter a hospital in Northern Ireland. He said that his government had asked the British government to apply to the United Nations for a peace-keeping force, and to see that police attacks on the people of Derry would cease immediately. The broadcast was received with jubilation in the Bogside, where the arrival of Irish troops was eagerly anticipated. It was greeted with extreme annoyance by Major Chichester-Clark, who now sent B Specials into the streets of Derry.

The London government was also watching events closely, and on the afternoon of 14 August, just before the B Specials became engaged in the Bogside battle, British army units arrived in Derry and took over from the R.U.C. They were prepared to halt as soon as they should meet the Irish army, but they reached the Bogside unimpeded, and were welcomed because, even if they were not the Irish army, at least they replaced the R.U.C. The Citizens Defence Association, in the person of its vice-chairman, Mr Paddy Doherty, negotiated with the army. A guarantee was given that neither troops nor police would enter the Bogside, and peace was achieved.

In the meantime, however, the situation had become even more serious elsewhere. On Wednesday night there was some confused trouble in Belfast – partly in response to the Bogside's appeal for action that would relieve the pressure there. There were attacks on police stations, some baton-charges by the police, and some building of barricades in the Falls Road area. The barricades, mainly of fairly flimsy materials, were soon alight. On Thursday, in Belfast as in Derry, the B Specials were turned loose on the streets as well as the regular R.U.C. The Specials distributed weapons to civilians, and at about half-past ten in the evening these deployed from the Shankill Road, led by men wearing white arm-bands, and moved in two directions into the nearby Catholic areas of Ardoyne and the Falls Road. As they reached the first Catholic houses they began burning them, while the people who had lived in them fled. The Belfast Citizens Defence Association, formed like that in Derry in the preceding few weeks, checked the invaders in the small streets between the Shankill and Falls roads. Others began building massive barricades. The civilian attackers then withdrew, and the R.U.C. and Specials advanced on the Falls barricades with armoured cars, automatic rifles, and machine-guns, firing into the night as they came. As they cleared the way ahead, behind them the civilians systematically fired street after street of little working-class homes, until five hundred houses were ablaze in central Belfast. The firing so far, because of the virtual absence of firearms from most of the Catholic areas affected, had all been on the one side, but as the Specials and R.U.C. moved into the Lower Falls area they were met by gunfire. The few weapons available in the Falls area were deployed against them with some effect while the barricades were strengthened, until the ammunition was exhausted. The block of flats known as

Divis Street Towers was in the centre of this action. A soldier on leave from the British Army who had gone to the top of the tower-block was killed by a burst of machine-gun fire from the invaders, who also killed a nine-year-old boy in his bed in one of the flats. Two of the attackers were also shot dead. As women and children fled from burning houses, some in their night-clothes, and as the small store of ammunition in the Falls area was expended, it seemed if if complete disaster was inevitable. Desperate appeals went across the border to Dublin. Mr Frank Gogarty, chairman of the C.R.A., said in the early morning: 'For Christ's sake tell someone to intervene. Tell someone in Dublin. There will be another four hours of murder here.' Fighting continued into the daylight hours and on into the afternoon. By this stage women and children were arriving in Dundalk, Dublin, and at reception centres established by the army across the border, many of them appealing desperately for *guns*, while men and boys fought machine-guns with stones and bottles in the Belfast streets. In Belfast, as in Derry, the fighting was halted by the arrival of units of the British army who arrived at about half-past seven in the evening in the Falls and Shankill roads, and advanced cautiously into the bizarre scene: rubble, barricades, blazing factories and houses. More than four hundred people had been wounded in the night and day of conflict, and seven were dead.

As in Derry, the British soldiers who replaced the police came to an arrangement with the Citizens Defence Committees, and did not cross the barricades into the defended enclaves. The ghettos of Belfast are less compact, more dispersed, than the Derry Bogside, and therefore much less easily defended. Many areas had been abandoned, and acres of houses had been burnt out: whole streets in the area between the Shankill Road and the Crumlin Road. Along the Crumlin Road itself, and more widely in isolated instances all over Belfast, there had been a great deal of selective burning-out of Catholic-owned or Catholic-occupied houses or shops. Fear now fed upon fear, and the movement begun in October now moved into its third phase.

'Free Derry' and 'Free Belfast' existed as self-governed areas behind formidable and permanent-looking barricades for weeks, while negotiations went on between the various committees and groups which represented or sought to represent these areas and the British army and, later, the R.U.C. Negotiations of other kinds, at other levels, went on too. Mr Callaghan, the British Home Secretary, came to Northern Ireland on 27 August, and was enthusiastically received by the people of Free Belfast and Free Derry. Mr Lynch followed through his broadcast and set up his hospitals and refugee camps, which were occupied for a time. The Dublin Minister for External Affairs went to New York, in pursuance of an Irish government request that the Northern Ireland situation be placed on the agenda of the Security Council of the United Nations. He did not succeed, but he received a hearing (which was a success of a kind) and made a speech in which he saw the partition of Ireland as the root cause of the troubles of the north. In an operation of extraordinary ineptitude, the Irish government also hastily seconded press officers and public relations officers from various state agencies and sent them to Irish embassies abroad to supply masses of anti-partitionist literature (much of it surviving from the propaganda campaign of twenty years earlier) for the waste-paper baskets of the world's press and foreign ministries.

The British government had now intervened directly in Northern Ireland and was putting considerable pressure on Major Chichester-Clark's government to make drastic changes in the structure and organization of the politics of the area. The Cameron Commission's report, extremely critical of the government and its agents in its analysis of the causes of disturbances in Northern Ireland, left little scope for a renewal of strong 'law and order' methods, and the report of the Hunt Commission of Inquiry into the police forces of Northern Ireland recommended drastic changes. And some changes were guaranteed in what has come to be known as the Downing Street Declaration, resulting from Major Chichester-Clark's visit to Mr Wilson in the week following the Belfast fighting when, so far as certain reforms were concerned, Stormont's freedom of action was taken away. One of the first actions taken by General Freeland, the British commander, when his troops moved in was to strip the R.U.C. of their heavier armament. More drastic changes in the police were soon put in train, partly in line with the Hunt report. The B Specials were to be abolished, and a new force, to be known as the Ulster Defence Regiment, was to be formed for security duties. Reforms in the matter of voting systems, housing, discrimination, and other matters of long-standing grievance were to be hurried through. In October, Northern Ireland was debated in Westminster, which thus took up the powers it had reserved in the Government of Ireland Act, 1920.

But the situation showed little sign of returning to any kind of normality. As the British government began to assume more and more responsibility for the Northern Ireland situation the Unionist right, in its frustration, assumed more and more the rebellious stance of 1912. There was a long period of negotiation about the very solid barricades behind which 'Free Belfast' continued its self-governing existence. Some barricades (as a bargaining point) were put up in the Shankill area too, and the Shankill militants demanded that the Catholic defences be lowered and their area opened again to the police as well as the army. The Citizens Defence Committees, however, were extremely reluctant to take down the barricades without full and satisfactory guarantees of army protection against their neighbours. The situation, through September and October, remained explosive. Gas was used to disperse a Protestant crowd on 7 September in Belfast, and on the following day a Protestant was shot dead, after which a number of Catholic families, fearful of reprisals, left their homes. In the middle of the month the British army, with the collaboration of the Bishop of Down and Connor, Dr Philbin, succeeded in persuading the reluctant defence committees to begin dismantling the barricades. The army had in the meantime constructed what was euphemistically termed a 'peace line' – a 'Berlin wall' would be a better description – to seal off the Falls from the Shankill. At the end of the month this was breached by a Unionist mob which burnt out some more Catholic houses, and a fortnight later a new attack was made. This time the R.U.C. (who, of course, still functioned in the Protestant areas, where they were regarded as natural allies) tried to prevent the onslaught on the Catholics of Unity Walk: the mob was armed and an R.U.C. constable was shot dead. The army now moved in, to be greeted by a fusillade of fire from the Protestants who brandished Union Jacks. The army moved in to occupy the Shankill Road, but from now on it had to deal with the hostility and resentment of the U.V.F., who felt they had been deprived of their lawful prey and that 'loyalists' should not be subject to army control. At the end of September, too, a Protestant man was brutally killed by a mob in Derry. The violence was sporadic, but constantly threatened to flare up into something on the scale of August. It soon became clear that the troops who had been moved in at the height of that crisis must stay for a long time and in considerable numbers. Belfast and Derry settled down to being occupied cities, with barbed wire, sandbags, armoured cars, patrols of heavily armed troops, and all the outward appearance of communities at war.

The reforms yielded by Stormont were grudgingly conceded, under duress from the civil rights movement on the one hand and from the British government on the other. They were not only grudging: where possible they were watered down to render them as ineffective as possible. For example, the terms on which the new Ulster Defence Regiment was recruited departed from two of the most important recommendations of the Hunt Committee – those respecting the number to be enrolled and the qualifications required for entry – so that the new force appeared to be remarkably like a new version of the old B Specials. On the other hand, the British commitment to measures of reform was firm, and Major Chichester-Clark appeared to accept this (he had indeed no choice) even if he had to try to bring a very reluctant party with him. As usually happens in such cases, however, reforms slowly and reluctantly granted under duress soon cease to mean very much in themselves: people who have been too long refused a little, when they win it through their own efforts, begin to demand a lot. And what the able new representatives of the minority in Northern Ireland were now beginning to demand was, in effect, that the whole basis of the relations between the two communities should be changed. The forces of conservatism began to draw together.

While the Republic had been slow to be deeply affected by the events in the north, the desperate days of August had profound repercussions there. Many people who had subscribed unthinkingly to a policy of reunification based on the proposition that Ireland was one nation were suddenly faced with the realization that it was at least one small island. Even those who were not interested in reunification had brought home to them that an upheaval such as was happening in the north must affect the country as a whole in some ways. Admiration for the early achievements of the civil rights movement and for its moderate leadership – which was widespread – was matched by distrust and fear of its radical leaders, especially when these attacked the policies and attitudes of the southern government almost as vehemently as they did those of the northern. This was most marked within the ranks of the ruling Fianna Fail party, which became quite schizophrenic as the northern struggle revealed its own internal contradictions. The malaise was manifest in several ways, of which perhaps the least important was a mean display of fear and hatred of Miss Devlin among many of the backwoods ward-heelers of the party. But more dangerous embers were fanned into flame.

Ministers and other members of the government party revived the memory of the time when it had been 'the republican party' and were determined, on the one hand not to fall in with the policy of 'appeasement' which Mr Lynch had narrowly carried in the cabinet, and on the other hand not to be outdone in old-fashioned nationalism by any group in the north. The I.R.A., since the end of its unsuccessful border campaign of the 1950s, had held to its non-violent, socialist-inclined, policy. It had not played any leading part in the civil rights campaign, but it had not opposed it. Members of the I.R.A. and of the political republican movement had acted as stewards or had played other minor parts in the street agitation of 1968–9, and had on one or two occasions (as in the mid-course of the Belfast to Derry march in January) provided discreet (and unasked) protection when it seemed that unarmed civil rights demonstrators might be exposed to armed attack. But they had maintained the policy of restraint to the extent that in Belfast, where by long tradition one of their functions had been to defend the Catholic areas against the ever-present danger of pogrom, the nationalist streets were virtually unarmed when the August attack came. The few guns available were used with some effect, but the movement was critically divided as a result of that experience and of the recriminations of the population whose homes had been exposed without defence to a police and Paisleyite mob. The policy of restraint and of pursuing social policies was largely a southern one: the fury of resentment against it now was largely northern. There was a widespread feeling in the north that it must never happen again. Next time (and a next time was anticipated) there must be weapons for defence.

In this atmosphere of recrimination, fear, and renewed militancy in the north, contacts began between members of the northern defence committees and members and representatives of the Dublin government. Mr Lynch, after the hint of militancy in his 13 August broadcast, which was followed through to some extent in the next few weeks, soon reassessed the position and realized that, unless he were to abandon the policies followed since the late fifties, he had in fact little room for manoeuvre. Because the Northern Ireland problem remains essentially a colonial problem, the paradox which was to startle British opinion in October, when Belfast Protestants from under the Union Jack fired on British soldiers, was more apparent than real. The reality was perceived more than half a century previously by Pearse, who wrote, speaking on behalf of nationalist opinion:

When the Orangemen 'line the last ditch' they may make a very sorry show; but we shall make an even sorrier show, for we shall have to get Gordon Highlanders to line the ditch for us.[81]

202

Mr Lynch perceived the reality too. Although he might protest that the Irish government could not stand by while Irish people were being killed in the north, he soon realized that in private he could but acquiesce in Mr Wilson's actions, and hope perhaps to exert some influence on them. His government's programmes of economic expansion, the free trade agreement with Britain, and other arrangements of the kind had left him with no real independence of action. He could ask only, and without immediate prospect of success, for the 'Gordon Highlanders' in this case to wear blue U.N. helmets. If he had responded immediately to the Derry crisis, sending troops into the Bogside (and taking a gamble with a great many lives in Ulster), the situation might be quite different. But this was not a possibility now: the British army had moved in. Mr Lynch began to change the tone of his statements and within a month made a speech in Tralee, Co. Kerry, in which he abandoned the old anti-partitionist line. He no longer pointed to the border as the main issue: this was, he said, peace, with justice and equality. He renounced the use of force to solve the Irish problem. Major Chichester-Clark responded by a speech to Unionists in which he acknowledged the right of republicans, north and south of the border, to advocate the reunification of Ireland by peaceful means, and in which he insisted on the need for putting through the reform programme. Mr Lynch, speaking at a debate on Northern Ireland in the Dail in October, suggested some form of loose federal arrangement by which Northern Ireland could maintain its economic and financial links with Britain while entering into political links with the Republic. The heads of the three governments were clearly drawing together towards a considerable measure of understanding which would separate them all as much from the radical wing of the northern movement of revolt as from the blind reaction to it.

But Mr Lynch's colleagues did not all follow him down this road. His Minister for Agriculture, Mr Neil Blaney, whose constituency in Donegal adjoined Derry, made speeches in which he said that Fianna Fail policy did not absolutely rule out force.

Mr Blaney had a great deal of support and sympathy in Derry, where he had shown himself frequently during the troubled year, and had offered aid and comfort of various kinds. Mr Kevin Boland too, the Minister for Local Government, was widely known to be deeply dissatisfied with Mr Lynch's failure to identify his government's policy in some more positive way with the cause of the northern nationalists. It was not at this stage so widely known that the sympathies of the Minister for Finance, Mr Charles Haughey, lay in this direction too.

The winter and spring were filled with clandestine as well as open activity. There were new developments and new alignments. The all-out attack on the Belfast ghettos in August and the arrival on the scene of the guns and armoured cars of the British army had changed the nature of the confrontation. The importation of arms and the raising of the money necessary for this went ahead in various ways. The U.V.F. already had fairly ready access to supplies of arms in the north – in particular those held by the B Specials. An important part of the new reform programme was concerned with this problem: the R.U.C. was technically 'disarmed', and the B Specials were disbanded and, theoretically, disarmed. For a time, indeed (the best part of a year), the disarming of the R.U.C. was fairly effective. The service pistols which had been the standard issue were withdrawn, as well as the heavier weaponry which had been taken from them as soon as the army assumed control. It was not until late 1970 that a redistribution of weapons (mainly Walther pistols) began to the R.U.C. The disarming of the auxiliary and irregular forces of Unionism, however, was little more than nominal. These could take advantage of the fact that the whole detailed apparatus of the Orange state remained to a large extent at their disposal and that they could continue to rely upon the complaisance of both police and magistracy. The U.V.F. and the disbanded Specials simply applied for and received gun-licences. Many of the disbanded units of the Specials retained their corporate identity as new 'gun clubs'. By the end of 1970, the Specials too remained fully armed, legally. And irregular forces of the right, hinted at in threatening speeches by some right-wing Unionist politicians, continued to drill and to prepare for action. From time to time the U.V.F., frustrated by the British intervention in the north, made forays into the Republic. They blew up or damaged with explosives some public monuments in the winter of 1969–70, but although at that time they issued threats to 'burn Dublin', these were not seriously put into effect until the spring of 1971, when several million pounds' worth of fire damage was caused to a number of Dublin department stores.

The Catholics, especially those in Belfast who feared for their homes and their lives after August, could not legally obtain arms as could their opponents. They made strenuous efforts, directed in part by some of the Citizens Defence Committees, to obtain them by other means. A great many people in the Republic, in Britain, and in America were willing to help them. These included some people associated in one way or another with the Dublin government. Mr Blaney and his friends in the government itself had, from the very beginning, taken a keen interest in the northern developments. This group within the Irish government was one closely associated with property interests and with the business groups whose money had poured into Fianna Fail public and private funds for a number of years. They cannot have regarded with any pleasure the radical and socialist leadership which had been thrown up by one wing of the civil rights movement, nor indeed the eclipsing of Fianna Fail's Nationalist party allies in west Ulster by even the 'moderate' leaders.

The Blaney group therefore tried to move, politically, across the border and take over a position within the civil rights movement. When large amounts of money were being raised in different ways, late in 1969, by agencies in both north and south, to help those who had been affected by the troubles of August, the Dublin government tried to channel all such aid through the Irish Red Cross (in which it had good peronal connections), where control could be exercised over the funds. A grant was also made by the government from public funds, some of which was spent on relief of distress. Who controlled what, however, soon became a matter of some obscurity, since in their dealings with him and with each other Mr Lynch's ministers were not as frank as they might have been.

The political moves in Northern Ireland were associated with the appearance of a weekly newspaper, *The Voice of the North*, the first issue of which appeared on Sunday, 12 October 1969. This, printed in Cavan on the southern side of the border, professed to be a paper of the northern civil rights movement. Mr Seamus Brady, a journalist who had been, among other things, a speech-writer for Mr Blaney, and who left the Dublin Government Information Bureau in mid-October, was the person mainly responsible for the production of the paper, but Mr Aidan Corrigan was closely associated with him. The paper was financed through one of the funds passing through bank accounts in false names which later became the subject of extensive investigations in Dublin. It carried propaganda for the militant, or Blaney, wing of Fianna Fail, with strong sectarian overtones. It was unsuccessful in its task of winning a position in Northern Ireland for the political group it represented, although for a time some civil rights leaders in Belfast were enticed into collaboration.

Gun-running was also organized on a large scale in the winter months. This was done by various groups. Bank robberies were carried out at intervals, on both sides of the border, at intervals in the winter and spring. Some of these have been attributed to a small group known as Saor Eire, and it is inferred that the stolen money was intended in part for the purchase of arms. A policeman, Garda Fallon, was shot dead in Dublin in the early part of 1970 while attempting to apprehend a group of bank-robbers.

In August and later, intelligence officers of the Irish army were active in Northern Ireland. Their activities, unlike those of the police special branch (who collaborated to a considerable extent with the R.U.C. and the British police), were autonomous. One of them, Captain James Kelly, who was in Belfast and Derry during the August fighting while on leave, by his own testimony formed strong sympathies with the citizens defence committees and felt committed to help them obtain arms. His superior officer, Colonel Michael Hefferon, Director of Army Intelligence, first prohibited him from operating further in Northern Ireland, and then advised him that his resolve to help the defence committees obtain arms was incompatible with his duties as an army officer. The army was, however, officially involved in discussion of 'contingency plans' for the north, and was in touch with the northern defence committees. For one short period, about the end of September, men from the Derry Bogside received military training from the army at the camp in Dunree, Co. Donegal. It seems clear that, apart from the intrigues and deceptions within and between the government and its members, there were shifts and changes and uncertainties in the Dublin formulation of policy in the six months after August. Secret agents were numerous and extremely active, and these included British agents, some of whom gathered intelligence, others influenced decisions. Quantities of arms were purchased, mainly in continental Europe, and elaborate arrangements for their importation to Northern Ireland were made.

All this led, in May 1970, to the beginning of a prolonged public political crisis in the Republic, when Mr Lynch, having accepted the resignation of one minister on grounds of ill-health, dismissed Mr Haughey and Mr Blaney from his government, and accepted the resignation of Mr Boland and some junior ministers. After preliminary hearings – at which no *prima facie* case was found against Mr Blaney – Mr Haughey, Captain Kelly, Mr John Kelly of Belfast, and Mr Albert Luykx, a businessman of Belgian origin, were charged with conspiracy (to contravene the act which prohibits the unauthorized importation of firearms). The trial was stopped by the judge after he had had an altercation with counsel for one of the accused. A second trial ended in acquittal for all four, on 23 October 1970. In a further week-end of crisis Mr Haughey and Mr Blaney tried to take over the leadership of the Fianna Fail party from Mr Lynch, appealing to the old spirit of the 'republican party'. They failed, and when a motion of confidence was put in the Dail on 4 November they voted with the government. Mr

207

Boland, however, resigned his seat. The defeat of the militant group in the government party was clearer and more over-whelming at the noisy, violent and bitter annual conference of the party in February 1971.

Mr Lynch, meanwhile, with the support of the majority of his own party in the Dail, as well as that of the two opposition parties, went on to establish a policy of collaboration with the British government and with Major Chichester-Clark's government to oppose violence as a means of ending the partition of Ireland, to support the British military presence in the north and the reform programme of the Downing Street Declaration, and to move towards a closer association with Britain in European and other matters. His immediate reaction to the acquittal in the arms case had been to say that, while the verdict was 'Not Guilty' on the charge of conspiracy, there was no doubt of an attempt to smuggle arms, and that the dismissed ministers had been involved. He pursued the matter further by arranging for the Dail committee of public accounts to investigate the dispensing of the monies provided from public sources in the Northern Ireland Relief Fund.

In the north, too, another commission of inquiry had been announced immediately after the August troubles – the Scarman commission, presided over by a judge of that name, which was to begin the long process of taking evidence on the disturbances of the summer. Among the other aftermaths of the fighting, Miss Devlin was sentenced by a Derry magistrate to six months' imprisonment for her part in the Bogside action. Her arrest in June 1970, as she was on her way to Derry, and her imprisonment to serve this sentence, sparked off the worst week-end of rioting since August 1969: five people were killed. In the meantime, while on the surface it seemed that the presence of large numbers of troops and the implementation of some reforms had had a calming effect, tension remained high, and most observers feared another outbreak, possibly much worse than August, in the summer of 1970. As had so often happened before in Ulster, moderation tended to give way to a confrontation of extremes. In January two Stormont Unionist

M.P.s resigned. Mr Richard Ferguson, late in 1969, had announced, in the interests of moderation, his resignation from
the Orange Order. Since then there had been a number of
threats to his life – which in the climate of the time and place
were to be taken seriously. He decided to resign from parliament because of these. The other resignation was that of
Captain O'Neill, who departed from the political scene in
Northern Ireland. Both seats were contested by Unionist and
other candidates when the by-elections were held in April, and
both were won by 'Protestant Unionist' candidates. The figures,
which illustrate the extent to which Protestant unionist opinion
had moved to the right since the Stormont general election of
1969, were:

In the constituency of Bannside, on an 80 per cent poll:

Rev. Dr Ian Paisley, Protestant Unionist	7,981
Mr Bolton Minford, Official Unionist	6,778
Mr Patrick McHugh, Northern Ireland Labour Party	3,514

In the constituency of South Antrim, on a 71 per cent poll:

Rev. William Beattie, Protestant Unionist	7,137
Mr William Morgan, Official Unionist	6,179
Mr David Corkey, Independent	5,212
Mr Adrian Whiteby, Northern Ireland Labour Party	1,773

Dr Paisley, and a clerical colleague, had now followed some of
the civil rights leaders from the streets into parliament, where
his tone began, from this point on, to moderate somewhat. In
an interview which he gave to the *Ballymena Observer* after his
election, Dr Paisley gave some indications of his political position:

Is it right for a minister to be in politics? A minister is first of all a
Christian, and I believe that Christianity is not something that has
any reservations on the departments of its activities. He should be a
Christian in his home, in his business, in society and in politics.
Politics is a very important part of society. If Christianity has anything to give to the world surely, in the field of government, it has a
very important contribution to give.

209

In normal times I do not think that a Christian minister should stand as a Member of Parliament, but when the situation is such as it is in Ulster today, when the very heritage of our Protestantism is at stake, Protestant ministers, I feel, should be giving a lead to their people. ...

... I think that Stormont must get back the security of Northern Ireland into its own hands. I believe that all the 'No Go' areas and Republican enclaves that have been established in various parts would never have taken place had Ulstermen been handling the situation. ...

... I think that Henry Clark's criticism of the fact that we did not have 'British' on some of our election literature – I think 'British heritage' was mentioned on some – was only a political gimmick. It was the act of a despairing man grasping at a straw to try and extricate from sinking. Our flag is the Union Jack, and I think that declares exactly where we stand. I believe that Ulster's future is with Great Britain, but I distinguish between loyalty to the Throne and our attitude to any particular political party which may be in power. The voters of Ulster owed no allegiance whatsoever to the Government in the two contests – in fact they defeated that Government – but still they claim to be loyal citizens because their allegiance was to the Crown and Constitution and not to any political party. ...

... I do not agree that the Westminster Government is considering suspending Stormont, and I think this has been confirmed by a statement by Mr Callaghan on the result of the Bann Side, in which he has come out to say that Northern Ireland constituencies have the right to choose who they want and they have no other option but to support the Government at Stormont provided it is prepared to accept basic British standards. Such standards have never been an issue at any election. We believe in the same standards. I have always thought that the first standard Britain believed in was democracy; two, that justice is to be done and seen to be done in the courts of the land; three, that there is no discrimination against a man's religion; four, that the Queen's Writ should run everywhere. At present what I am campaigning for are British standards and condemning a Government which is not prepared to see that British standards are established all over the Province.

The British general election in June gave a greater opportunity to test and measure the movement of opinion in

Northern Ireland, since the twelve Westminster seats, ten of which were held by Unionists, one by Mr Fitt, and one by Miss Devlin, were contested. 'Unity' candidates, representing some nationalist or civil rights groups, stood for some of the seats. While the Conservative and Unionist party did well in the United Kingdom as a whole, winning the election, in Northern Ireland the Unionists lost ground, and returned only eight members to the new parliament in Westminster. In West Belfast, Mr Gerry Fitt, who had gained 26,292 votes in 1966 against Mr James Kilfedder's 24,281, now increased his vote to 30,649 against 27,451 for a different Unionist opponent, Mr Brian McRoberts. In Mid-Ulster, Miss Bernadette Devlin defeated Mr Neville Thornton, Unionist, by 37,739 votes to 31,810, in spite of the intervention of two other candidates, Mr Michael Cunningham ('Independent Unity and Farmers' candidate') who received 771 votes, and Mr Phelim O'Neill ('National Socialist') who received 198. Miss Devlin's vote in the previous year's by-election had been 33,668. In the constituency of Fermanagh and South Tyrone, the Unionists lost the seat when Mr Frank McManus ('Unity') defeated the Marquess of Hamilton by 32,832 to 31,390. And in North Antrim the Unionists lost another seat to Dr Paisley, who won 24,130 votes, as compared with 21,451 for the Unionist Mr Henry Clark, 6,476 for Mr Patrick McHugh (Labour), 4,312 for Mr Alasdair McDonald (National Democratic party), and 2,069 for Mr Richard Moore (Liberal).

The new British government indicated that on the matter of the Northern Ireland reforms its policy was the same as that of its predecessor. In the meantime tension heightened again in Ulster as the summer marching season approached. The militant Orange groups insisted on their right to march, and, in some cases, to take routes which would bring them past Catholic areas which had suffered severely in the previous year's burnings. The new British Home Secretary, Mr Reginald Maudling, issued requests for moderation, but it was decided not to interfere by ban with the marches. Serious trouble began on the week-end beginning on Friday, 26 June, when Miss Devlin was

arrested and imprisoned while on her way to address a final
meeting of her supporters in Derry (after which she had proposed to surrender herself to the authorities to begin serving her
sentence). Rioting began in Derry and went on into the night,
with petrol bombs being thrown again in the Bogside. Ninety-
two soldiers were injured. On the afternoon of the following
day, Saturday, what were to develop into more serious disturbances began in Belfast. Some of the areas affected were
those of the troubles of the previous August. An Orange parade
which took a route into Catholic areas on the Springfield Road
attacked a Catholic crowd, and the army intervened with C.S.
gas. Trouble flared elsewhere, in connection with the Orange
celebrations of what is known as the 'little Twelfth', as the
parading and party songs added to the tension in the city. For
the first time, the fighting spread across the river to east Belfast,
after an Orange band returning from the day's celebrations to
Ballymacarrett put on a provocative display outside St Mat-
thew's Roman Catholic church there. This was the centre of a
small Catholic enclave in the middle of a predominantly Protestant area, and, after exchanges had gone on between the two
sides for some time, the Catholics became alarmed as an armed
mob gathered to invade their community as the larger Catholic
communities in west Belfast had been attacked the previous
year. Help was sought and was provided by an I.R.A. unit
which moved into the grounds of the church. When, in the
middle of the night, the large Protestant mob, armed like that of
August, invaded the area and began burning buildings, the
I.R.A. group opened fire, first aiming their rounds high in the
hope of frightening off the attackers. These rounds, plunging
down behind the attackers into the Protestant streets beyond,
appear to have given many people the impression that the fire
was coming from the tower of the church, as was widely re-
ported in the following days. When the warning shots failed to
drive back the U.V.F.-led assault, the rounds were aimed lower,
and the attack was beaten off with casualties. All over Belfast,
however, the situation seemed to go out of control through the
night, as over a hundred buildings burned – some set off by

battery-operated incendiary devices – and troops opened fire with machine-guns from armoured cars. On Sunday the rioting and fighting continued in several parts of Belfast and was renewed in Derry. Two soldiers were injured by gunfire on the Springfield Road. Over the week-end six civilians (five of them Protestants) were killed, and many more were injured with gunshot wounds, by far the heaviest casualties being those of Ballymacarrett.

This week-end of violence was publicly interpreted in two different ways. The anti-Unionists argued that, in the state of tension which existed, all Orange parades should be banned for July 1970. The Unionist right saw the fighting as part of a plan to mount armed attacks on Orange processions, and they insisted that the government must not yield to this threat: the marches must go on. The main parades in 1970 were due to take place on Monday, 13 July. Clearly, this was not a matter for Stormont alone, and a number of Orange leaders went to London to see Mr Maudling. It was decided that preliminary and minor parades would be cancelled, but that the main marches would proceed. In the meantime, it was apparently decided that a display of 'law and order' might appease the militant right, and an extraordinary operation was mounted on the Falls Road.

Just about half-past four on the afternoon of Friday, 3 July, a party of soldiers and police in a number of vehicles moved rapidly into Balkan Street in the Falls area, and began a search. They found fourteen guns in the house which they had entered. In the meantime, the street had been cordoned off, and a crowd had gathered. As the soldiers withdrew, stones were thrown at them, and they replied with canisters of C.S. gas. Within half an hour about two and a half thousand troops had been deployed along the streets leading into the Falls area, and helicopters appeared overhead, broadcasting through loud-hailers the information that a curfew was beginning. It was plain that a prolonged and large-scale search of the whole area was planned. As the troops moved in stage by stage towards the centre of the Falls enclave in the course of the evening and night, the I.R.A.

213

force within the area put into effect the hasty reorganization and rearming which had taken place since August, and, behind a screen of unarmed men and boys who impeded the soldiers with stones and petrol bombs, they mounted an armed resistance. This, carried out in part with machine-guns, continued for a number of hours into the night in a haze of C.S. gas. Gelignite bombs were used against the army vehicles. Resistance gradually diminished, and by Saturday morning the British were in full control of the cordoned-off area of streets. The 'curfew' was rigidly enforced, and the people of the area were confined to their homes, through which the soldiers moved systematically. Some of the soldiers behaved civilly; others smashed and looted. During the night four men were killed by the soldiers: one was run down by a Saracen armoured car and three were shot. From Friday afternoon until Saturday afternoon the people were confined indoors: then, in response to numerous protests, the army gave permission for some to come out of doors, only within the 'curfew area', between five o'clock and seven for the purpose of buying food, milk, and other supplies. Many of the houses had been without food. The curfew was then renewed, but it collapsed on the following day, Sunday, under pressure from women, who organized themselves within the area and without, and breached the curfew zone from both directions in march-columns of up to three thousand. The search operation resulted in the discovery of considerable quantities of ammunition, but a relatively small number of weapons.

On Sunday, 12 July, the eve of the day which had been chosen for the main Orange parades, which, many people feared, would lead to a bloody outcome, 11,000 soldiers, after heavy temporary reinforcement, stood by in Northern Ireland. Mr Lynch, in Dublin, broadcast to the nationalists and anti-Unionists of the north. He appealed to them not to interfere in any way with the Orange processions the following day; he assured them that their own security was now guaranteed by Britain, and that his own government was 'the second guarantor'; he referred to Ireland's 'two great traditions' – one of which was having its main celebration the following day – and he spoke of the role of the British army in the north:

> I very much regret the injuries suffered by British soldiers during the course of the duties imposed on them in the north of Ireland; these young British boys find themselves in a situation which must seem to them inexplicable.

The northern problem, he said, was an Irish problem, to be solved by Irishmen. The marches passed off peacefully on 13 July, and on the 23rd all marches were banned for the next six months. Although there was another outbreak of street-fighting in Belfast on 5 August, in which there were again exchanges of gunfire, it seemed to some by the end of summer that violence was at last beginning to diminish. In fact the armed clashes at the beginning of July had introduced a new phase of the northern upheaval.

In parliamentary politics, as outside them, there were new alignments. The struggle within Unionism produced a temporary break-up of the party: Mr Craig and some others on the right were expelled, while the appearance of the 'Protestant Unionists', Dr Paisley and Mr Beattie, in parliament added to the strength of the right-wing opposition, which kept up a steady pressure on Major Chichester-Clark and his government. The agreements reached by the anti-Unionist opposition, by which 'Unity' candidates had been put forward in some constituencies in the general election, was followed in August by the formation of the 'Social Democratic and Labour Party', with, as its provisional executive, Mr Gerry Fitt, Mr Paddy Devlin, Mr Austin Currie, Mr John Hume, Mr Ivan Cooper, Mr Patrick O'Hanlon, and Senator Patrick Wilson. As all these were already in parliament, where they had represented somewhat different groups, this new organization had an advantage over the new 'Alliance Party', representing 'moderate unionism', which attempted to cater for conservatives of both Protestant and Catholic confessions who feared and opposed the populism and radicalism of right and left. Some parts of the reform programme proceeded, very slowly. Its effects were first

215

felt in the reorganization of the police, but the replacement of the gerrymandered local authority in Derry by a government-appointed commission also began to have an effect, most noticeably in the rapid rehousing of the people of that city. The old Bogside of 1969 and earlier began to disappear as new houses and flats were built, on wider streets. By the beginning of 1971, however, it was clear that most of the changes so far produced in Northern Ireland by two years of agitation and confrontations were minimal, except in one respect: the guns which, as ever, controlled the streets, were not now at the disposal of Stormont but were the guns of the British army.

Two main groups were prepared to oppose this development by violent means. The Unionists of the right, with a strong political wing in parliament and with a secret armed force, the U.V.F., bitterly resented Britain's interference in what they reckoned to be their affairs. Their attachment to the union was on their own terms, and they represented what had been a dissident and disruptive force *before* the civil rights agitation had begun. For the moment there was an alliance between the radical and populist – and violent and sectarian – forces of the working-class right and the business and professional groups (represented by, for example, Mr Faulkner), who opposed those elements in the civil rights movement which seemed to threaten an all-Ireland republic, and who opposed also both the British intervention and the landlord class that had for so long ruled in the north. The alliance might be compared to that in the south by which the Irish Free State had been established fifty years earlier, and it was probably equally unstable. Its first target was the traditional ruling group in Northern Ireland, represented by Major Chichester-Clark as by his relation and predecessor Captain O'Neill. Its second target must be the British intervention.

The other group which was prepared to oppose the imposition of British will was the I.R.A., with its allies. These, as they rearmed, became increasingly important again in a situation which, little more than a year ago, appeared to have excluded them. The actions at Ballymacarrett and the Falls at the beginning of July had seemed to a great many people in working-class Belfast to teach a lesson quite different from that taken by middle-class moderates: it was that I.R.A. guns could protect their homes and families. As a result, the discredited I.R.A. began to recover credit rapidly in some parts of the city. The organization itself was deeply divided, essentially on the question of tactics, but the more traditional ('green' as distinct from 'red') style of the 'Provisionals' prevailed in most parts of the north over the new social-concern style of the 'Officials' – who did however retain their position in one important area in Belfast, the Lower Falls. The "Provisionals' also stepped up recruiting in the Republic, and were able to draw on the dwindling reservoirs of old-style separatist sentiment, especially in some parts of the west – notably Donegal, Mayo, Clare, and Kerry. The I.R.A. now began to attempt, with some prospect of success, to do what right-wing Unionists had accused it of doing from the start: to take over the civil rights movement and use it for its own ends. An opportunity was provided at the end of November, when various civil rights groups had decided that they must take to the streets again because of what they saw as the whittling-down of the reform programme. A civil disobedience campaign was planned, to begin in County Fermanagh with a march, in contravention of the six-month ban on parades, in Enniskillen on 28 November. As a number of the sponsors of this campaign drew back at the last moment, the Enniskillen march, which duly took place in the presence of a massive show of force from the British army and the police, passed off relatively quietly.

The familiar atmosphere of suppressed violence had, however, returned to Northern Ireland by the end of 1970. Sectarianism was not at this stage the issue: the two I.R.A. groups had patched up a truce and a general agreement on territorial demarcation, and there was also a considerable measure of collaboration (particularly in the matter of arms exchanges) between them and the U.V.F. The I.R.A. felt that if they could win the confidence of the people and a fair measure of control of 'their own' streets in Belfast especially, they could move

217

towards the overthrow of the Stormont government. The
U.V.F. had a similar short-term objective – the overthrow of
Major Chichester-Clark – and they too were preparing for a
campaign similar to that which had brought about the downfall
of Captain O'Neill in 1969. The renewal of street fighting in
January 1971 was associated with the new I.R.A. tactics in Belfast – to strike back whenever one of the ghetto areas was again
entered by the British army in connection with an arms search
or otherwise. A search for arms on the Kashmir Road led not
only to fighting between the army and groups of men and
youths, but also to savage fighting between the two groups of the
I.R.A. Retaliation by the 'Officials' for the arms search was followed by widespread attacks on the British in other areas of Belfast by the 'Provisionals', and a territorial dispute, coupled with
a dispute over tactics, led to the internal I.R.A. warfare. The renewed violence was complex. At the end of January there was
an outbreak of gun-fighting on the Protestant Shankill Road,
between Protestant militants and the British army. The week-
end of Friday, 5 February 1971, was the worst in Belfast since
1969: gunfights, burnings and explosions were widespread. Gelignite and nail-bombs were widely used against army vehicles,
and a combination of gelignite-bombs and petrol-bombs was
effective in putting armoured cars out of action. The army
began to suffer casualties, in dead as well as wounded. As the
sporadic outburst of fighting continued, Major Chichester-
Clark's political position, caught as he was between the right
wing of Unionism demanding repressive measures, and the
British government refusing to permit them, became precarious.
A campaign of sabotage, similar to that which brought down
his predecessor in 1969, was not proving successful, in spite
of the open activities of the I.R.A. The killing of five men,
two of them B.B.C. technicians, travelling in a Land-Rover
up to the television booster station on Brougher Mountain
in Co. Fermanagh, had a considerable effect on public opinion
when it was attributed to an I.R.A. land-mine. The circumstances remained obscure however: the I.R.A. did not, as was their

usual custom, claim responsibility for the killing, whose victims included three men from Kilkeel, Co. Down. But it was the coldly calculated killing of three young soldiers (two of them brothers) who were shot in the head, that finally brought down Major Chichester-Clark. This was immediately attributed by the Minister of Home Affairs, Mr Taylor, and by much of the press, to the I.R.A. It served the purpose of the Unionist right wing, as the Prime Minister's parliamentary support melted away. He made one final effort – a visit to London to seek some way out – but on Saturday, 20 March 1971, he resigned.

Major Chichester-Clark's resignation marked the final breakdown of the system by which Northern Ireland had been governed since 1920. His successor, who brought back members of the Unionist right including, symbolically, the first of the O'Neill ministers to have been dismissed, now restored to his old ministry, was Mr Brian Faulkner.

Notes

1. *Reflections on the Revolution in France* (Pelican Classics, ed. C. Cruise O'Brien, p. 100).
2. St John D. Seymour, *Anglo-Irish Literature 1200–1582*, p. 99.
3. D. B. Quinn, *The Elizabethans and the Irish*, p. 119.
4. Version as printed by C. Gavan Duffy, *The Ballad Poetry of Ireland* (Dublin, 1845), p. xvi.
5. Gavan Duffy, *Ballad Poetry of Ireland*, p. 248.
6. P.R.O.I. Rebellion papers 620/24/106, quoted in H. Senior, *Orangeism in Ireland and Britain 1795–1836*, pp. 44–5.
7. Nat. Lib. I., Lake MSS 56, quoted in Senior, p. 67.
8. A. Bryant, *The Age of Elegance*, p. 267.
9. C. S. Parker, ed., Robert Peel, *Private Papers*, vol. 1, p. 81; Senior, p. 180.
10. Senior, p. 268.
11. John Mitchel, *Jail Journal* (Dublin, Gill edn, n.d.), p. 69.
12. W. S. Churchill, *Lord Randolph Churchill*, vol. 2, p. 59.
13. A. T. Q. Stewart, *The Ulster Crisis*, p. 22.
14. D. Ryan, 'James Connolly', in *Leaders and Workers,* ed. J. W. Boyle, p. 70.
15. J. W. Boyle, 'Belfast and the Origins of Northern Ireland', in *Belfast: the origin and growth of an industrial city*, ed. Beckett and Glasscock, p. 141.
16. P H Pearse, *Political Writings and Speeches* (Dublin, 1924), p. 94.
17. R. MacNeill, *Ulster's Stand for Union*, p. 51.
18. D. Gwynn, *The History of Partition* (1912–1925), p. 46.
19. ibid.
20. ibid.
21. Gwynn, pp. 48–9.
22. Stewart, p. 63.

23. Stewart, p. 62.
24. Gwynn, p. 58.
25. H. Nicholson, *King George the Fifth*, p. 226; Stewart, p. 80.
26. Gwynn, p. 73.
27. Pearse, *Political Writings*, p. 185.
28. I. Colvin, *Carson*, vol. 2, p. 241.
29. Stewart, p. 136.
30. Stewart, p. 150.
31. Sir J. Fergusson, *The Curragh Incident*, pp. 149–50.
32. From a ballad of the republican movement after 1916.
33. Gwynn, p. 145.
34. A. Griffith, in introducing Mitchel, *Jail Journal* (Dublin edn), p. xiv.
35. *Dáil Éireann: Minutes of Proceedings of the First Parliament of the Republic of Ireland, 1919–1921*, p. 22; B. Chubb, *A Source-book of Irish Government*, p. 51.
36. R. MacNeill, p. 279.
37. J. W. Boyle, in *Belfast*, p. 143.
38. *Hansard*, 15 February 1922.
39. Government of Ireland Act, 1920 (10 and 11 Geo. 5, ch. 67); Chubb, p. 5.
40. Articles of Agreement for a Treaty between Great Britain and Ireland, 12; Chubb, p. 14.
41. Government of Ireland Act, 5. 1; Chubb, p. 8.
42. D. P. Barritt and C. F. Carter, *The Northern Ireland Problem*, p. 84.
43. *Parliamentary Debates*, *N.I.*, vol. 16, cols. 1091–5 (24 April 1934).
44. *Fermanagh Times*, 13 July 1933.
45. *Londonderry Sentinel*, 20 March 1934.
46. St John Ervine, *Craigavon: Ulsterman*, p. 516.
47. Government of Ireland Act, 75; Chubb, p. 11.
48. *Bunreacht na hÈirann*, Chub, p. 21 and pp. 57–9.
49. The Ireland Act 1949 (12 and 13 Geo. 6, ch. 41); Chubb, p. 28.
50. See D. O'Sullivan, *The Irish Free State and its Senate*, p. 585.
51. *Dáil Debates*, vol. 74, cols. 1285–6.
52. Barritt and Carter, p. 130.
53. *Irish Times*, 12 April 1951.
54. ibid.
55. ibid.
56. *Dáil Debates*, vol. 125, col. 898.

57. *Belfast Telegraph*, 10 May 1969.
58. *Economic Development* (Stationery Office, Dublin, 1958), p. 227.
59. D. Barrington, *Uniting Ireland*, p. 24.
60. Speech at Tralee, Co. Kerry, 29 July 1963.
61. *Ulster Year Book 1966/1968*, p. 11.
62. *Report of the General Assembly*, 1950, p. 90. See Barritt and Carter, p. 29.
63. *Irish News*, 13 April 1948.
64. *Fermanagh Facts* (Fermanagh Civil Rights Association, 1969), p. 28.
65. *Fermanagh Facts*, p. 35.
66. *Ulster Year Book 1966/1968*, pp. 23, 25, 28. See also 'Human Rights in Northern Ireland', *Review of the International Commission of Jurists* (Geneva), June 1969.
67. *Fermanagh Facts*, p. 2.
68. *Northern Ireland: the Plain Truth* (Campaign for Social Justice in Northern Ireland, 1969), p. 21.
69. *Disturbances in Northern Ireland: Report of the Commission appointed by the Governor of Northern Ireland* (Cameron Commission Report), pars. 27, 28.
70. Cameron Commission, par. 31.
71. From *Utopia*.
72. T. F. O'Rahilly, ed., *Measgra Dánta*, part 2 (Cork, 1927), pp. 126–7.
73. Cameron Commission, par. 41.
74. From Yeats, 'Meditations in Time of Civil War', *The Tower* (1928).
75. B. Egan and V. McCormack, *Burntollet*, p. 19.
76. Egan and McCormack, p. 23.
77. Egan and McCormack, p. 26.
78. Statement of Mrs Teresa Donnelly. See Egan and McCormack, p. 59.
79. Egan and McCormack, p. 60.
80. Cameron Commission, par. 177.
81. Pearse, *Political Writings*, p. 186.

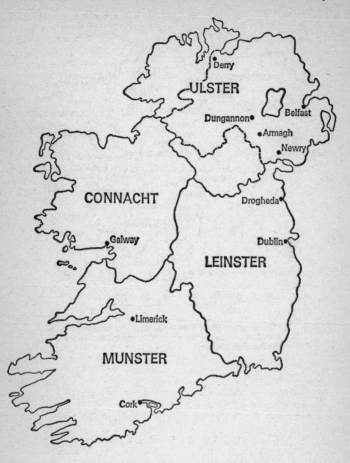

1. Outline map of Ireland showing the four provinces. The broken line indicates the present boundary of Northern Ireland.

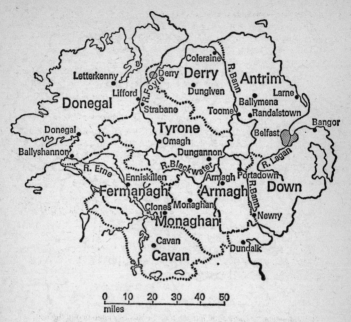

2. Outline map of Ulster showing some places mentioned in the
   text. The counties of Donegal, Cavan and Monaghan are in
   the Republic of Ireland.

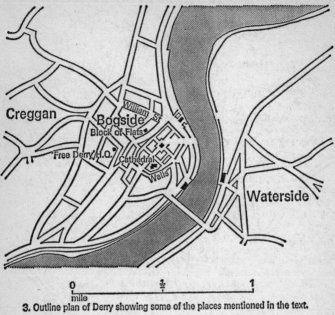

3. Outline plan of Derry showing some of the places mentioned in the text.

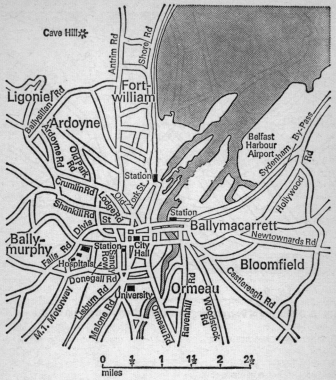

4. Outline plan of Belfast showing some of the places mentioned in the text.

Index

235

Index